ADVANCING THE RULE OF LAW ABROAD

NEXT GENERATION REFORM

RACHEL KLEINFELD

CARNEGIE ENDOWMENT
FOR INTERNATIONAL PEACE

WASHINGTON DC ▪ MOSCOW ▪ BEIJING ▪ BEIRUT ▪ BRUSSELS

Carnegie Endowment for International Peace
1779 Massachusetts Avenue, N.W.
Washington, D.C. 20036
202-483-7600, Fax 202-483-1840
www.ceip.org

To order, contact:
Hopkins Fulfillment Service
P.O. Box 50370, Baltimore, MD 21211-4370
1-800-537-5487 or 1-410-516-6956
Fax 1-410-516-6998

Cover design by Jocelyn Soly
Composition by Beth Schlenoff
Printed by United Book Press

Library of Congress Cataloging-in-Publication Data

Kleinfeld, Rachel.
Advancing the rule of law abroad : next generation reform / Rachel Kleinfeld.
p. cm.
ISBN 978-0-87003-348-3 (pbk.)—ISBN 978-0-87003-349-0 (cloth) 1. Law reform. 2. New democracies. 3. Rule of law. 4. Law—American influences. 5. Law—European influences. I. Title.

K559.K59 2012
340'.11—dc23

2012001516

TABLE OF CONTENTS

ACKNOWLEDGMENTS

This book owes its existence to Tom Carothers, who well over a decade ago began to support my journey in the rule-of-law field. His insight, wisdom, and willingness to put up with an extremely long writing process have allowed these words to finally see the light of day. I also owe great thanks to the Carnegie Endowment for International Peace, particularly Ilonka Oszvald and Jocelyn Soly, who painstakingly worked through the copyediting and cover design of this book.

The seeds of this writing began a decade ago at Oxford University. I owe immense thanks to the trust of Kalypso Nicolaidis, my adviser who not only oversaw my doctoral thesis in this area, but believed that I still might finish despite my decision to move back to America and start a nonprofit organization a year into the writing. Her patience, good-humor, and intellectual partnership have been a gift.

My thinking in the rule-of-law field has been spurred by many great intellects and practitioners. From my earliest days I have been influenced by my father's fierce intelligence and his life-long service to the law, which provided inspiration—and fodder for decades of dinner-table debates. I also thank both my father and mother for their libertarianism, which allowed me to spend youthful years gallivanting through countries that lacked much rule of law—experiences for which I will thank them for the rest of my life. Two who deserve special mention are Richard Messick of the World Bank and Wade Channell from USAID. Their willingness to read early versions of the manuscript and provide feedback has strengthened the work, and I have learned a great deal from their own writings and our manifold conversations over the years.

I have also enjoyed talking through these issues with many members of the Truman National Security Project community, from those working on the ground in Afghanistan and Iraq, to those in the trenches at the U.S. Department of State, Department of Defense, National Security Council, and other government agencies. Since the Truman community always engages in lively debate, I will not name names of those who might disagree with these conclusions—but I deeply appreciate all of their thoughts, grounded insights, and targeted questions. Their work in some of the most dangerous parts of the world—and some of the toughest parts of Washington, D.C.! —inspires and humbles my own efforts.

The research for this book drew on scores of interviews in countries around the world. I thank all those who provided their time to answer my many questions. Their names appear throughout the notes, but some who offered deeper insight (and second and third interviews) demand particular mention, such as Sebastian Pompe in Indonesia, Aurel Ciobanu-Dordea in Romania, and Fatos Bundo in Albania. While in most countries I worked without a translator, in Indonesia, John Riady provided that service—as well as handling all logistics, setting up meetings, and swiftly becoming a fellow thinker and colleague. I've rarely met such a fast learner or such a skilled compatriot at the art of getting things done while stuck in the midst of Jakarta traffic! I am grateful for his help, savvy, and intelligence.

This book owes its existence to experiences I had in rural India, Russia, and Eastern Europe, where the fabric of rule-of-law societies had frayed. These experiences sent me on a nearly twenty-year journey to discover how to improve the security, enhance the development, and increase the empowerment and human rights of people around the world who struggle under societies without liberty under law. It is easy to write about these issues; it is hard to fight them from the ground up. This book is dedicated to all those working for justice and dignity under the rule of law—may their struggle be rewarded, and may the United States stand on their side.

FOREWORD

When one speaks to an audience in a country moving away from authoritarian rule about possible paths ahead, the surest way to elicit wide agreement and interest is to highlight the importance of the rule of law. Whereas references to democracy or market economics will provoke a debate about their value and appropriateness for the society in question, the rule of law commands near-universal respect. Different audience members may understand the term in different ways—some will hear anticorruption, others the need for basic personal security, and still others will interpret it as a broad but powerful quest for justice—but they will not question the importance of the basic enterprise.

In parallel fashion, although Western policymakers and aid practitioners trying to assist postauthoritarian transitions often squabble over models and sequences of political and economic development, they are almost always unanimous in agreeing that rule-of-law development should be a priority. As I wrote in the 1990s, when the international community was starting to support political and economic transitions in every corner of the world, the rule of law has come to be seen as the "elixir of transitions." That is to say, it is perceived as a necessary foundation for the success of all other elements of the transitional package—political, social, economic, and humanitarian.

The result has been a mushrooming of efforts to foster the rule of law in a remarkably large and diverse group of countries. Throughout the developing and postcommunist worlds, one finds a welter of specific undertakings advanced under the rubric of rule-of-law development. These include attempts to promote transitional justice, judicial and police reform, legal aid, access to justice, alternative dispute resolution, legal education, and much else.

Unquestionably many of these efforts are valuable and have produced positive effects. But the experience has often been daunting. Russia has attempted myriad rule-of-law reforms for twenty years and absorbed significant amounts of Western assistance in the effort, yet law in Russia remains associated as much with the abuse of power as the regulation of it. El Salvador has been an early and continuing recipient of substantial amounts of rule-of-law assistance from abroad, but is beset today with devastating levels of criminality. Nearly two decades of varied attempts to help Cambodia with transitional justice and basic legal reforms have produced only very modest results.

Why has the rule-of-law endeavor proved so difficult? Despite powerful public support for the idea in countries around the world, reform efforts inevitably confront the fact that the technical elements of strengthening legal systems are only a minor part of undertakings that must confront the enormous challenges of creating meaningful limitations on political power holders, changing how governments relate to citizens, and altering fundamental norms that govern how citizens interact with each other.

Rule-of-law reformers increasingly recognize these realities and have learned many lessons about what works and what doesn't. Aggregating, capturing, and synthesizing this knowledge is a difficult but critical task. This book does just that.

Drawing on deep-reaching comparative research and sharp analytic insights, Rachel Kleinfeld persuasively argues that rule-of-law reform is poised to advance from an initial, somewhat exploratory generation to a more knowing and effective second generation. She builds her case by moving systematically from a reconsideration of competing ideas about the rule of law and a broad look at the overall set of available policy tools to an incisive analysis of which particular configurations of these tools are most likely to be effective in different types of cases. She proceeds from a full awareness of the difficulties that rule-of-law reform often encounters, but maintains a notable conviction that the international community can do better.

Having addressed rule-of-law issues in a series of works coming out of its Democracy and Rule of Law Program since the 1990s, the Carnegie Endowment for International Peace is pleased to publish this important contribution to a field that remains as crucial and compelling today as when it emerged in the international policy agenda decades ago.

—Thomas Carothers
Vice President for Studies
Carnegie Endowment for International Peace

CHAPTER ONE

INTRODUCTION

As this century comes to a close, I think historians will say that one of the great advances in our civilization during this last 100 years has been the gift of law to people across the world.

– U.S. Supreme Court Justice Anthony Kennedy[1]

These sequestered nooks are the public offices of the legal profession, where writs are issued, judgments signed, declarations filed, and numerous other ingenious machines put in motion for the torture and torment of His Majesty's liege subjects, and the comfort and emolument of the practitioners of the law.

– Charles Dickens, The Pickwick Papers

In the winter of 1992, I traveled to St. Petersburg to live with my brother, who was working with the city's first Russian-American theater company. Its office was located just above one of the favorite nightspots of the rising Russian mafia. Every day, we would walk to work past kiosks that had been burned out the night before—a message to shopkeepers to pay their protection money. At night we would try to avoid the burly men who had already kidnapped two of the actors, releasing them late at night, stripped, in a forest. We were among the first Americans living in the city since the Soviet Union's demise, and the *mafiosi* assumed we were rich. One day, a gangster pulled a few of the troupe aside and offered them a nuclear submarine—for a bargain price. The man was far off the mark about actors' material resources as well as their desire for a weapon of war, so we'll never know if his offer was real. But it was plausible, in those cowboy capitalist days after the fall of the Soviet Union, when anything and everything seemed to be for sale.

When the rule of law breaks down in any country, the effects are felt around the world. A nuclear submarine swimming through international waters might be noticed—but it's plausible that a Russian border guard, having just received more than his yearly wage in a one-off payment, could turn a blind eye to smugglers leaving the country with small arms or even nuclear waste from which a dirty bomb could be built. Jails in Washington, D.C., house Central American gang members whose empires spread from El Salvador to our nation's capital—and whose dominions are fed by cheap guns purchased in our own states.[2] Street corner stands in Thailand do a bustling business in pirated videos, cutting into Hollywood's bottom line. Corruption infuriates Tunisia's frustrated, unemployed youth, and once the spark catches, the entire Middle East is aflame.

Rule-of-law deficiencies in other countries—whether just across a border or separated by distant seas—have led the United States and a host of other countries and international institutions to try to promote improvements in the rule of law within foreign nations. These efforts are sometimes called "rule-of-law assistance." But the term is a misnomer, suggesting that aid is the only way to engage other countries in this sphere. Instead, this book will use the term "rule-of-law reform" to encapsulate the full range of methods used—from diplomacy and aid to membership requirements in NATO, the North Atlantic Treaty Organization—to help other countries improve their rule of law.

In 1998, scholar Thomas Carothers published what was then a path-breaking article on *The Rule of Law Revival*, recounting the possibilities, progress, and problems of the burgeoning field. Yet fourteen years later, little has changed. Like the movie *Groundhog Day*, rule-of-law practitioners and scholars keep waking up to the same predicaments, noting them in the same working papers, and then going back to do the same things. Despite its importance, the field of rule-of-law reform has remained in conceptual infancy, unaware of its own history, and as the saying goes, bound to repeat it.

Yet recently, change has begun poking through like crocuses in springtime. Just as Bill Murray's character finally broke out of his endless loop, rule-of-law practitioners and scholars have begun to make progress in altering the thinking and programs on the rule of law. This book describes this nascent second-generation movement of rule-of-law reform and provides further scholarship to support it. It focuses primarily on U.S. efforts. But work to promote the rule of law abroad is a global activity in which other countries and international bodies engage in a generally similar set of tactics. And many of the broad ways of thinking about rule-of-law challenges and strategies apply equally to a range of countries, aid agencies, and international bodies engaged in rule-of-law promotion, even though they have different histories and administrative arrangements. For that reason, this book offers examples from both U.S. and non-U.S. actors to showcase similar methods in what is a global field with widely shared characteristics. It also draws on examples from outside the United States to illustrate some strategic options that are less prevalent in America and more developed elsewhere. By contrasting what is known now with what has been done in the past, we can make headway on an important area of reform that has bedeviled the international community for years.

Why Are So Many Countries Trying to Spark Rule-of-Law Reform in Other Countries? And Should They Be Trying?

A respected éminence grise of the U.S. foreign policy establishment once told me, "No serious security threat can come from a country where you can't drink the water." His advice may have been well taken in the twentieth century, when it could have helped us avoid the war in Vietnam and a host of ill-conceived excursions into Latin America. But in today's globalized world, countries are not the only actors. The Twin Towers were brought down by people organized in places like Sudan,

Pakistan, Yemen, and Afghanistan—all areas where imbibing from a tap is ill-advised. Today's foreign policy leaders simply face a new reality.

For much of the nineteenth and twentieth centuries, a handful of countries controlled most of the space on the map. Through colonial relationships or paternalistic proclamations like the Monroe Doctrine, these "great powers" kept the peace and controlled the borders from yesteryear's Ceylon to Suriname. That world began to fall apart in the 1950s as decolonization got under way. For the next few decades, U.S. and Soviet proxy regimes and the legacy of colonial systems kept the lid on scores of new countries as they emerged headily into independence. Difficulty traveling between Soviet and Western spheres, and the costs of migrating from the Third World to anywhere else, kept most rule-of-law problems local and avoided major spillover.

But cracks began to show almost immediately. Communist movements in Latin America in the 1950s, Middle Eastern terrorism in the 1970s, and the drug trade in the 1980s impelled the United States to begin training police in scores of countries to head off threats before they reached U.S. borders. In the 1970s, publics in Europe and the United States became passionate about human rights and demanded that their governments promote such rights as part of their foreign policies. By the early 1990s, scholars of aid effectiveness started linking a country's ability to enforce contracts to its ability to develop economically—and the basket of issues that would become known as the rule of law quickly became important to the development community as well.

Meanwhile, the Soviet Union fell. The United States pulled back its State Department presence around the world when the Russians reduced their own footprint—and suddenly, dozens of states that had held together thanks to the centripetal forces of that great-power rivalry began to break apart. Organized crime began to rival—and at times fuse with—governments as the drug trade grew, communist states privatized, and the Balkan wars spawned large-scale smuggling operations. Al-Qaeda, nurtured by the Saudis and Americans to fight the Soviets in the 1980s, began to metastasize within a series of states too weak to root it out. Countries such as Yemen emerged from civil wars with weak governments and strong societies, in which the rulers often controlled little beyond the capital city. As had happened during the Middle Ages and the centuries surrounding the fall of Rome, blank spaces began to appear on the map, where the writ of government failed, and highwaymen ruled once again.

In most countries where the United States and others are working to improve the rule of law, governments are too weak to monopolize violence or are unable to create mechanisms of control for their police and judiciaries. People are preyed upon by criminals and traffic cops. Businesses cannot grow too large for fear of mafia-style shakedowns. Justice is sold to the highest bidder. In other countries, autocrats continue to rule. Individuals need to be protected against an overly strong, encroaching state—the same problem that led Enlightenment liberals and ancient Greeks to promote the idea of the rule of law in the first place. But even in apparently formidable autocracies, internal rot has often taken hold of public services. A shell of order and control held together by force hides a feeble state apparatus eaten away by corruption and ineffectiveness. And, whether the problem is terrorist recruitment, pirated movies, or corruption so serious that it breeds revolution, these rule of law failures often become the policy nightmares that bedevil countries in the developed world. Thus, the United States and other countries have decided that myriad difficulties can be solved only if they help catalyze rule-of-law improvements abroad.

The question that keeps arising is: How? Because the reality is clear: The United States, along with most others working in the field, is not very good at promoting the rule of law abroad. After decades of work and billions of dollars, the track record of successful rule of law promotion efforts is paltry. In his comprehensive study of police reform, David Bayley found that: "As a general proposition, American foreign assistance has not been shown to contribute significantly or consistently to reforming police institutions abroad, still less to the creation and stabilization of democratic governments."[3] A General Accounting Office (GAO)[4] study of U.S. democracy assistance to Latin America and the Caribbean from 1992 to 2002 found that after over a billion dollars spent, the programs had "a modest impact," while its study of U.S. rule of law programs in the former Soviet Union for the same period found "limited impact" with the newly independent states scoring "poorly in the development of the rule of law and, as a whole . . . growing worse over time."[5] Scholar Stephen Golub notes that "what stands out about rule of law assistance . . . is how difficult and often disappointing such work is." Even successfully implemented tactics, such as an improved constitution, are often undermined by later failures in implementation and enforcement.[6] Moreover, U.S. efforts fail in part for structural, systemic reasons that are difficult to change, such as convoluted systems of funding and accountability that have accreted over time within the diplomacy and aid apparatus, often as a result of congressional rulings. As one piece of legislation has been built atop another, and old programs have been repackaged to fit new needs, the United States has created a series of Rube Goldberg-style contraptions for promoting the rule of law abroad that would cause any strategist to despair.

It is easy to think, after reading such findings, that the United States should get out of the business of trying to affect the rule of law in other countries. But history flies in the face of a passive stance. The United States has been intervening in other countries' judicial, penal, and police systems for more than a century, since its early incursions into nearby Latin America at the end of the nineteenth century. What the past century has shown is that, whether good at it or not, and regardless of the ideology of any particular administration or Congress, the United States is going to continue trying. No matter the track record, Americans continue to rediscover that solutions to their security problems, hope for human rights improvements, and the bedrock of economic development require rule-of-law improvements in other countries. Meanwhile, nearly every interaction between the United States and another country affects that country's rule of law—even when it is an unintended consequence.[7] Decisions on whether to undertake military-to-military training missions, sign a free trade deal, or conclude a treaty all influence a country's rule of law. When the United States engages in typical diplomatic action, it may choose to shore up dictatorial leaders, and thus unconsciously promote inequality in the law—or it may reward democratic governments and be seen by local reformists as standing by their side. The United States allows corruption in procurement and inadvertently shows that national interest trumps the rule of law, or it cracks down, even at the cost of not getting money out the door as quickly, and sends a very different message. The United States has no choice but to have an impact—it can choose only whether to be conscious and deliberate about the kind of impact it has.

History shows that the United States is going to engage in rule-of-law reform abroad whether it has working institutions skilled at doing it or has to slap something together on the fly with the policy equivalent of duct tape. And since the United States is going to do it, it should make every effort to get better at it. Improving the track record requires the United States to understand its history, think about what it is actually trying to accomplish, and learn from its mistakes in order to strategically engage in a field that matters, in a way that has a chance of success.

What Is the Rule of Law?

What is this miracle cure that seems so important to so many foreign policy goals?[8] For decades, rule-of-law reform took place without much of a definition at all, based on the idea that "you'll know it when you see it." Instead of a definition, governments and donor agencies simply elucidated the institutional characteristics they thought were necessary for a country to have a modern legal order—and then set about helping a country build, or improve, each area.[9] For example, when seeking to quantify U.S. rule of law activity, the General Accounting Office explained:

> Throughout this report, we use the phrase "rule of law" to refer to U.S. assistance efforts to support legal, judicial, and law enforcement reform efforts undertaken by foreign governments. This term encompasses assistance to help reform legal systems (criminal, civil, administrative, and commercial laws and regulations) as well as judicial and law enforcement institutions (ministries of justice, courts, and police, including their organizations, procedures, and personnel).[10]

Scholar Stephen Golub provided an excellent taxonomy of this first-generation definitional style:

- A focus on state institutions, particularly judiciaries.
- This institutional focus is largely determined by the legal profession, as represented by a nation's jurists, top legal officials, and attorneys, and by foreign consultants and donor personnel.

- As a result, a tendency to define the legal system's problems and cures narrowly, in terms of courts, prosecutors, contracts, law reform, and other institutions and processes in which lawyers play central roles.
- Where civil society engagement occurs, it usually is as a means toward the end of state institutional development: consulting nongovernmental organizations (NGOs) on how to reform the (narrowly defined) legal system, and funding them as vehicles for advocating reform.
- A reliance on foreign expertise, initiative, and models, particularly those originating in industrialized societies.

These features translate into funding a distinct array of activities, including:

- constructing and repairing courthouses;
- purchasing furniture, computers, and other equipment and materials;
- drafting new laws and regulations;
- training judges, lawyers, and other legal personnel;
- establishing management and administration systems for judiciaries;
- supporting judicial and other training/management institutes;
- building up bar associations; and
- conducting international exchanges for judges, court administrators, and lawyers.[11]

With the addition of access to justice programs and anticorruption initiatives, this definition still rings true. However, it leads to multiple difficulties—not the least of which is the fact that each of these laws and institutions of justice could be reformed, without much rule of law resulting—or rule-of-law improvements could come about despite "outdated" institutions and laws.

Consider, for instance, a 2004 analysis of a rule-of-law reform program run by the European Union's aid agency. The EU's definition of its activities, like American first-generation rule of law assistance, emphasizes creating judiciaries that are "independent, well staffed and well trained, well paid, efficient, respected, and accessible to people. The self-governance of it should be real, including the non-interference of the other branches of power in the training of judges in a special Judicial Institute, the work of their self-governing bodies, and their appointment, as well as the work of courts."[12]

These desires seem very reasonable. Of course, a state based on rule of law should have independent judges, who are well paid, whose appointments are apolitical, and who decide cases efficiently. But when applied to the federal judiciary in the United States, nearly all of these assumptions are violated. The U.S. federal bench is, of course, independent—but the reality is that judicial appointments are heavily political, and many observers read political ideologies into the more controversial decisions. Judges are well compensated compared with the median U.S. income, but among their peer cohort, salaries are quite low—in fact, the judges often make less than their law clerks just out of school will receive upon their second year in a corporate law job. In some regions, such as on the United States Court of Appeals for the Ninth Circuit, case backlogs are immense, and justice is exceedingly slow in comparison to other appeals courts. It is fair to say that the Ninth Circuit would never be upheld as the Platonic ideal of the rule of law. However, presumably if the United States could help other countries get to the point of having courts similar to the largest appeals court in America, it would be satisfied by their rule-of-law development. If that is the case, then what is America looking for when it reforms legal institutions and rewrites laws? To put it bluntly, as the World Bank did, this definitional style "poses certain special problems for measurement, not the least of which [*is*] the lack of any consensus on what a well-functioning system looks like."[13]

Institution-based definitions have led rule-of-law reformers into multiple traps. First, by implicitly focusing on laws and institutions as the areas of a state in need of reform, institution-based definitions limit the conceptual space for treating rule-of-law reform as a cultural or political problem. Reform programs focus on flaws within the traditional institutions of justice—the courts, police, prisons, laws, and lawyers. However, many rule-of-law problems are located primarily not in these legal bodies, but in the broader relationships between the state and society. For instance, rule-of-law reforms in legal institutions may do nothing about corrupt parliamentarians, a president who telephones his desired decisions to nominally independent courts, or a violent, gang-ridden culture.

First-generation definitions that focus on laws and institutions have corralled practitioners into a manner of thinking that is structurally unable to consider *why* the judicial, penal, and law enforcement systems are in such a degraded state, who benefits, and what must be done to change the causal mechanisms that are implicated. It treats reform as apolitical, without considering that vested interests may make reforming one institution far more difficult than another. While some rule-of-law flaws may indeed result from a lack of training or resources, many problems that appear to be funding-based are at root actually political decisions about which agencies to fund, and which to starve. World Bank rule-of-law programs in Peru, for instance, unraveled because all the institutional reform in the world could not overcome the desire of the government *not* to be governed by the rule of law.[14]

Along these lines, the standard first-generation package of rule-of-law reforms is far too circumscribed to address the real problems faced by transitioning countries, particularly those recovering from war, such as many African states. In countries with weak states and strong non-state actors such as insurgencies or organized crime, the impact of rewriting laws, creating a more efficient and less corrupt court system, or even providing the police with new equipment is likely to be rather negligible when few cases ever make it to court. The objective must be larger: to create or reinstate citizens' faith in the state as a problem-solving mechanism rather than vigilante justice. This may entail institutional reform, of course—but sights must be set more broadly, and articulated to the public in a bigger way, to create the needed buy-in.

In other cases, legal institutions may be a poor means to have an impact on problems that are actually societal or cultural. For instance, the United States has tried for years to help Albania reduce its corruption. There is no shortage of political causes for such corruption, but a study by a U.S. Agency for International Development (USAID) contractor also uncovered profound cultural causes. A ten-city survey found that more than two-thirds of Albanians felt that "a student who gives his teacher a gift in the hope of receiving a better grade" is either not corrupt or is justified, while the same share condemned a flower seller for corruption for raising prices during the holidays—and nearly half thought such a flower seller deserved punishment.[15] Clearly, the capitalist international community has a different notion of corruption than Albanians socialized under decades of communism. These cultural ideals will not simply be swept aside by institutional modifications that are up against far deeper cultural values.

Second, an institutional focus tends to narrow the methods the United States uses to improve the rule of law in other countries. By defining the rule of law as institutions, the United States implicitly limits its tool kit for catalyzing change. The most straightforward way to reform institutions appears to be to provide funding and technical advice to institutions, so rule-of-law reform is seen as the province of development practitioners. This downplays other means of leverage. For instance, politicians and diplomats might use major speeches and other diplomatic carrots and sticks to affect the incentives of local politicians—as when Vice President Joe Biden spoke publicly in Moscow urging Russia's leaders to reduce corruption.[16] Governments can also use the lure of belonging to international institutions with rule-of-law membership requirements to shape incentives and socialize professional communities in other countries—as the World Trade Organization process might be able to do. In fact, for the European Union, membership in the EU is its main method of catalyzing change. Such membership requirements—to NATO, the WTO, and other international bodies in which the United States has a say—need to be included in U.S. thinking about how to leverage change, too. While most rule-of-law reform writings to date focus on the effects of American money and technical assistance, these diplomatic and institutional tools are often key means to improve the rule of law in other countries.

Third, from an implementation standpoint, institution-based definitions lead too easily to institution-modeling, an approach that fails the basic test of strategy: matching resources to ends. In too many countries, reformers approach program creation by looking at each legal institution or law, comparing it to its Western counterpart, and then trying to create "improvements" until they match. Such a "strategy" does not consider the political and cultural pressures that deform institutions, as already discussed. Nor does it take into account available domestic resources, such as internal reformers already working in an area, or local demand for reform that may make a field more susceptible to outside intervention. And it lacks a sense of punctuated time, treating all eras alike, rather than recognizing that there are windows of opportunity and moments of political and social change in which reform is more likely to take root.

Finally, institution-based definitions make it difficult to distinguish between institutional reforms necessary for building the rule of law and changes to legal institutions for other purposes—that is, preferring one bankruptcy law over another simply because the former is more similar to U.S. statutes, despite a French or Germanic system being equally valid for a state based on rule of law. This problem may seem minor—but, in fact, it has resulted in serious headaches for reforming countries. Laws that are changed and rechanged a few years later undermine legal certainty—one of the key goals of rule-of-law reform. The drafting process takes up the time of the often scarce legal talent in a given country. The legal practitioners of a reforming country must arbitrate between donor arguments that ultimately do not matter for the establishment of the rule of law. And the fights between various donors over different laws or institutional arrangements—when any might work for a rule of law state—lead to cynicism on the part of the reforming country, confusion among legal professionals, and wasted effort on behalf of everyone involved.

Moving to an Ends-Based Definition

Thanks to years of criticism from many scholars, a second-generation of rule-of-law reform has been emerging that improves greatly on first-generation efforts. This new style of reform begins with another style of definition—one long favored by scholars and political philosophers who focus on the end goals the rule of law serves within a state. Such a definition takes up the conversation that began with the ancient Greeks, when the concept of the rule of law was coined. The Greeks used the rule of law to describe a state in which government power was not arbitrarily exercised but was reined in as governments were forced to function through pre-written rules that applied equally to government and governed. Considering that "passion perverts the minds of rulers, even if they are the best of men," Aristotle and other ancient Greeks thought it was better for kings to rule according to law rather than through personal discretion.[17]

This style of definition was put on hold, along with the very ideal of the rule of law, during the ensuing centuries of divinely inspired monarchical rule. It returned to prominence during the Enlightenment, when making the ruler bow to law and infusing that law with the normative content of rights became a paramount idea in liberal thought.[18] A. V. Dicey, who attempted the first modern definition of the rule of law a century ago, defined it as three "kindred concepts," or ends, that a rule-of-law state should uphold: a government limited by law; equality under the law for all citizens; and the protection of human and civil rights.[19] Fifty years later, Friedrich Hayek traced the history of the rule of law and teased out another end he and his followers believed was previously implicit: predictable and efficient justice.[20] In scholar Judith Shklar's writing (conceived in the shadow of the Holocaust), the goal of the liberal state was to protect the weak from cruelty. For Shklar and other scholars such as Fareed Zakaria, protection from violence is a core goal of a liberal state based on the rule of law.[21]

What unites these thinkers is a definitional style that looks at the ends the rule of law is meant to serve within a country. Second-generation rule-of-law reform starts with such an ends-based approach, which allows reformers to focus on the goals that led them to undertake rule-of-law reform in the first place. Officials in the United States, for instance, do not stay up late worrying about how effective courts are in Afghanistan for the sheer sake of getting case backlogs in Kandahar to match those in Kentucky—they are concerned because the Taliban is regaining power by delivering effective justice that the population wants. An ends-based definition helps reformers consider this need for society to have efficient, effective justice delivery—rather than zeroing in on "court reform," which could easily end up funding the repair of a few buildings in Kabul, a meaningless exercise to the 70 percent of Afghan society that lives in rural areas.

An ends-based definition is no silver bullet. It has its own pitfalls, particularly the reality that such definitions are more work to actualize than a rote list of institutions that need reforming. Yet an ends-based way of conceiving of the rule of law does help practitioners avoid some of the traps that institution-based definitions fall into. Its very structure encourages broad thinking about the cultural and political roots of rule-of-law failures. It implicitly pushes reformers to look at the actual needs of societies, rather than apply cookie-cutter programs. It leans against technocratic thinking. And it easily clarifies the problem when multiple rule-of-law reforms will achieve an end equally well and are simply being fought over for parochial reasons.

The main problem with an ends-based definition is which ends to choose—and which to prioritize when they come into conflict. The rule of law has never had a fixed set of end goals; new reasons are added and removed depending on the era and the purposes of the proponent. Legal formalists, for instance, deny that human rights are required for the rule of law, while substantivist theorists claim that rights are central to the concept. The legal jurisprudential literature rarely discusses law and order as an element of the rule of law, while political thinkers from Locke to Shklar believe security from violence is central—and security remains key to U.S. engagement in rule-of-law reform.[22] For the United States and other international actors to begin using this second-generation method of rule-of-law definition, they will have to pick among competing sets of ends. Yet this need to choose among competing definitions should not be an insurmountable obstacle. A program of the Organization for Economic Cooperation and Development (OECD) and EU known as SIGMA, for Support for Improvement in Governance and Management, is already working toward such a definition and assessment style, as are the dozens of organizations that have banded together to create a World Justice Project Rule of Law Index. These assessments are convening around a set of ends that, though phrased differently, often separated in slightly different ways, and occasionally adding or removing an element or two, are generally agreed upon as creating the idea of a rule-of-law–based state:

- Governments are subject to laws and must follow pre-established and legally accepted procedures to create new laws.
- Citizens are equal before the law.
- Judicial and governmental decisions are regularized: They are not subject to the whims of individuals, or the influence of corruption.

- All citizens have access to effective and efficient dispute-solving mechanisms, regardless of their financial means.
- Human rights are protected by law and its implementation.
- Law and order are prevalent.

When these ends are stated clearly, it becomes obvious that the rule of law is not at all about having a particular set of institutions that conform to a particular, modern Western style. After all, the concept of a government limited by law was entrenched in England by the 1600s, long before the existence of modern rule-of-law reform activities such as the computerization of courts. Countries had honest government servants before the idea of ombudsmen was conceived. Citizens may be equal before the law in countries that have creditor-focused bankruptcy laws and in those that favor debtors. People can find fair and efficient adjudication of their disputes in Internet-equipped court buildings with heavy oak paneling, and from trusted village elders passing judgments deemed acceptable by the townspeople while sitting in the shade of a large tree.

Instead, this series of ends suggests that the rule of law is best seen as a relationship between a state and its society. The rule of law limits and defines the power of government, so that all are treated equally before the law, all are given the same chance for justice, all can expect non-arbitrary, honest, fair decisionmaking. And it allows the government to limit the actions of various members of society, so that minorities are protected from the majority, the vicious cannot overpower and prey on the innocent, and human rights are respected. In other words, as economic reform practitioner Wade Channell explained, the rule of law is not about law per se—it's about rule.[23]

Thus, at its root, the rule of law is defined by the checks and balances among structures of power within a country and the cultural norms and habits that define how public servants—from police to court clerks to politicians—treat citizens, how they are treated by those they serve, and how citizens act toward one another and society as a whole. Power and culture, not laws and institutions, form the roots of a rule-of-law state. That is the fundamental insight of second-generation rule of law reformers.

When the power structures and cultural norms are supportive, a country's laws and institutions will follow. When the norms and power structures don't support the rule of law, reforming laws and institutions can become like the cargo cult practice of building landing pads in the hopes of attracting airplanes with supplies that took hold among South Pacific islanders during World War II—cause and effect are switched.[24]

This second-generation movement is not yet united. For decades, practitioners have grumbled about issues of politics and culture over drinks after work—now, these criticisms have moved into agencies' more official realms. As I conducted interviews from Albania to Indonesia, I found practitioners on the ground observing problems, innovating toward solutions, and hitting on common methods—often without talking to one another or bothering to commit their thoughts to paper. Bureaucrats in the OECD, EU, European aid agencies, and USAID grope toward a common language to articulate new strategies. While culture has not yet been mainstreamed as an element of analysis, there is a clear, broad recognition within the community of aid givers that politics and power play a central role in development, and this work is beginning to seep into the rule-of-law field. For instance, the World Bank has established a Political Economy Community of Practice with more than 200 practitioners working to mainstream political thinking into development efforts and has discussed the importance of politics and power in a number of annual World Development Reports and strategy documents.[25] The authors of these reports have begun making statements such as: "Resource allocation is about choice and, as such, is fundamentally political" and "Projects are not likely to be successful when they fail to take fully into account the complex political and institutional realities on the ground—and thus the real incentives for implementation."[26]

The OECD and numerous European aid agencies have been moving over the past decade toward an understanding of politics as a driver of development change; Sweden's aid agency, for instance, has tied its conception of poverty to power since 2002; the Netherlands has a Strategic Governance and Corruption Analysis it uses to consider development programs; and the Norwegians have a similar political economy analysis (to which they add a special focus on legitimacy).[27] The UK aid agency Department for International Development began its "Drivers of Change" work in the early 2000s to look at the role of power in development, and DFID's 2006 and 2009 White Papers explicitly state that politics and power are key to development problems. Practitioners and scholars working in areas of development outside the rule-of-law field—from the UK-based development practitioner Sue Unsworth, to the World Bank–led movement for Problem-Driven Governance and Political Economy Analysis—are beginning to codify similar strategies.[28] This book is an effort to unite these various strands, explain their collective strategy in the context of historical efforts at rule-of-law reform, and describe why pushing politics and social norms to the forefront of rule-of-law efforts makes sense.

What Are We Actually Doing—and What Should Change?

For the past few decades, the first-generation rule-of-law reform tool kit has been remarkably stable. A large buffet of options is available, but the same menu is offered in every country in the world. First-generation rule-of-law reform programs generally work on:

1. Laws—Writing new commercial codes, adding human rights laws, altering or writing new constitutions.
2. Police—Providing equipment and more modern facilities. Computerization. Training (when conducted by the United States, generally in short, three- to four-week pre-set courses) on everything from handling drug-detecting dogs to human rights. Occasional structural reform.
3. Courts—Brick-and-mortar building projects. Computerization. Publishing laws. Judicial training programs and continuing education for judges.
4. Lawyers—Building, equipping, and creating curricula for law schools. Organizing bar associations.
5. Prisons—Generally, brick-and-mortar building projects to reduce crowding.
6. "Access to Justice"—Legal aid programs. Alternative dispute resolution programs that work outside traditional courts. The creation of specialized courts such as small claims courts.

7. Anticorruption—Training programs. Creating anticorruption agencies and ombudsmen. Laws to target corruption, such as "sunshine" laws and freedom of information laws.
8. Scattered efforts across other rule-of-law institutions, along the lines of increasing the number of notaries and building witness protection programs.

No one can fault any program on this list. The problem lies less in what the United States and other countries are doing than in the lack of strategic thought behind the deployment of any of these options. The first five are institutions and laws that should be made "better"—with no clear description, as noted earlier, as to what constitutes "better," or why they were not better in the first place. Access to justice and anticorruption programs do focus on ends—but having become standardized, they tend to be used on the ground with little thought to local realities, and little strategy for how to actually create change. Despite all the literature in the development community suggesting that moving to a more political, power-driven analysis of problems is necessary, actual programming and implementation has changed little in the last decade at a corporate level and has altered only moderately at the country level.[29]

Efforts to create change in these eight arenas generally use just two methods to leverage reform. The vast majority work through a method commonly known as "top-down reform": providing funds and technical assistance directly to foreign governments to amend rule of law institutions and laws. The entire practitioner field of rule-of-law reform is based largely around this top-down method of creating change. Private contractors run seminars on intellectual property laws in the new magistrates' schools that foreign donors help to fund. European lawyers descend on crumbling Ministries of Justice, armed with drafts of bankruptcy laws. U.S. judges fly to Rwanda for a week to give seminars on judicial independence.[30]

Some savvy practitioners began to augment these top-down development efforts with more indirect, bottom-up reform programs that support local civil society organizations advocating for citizens' access to justice, curbing corruption, or building constituencies for the rule of law.[31] Sometimes a bottom-up reform is undertaken at one remove, funding a U.S. or international NGO and giving it free rein to work with local civil society. These two methods of top-down and bottom-up reform are the most studied methods of intervention, and they form the methodology of most first-generation reform programs. But they are not the totality of options to improve the rule of law in other countries.

Two other methods that can be used to spur rule-of-law improvements in other societies include diplomatic means and what I will call "enmeshment." As U.S. Secretary of State Madeleine Albright explained in 2000, "The U.S. Government has long had a number of programs to develop [the rule of law's] various aspects in particular countries," but these development programs were "in addition to our diplomatic efforts to urge governments to respect and promote the rule of law."[32] Many rule-of-law building activities depend not on dollars spent on training and computers, but on these "diplomatic efforts," including positive and negative conditionality and rhetoric. For instance, when a country is egregious in its denial of the rule of law, the United States may use economic sanctions and other carrots and sticks to generate improvements. More often, it uses rhetoric: The *Washington Post*, for example, reported that President George W. Bush "began raising issues of the rule of law more prominently in telephone conversations with Putin late last fall after the arrest of Mikhail Khodorkovsky, Russia's richest man."[33]

Finally, the United States frequently works through exchange programs to affect the norms and cultures of other countries. Programs ranging from the International Military Education and Training (IMET) program to exchanges that bring foreign judges to meet with their U.S. counterparts are seen as ways to build knowledge and enrich cultural understanding of the rule of law in target countries. Very occasionally, the United States uses a stronger form of enmeshment to tie a country into law-based international regimes such as the WTO or NATO. And, of course, other international actors, such as the EU, use membership conditionality to an even greater extent. Through membership conditionality, socialization, and ongoing legal and structural intertwining, these international entities have the power to deeply affect the rule of law within another country.

What should diplomacy, membership conditionality, and top-down or bottom-up reform be targeting to change? After all, one of the problems of an ends-based definition is coming up with a suitable set of activities.

A first-generation reformer tasked with updating a country's laws can go about it with little additional thought. A second-generation reformer trying to catalyze change that will make a government limited by law has a much harder conceptual task. That is no reason, however, to choose the simpler model of definition (which is simply the programmatic equivalent of looking for your keys under the streetlight instead of where you might have misplaced them). Instead of a set of scattered programs that are focused around various institutions—immediately biasing toward institutional-modeling style reforms—it makes sense to look at rule-of-law reform as working to change four major parts of society: laws (including regulations and constitutions); institutions; power structures; and social/cultural norms (professional and popular). All rule-of-law work focuses on these four objects of change. Yet while most energy and intellectual effort for first-generation reform was placed on the first two—laws and institutions—second-generation reformers focus on the role of power structures and culture, and they push for reforms in laws and institutions only as a means to changing power and society.

At its heart, the rule of law is about the structure by which the government and governed determine the rules of society and hold each other accountable to those rules.[34] Therefore, work to reform the power structure within other countries focuses on building the checks and balances on power that form the bedrock of a rule-of-law state. Some of these power centers are "vertical"—they check government from below, such as through organized groups of concerned citizens, religious institutions, and other areas of legitimacy within society. Other power centers are "horizontal"—they might provide checks and balances between and within government agencies, such as internal investigative units among police, or the division of powers between an independent judiciary and other parts of government. Anticorruption programs have made a first stab in this direction, but without much conceptual framework to help guide their efforts.

Because only a despotic state can enforce all of its rules if they are not broadly accepted, the rule of law also requires a high degree of legitimacy to be effective. That depends on both citizen participation in making the laws and a culture that upholds the laws they have agreed to. Deepening a culture of lawfulness affects the norms that guide relationships between the state and society, and between various parts of the citizenry. The United States can use a host of different methods to build awareness among citizens of their rights, to build cultures that fight corruption, and to augment the honor and professional ethics of rule of law professionals.

While changing power structures and norms may require reforming laws and institutions, there is a fundamental difference from traditional rule of law reform efforts focused on institutional change as the end goal. Rather than reforming laws to make them more "modern" or tweaking institutional arrangements to make them appear similar to those in the West, reformers looking at power structures and cultural norms have clear goals that transparently serve rule-of-law ends. So, for instance, a first-generation contractor might work with local educators to develop a curriculum for a magistrates' school to make it look like a Western judicial curriculum. A second-generation contractor would work to create a curriculum that is focused on helping judges see their role as an independent check on the power of parliament and the president or prime minister, giving them the skills to be both trained judges and upholders of a more balanced power structure.

Together, these objects and methods of reform create a set of sixteen tactics that provide a broader palette for rule-of-law reformers to use. These tactics are described in depth in chapter 7, but graphically, they are represented in table 1.1.

Who Is Carrying Out Rule of Law Reform?

One of the fundamental reasons for U.S. difficulty in reforming the rule of law abroad lies in how these programs are structured at home. For a supposedly strategic goal, U.S. efforts are anything but strategic. Programs and policies have grown organically from multiple roots over a half-century, a history described in depth in the next chapter. The consequence of this organic growth is that development aid allocated to rule-of-law promotion flows through the traditional aid agency, USAID, as well as the Department of Justice, the State Department's Bureau of International Narcotics and Law Enforcement Affairs, and dozens of other entities. In fact, at least 7 Cabinet-level departments and 28

TABLE 1.1	TACTICS FOR RULE-OF-LAW REFORM			
METHODS OF CHANGE	**Top-Down** (Funding & technical assistance to rule-of-law institutions)	**Bottom-Up** (Funding & technical assistance to civil society)	**Diplomacy** (Pressure to force the government to institute change)	**Enmeshment** (Strong: Membership in international organizations; Weak: Socializing effects of exchange programs)
OBJECTS FOR REFORM	Power Structure			
	Culture			
	Institutions			
	Laws			

agencies, bureaus, and offices are involved in rule of law reform, from the Department of Defense to the Department of the Treasury.[35]

The funds spent on such reform efforts are modest in terms of the U.S. budget—but often quite significant within the targeted countries. Finding exact numbers is nearly impossible: "Rule-of-law reform" falls under many agencies, which pass money on to still other agencies, while assistance may be labeled anything from "democracy development" to "civil society reform." However, to provide a sense of scale: In the first decade after the Cold War, the United States spent more than $1 billion on rule-of-law promotion. By 2004, the United States was spending about that sum on rule-of-law reform each year.[36]

This rule-of-law promotion is carried out on multiple fronts. Government agencies undertake a small amount of direct work on the ground. And a portion of U.S. funding for rule-of-law work is provided through general funding for international organizations such as the United Nations (UN), OECD, and the World Bank. But most of this funding is allocated from the 35 aforementioned agencies, bureaus, and offices to an even greater number of nonprofit and for-profit contractors, as well as independent nongovernmental organizations such as the National Democratic Institute and American Bar Association that receive some government-funded grants.[37] The importance of third-party contractors and grantees to rule-of-law reform cannot be overstated—for an endeavor that the United States has said is crucial to its core foreign policy goals, nearly all work on the ground is carried out by private entities.

The multiplicity of governmental, intergovernmental, and nongovernmental conduits does provide flexibility—and some of this is important. In countries where U.S. activity, particularly diplomacy or aid funding, is curtailed by countervailing strategic interests, the existence of entities that can act independently from official U.S. policy provides important tactical flexibility. For instance, although the United States government officially supported Suharto's autocracy for many years, and all USAID projects had to be approved by the government, groups such as the Asia Foundation could work with civil society despite opposition from the Indonesian government.[38]

However, some of the overlap is simply a historical holdover, and the myriad agencies, funding lines, and contractors throw any hope of strategy to the wind. Decisionmaking over rule-of-law programs and goals is divided among the government agencies mentioned and their subsections. The Democracy and Governance office of USAID oversees some rule-of-law matters but functions separately from USAID's Economic Growth and Trade office, which deals with commercial law—and both of them are independent of the Office of Transition Initiatives, which works in countries immediately following conflict. Meanwhile, the Bureau of International Narcotics and Law Enforcement Affairs (INL) within the State Department (the main conduit for rule-of-law funding in that agency) acts independently from all of these USAID entities, as well as from the projected Bureau of Conflict and Stabilization Operations (CSO) that the State Department's 2010 Quadrennial Diplomacy and Development Review suggests should handle civilian deployments to unstable states where rule-of-law reform is likely to be needed. It also makes decisions separately from the Department of Justice, even though the latter derives much of its rule of law budget from INL. Regional bureaus within the State Department draw from different pots of money for rule-of-law reforms as well, with the exception of the Eastern European region, where a single entity in the State Department is in charge of allocating all rule-of-law funding for that area.[39] The Department of Defense is not supposed to be involved in most rule of law reform—except for the many congressional exceptions that have been carved out for DoD activities that *do* involve rule-of-law efforts. These loopholes include some of America's largest police training programs in Iraq and Afghanistan. The number of actors involved and their relative autonomy makes strategic planning, even within a single country, impossible; every agency, NGO, and contractor determines its own strategy. The idea of coordination among all of these bodies is risible.

And that is only development aid. But as we've already discussed, aid is one of many methods for spurring other countries to improve their rule of law. Diplomacy is another method—yet diplomatic decisionmaking often takes place on a separate plane from funding, among more politically powerful officials from the State Department, Treasury Department, and Justice Department (DOJ), as well as within the National Security Council, White House, and Congress. The State Department has a country strategy, which may or may not be accepted by the local embassy and USAID.[40] Other U.S. government agencies may have separate plans for a country and may be only loosely guided by the State Department—which is only now taking some degree of coordination responsibility for the other U.S. government personnel, such as the ICITAP (International Criminal Investigative Training Assistance Program) agents and DOJ leads in charge of police training who work out of a typical embassy. Personal relationships and the relative power of different agencies determine whether the State Department is coordinated with or can block another agency's program. Often each simply continues along parallel tracks. The same diffusion of power, responsibility, and strategy holds true for policymaking toward other methods of catalyzing rule-of-law reform—such as the decision to support another country's bid for NATO or the WTO, whose membership requirements and procedures affect member countries' internal rule-of-law structures. In the case of such membership bids, even more agencies may be involved—such as the Commerce Department or Treasury Department, as well as the Defense Department and the National Security Council.

Finally, the Department of Defense often makes its decisions on base location and other policies with little thought to the country's internal rule-of-law structures. That sounds just fine—after all, its basing or overflight decisions may rightly have little to do with a country's support for the rule of law and should instead be based on supply lines, logistics, and geopolitics. However, things can look different from a reforming country's perspective. Hypothetically, say that the United States is providing tens of millions of dollars in aid to improve the rule of law in Country X and that visiting congressional delegations are regularly lecturing the country's government on human rights abuses. Yet to fight a nearby war, the Department of Defense decides to open up a major transit station in the country, with billions of dollars in construction, many jobs, and at least a medium-term contract with the government in power for the duration of the war. As Country X's government might see it, tens of millions in rule-of-law aid, with myriad reporting requirements and strings attached, has suddenly been eclipsed by billions in construction contracts with far less oversight. Which arm of the U.S. government seems most powerful to Country X—and how seriously are they going to take the rule-of-law reform rhetoric emanating from Washington?

In other words, the U.S. system is so diffuse, and power is so divided, that the government cannot possibly choose one path to focus its efforts. Ideally, while multiple entities might be uncoordinated or even unaware of one another's existence, they would all be working toward the same endpoint: strong, stable, democratic, rule-of-law–based countries. But as discussed in the next chapter, not all the goals of rule-of-law reform go together. Often, U.S. implementers spend as much time battling with other U.S. agencies working at cross-purposes as they do fighting local domestic forces arrayed against rule-of-law reform.

This lack of strategy affects a stunning number of countries. In the first decade after the Cold War, the United States undertook rule-of-law reform programs in 184 countries.[41] In 2003 alone, it provided some form of police assistance to more than 150 countries—and that does not even count other rule-of-law reform programs.[42] There being fewer than 200 countries in the world, the United States has basically undertaken some form of rule-of-law reform in nearly every country outside of Western Europe.

Moreover, the United States and its 35 agencies are not the only actors in the field—it is one of multiple countries and international institutions that are pushing some version of rule-of-law reform abroad. As of 2010, the United Nations was conducting rule of law programming in more than 125 countries—up from 110 just two years earlier. Its inventory of rule-of-law initiatives, conducted because even the United Nations did not know all it was doing, found that the United Nations, like the United States, frequently had multiple arms working in the same country. In 2010, 35 countries (up from 24 in 2008) had five or more United Nations entities engaged in rule-of-law work within their borders, and in an additional 60 countries, three or more UN actors were conducting rule-of-law work.[43] As with the United States, the work performed by the United Nations spans a variety of fields—from deploying nearly 17,000 UN police officers (an increase of more than 100 percent in just two years) to assisting with constitution drafting. Since 2006, the United Nations has tried to improve its internal coordination of activities by creating a Rule of Law Coordination and Resource Group. But as it admitted in 2008, "Meaningful learning about the effectiveness of assistance has not kept pace with the amount of rule of law activity on the ground."[44]

The World Bank, along with other international development banks, is deeply engaged in rule-of-law activities. According to David Trubek, the World Bank spent $2.9 billion on 330 rule-of-law programs from 1990 to 2004. And such work has not slowed; in fiscal 2008, the World Bank spent $304 million on justice sector activities and claimed a portfolio of 2,500 projects.[45] Moreover, as with the United Nations and the United States, rule-of-law reform is not centralized within the World Bank. As it reports, its rule of law activities "take many operational forms and span all Bank operational instruments, including loans or credits, grants, technical assistance, and research. They also span a number of the Bank's operational divisions and units, since justice reform is a cross-cutting theme that involves issues of governance, anticorruption efforts, financial sector reform, private sector development, urban development, rural development, community-driven development, and land policy reform."[46] In other words, the World Bank's rule of law programming faces strategic challenges similar to those of the United States and the United Nations.

The EU and the OECD are also highly active in rule-of-law programming, with the EU having worked since the mid-1990s to improve the rule of law in its near abroad in order to prepare candidate states for accession to the Union. Both the EU and OECD have rule-of-law membership requirements as well as requirements for legal change among countries that wish to join their organizations. These requirements serve as diplomatic incentive-setting mechanisms through which the EU and OECD promote the rule of law—assisted by foreign aid and technical assistance programs that help countries seeking membership to make the rule-of-law transition. Their work on the rule of law in their near abroad has since spread to other EU aid and diplomatic activities in countries from the Middle East to Asia, with varying degrees of focus and success. Of the two organizations the EU has a far more centralized system of rule-of-law strategy—and its ability to think strategically shines through well-planned strategic documents. But translating thoughtful strategy into implementation has been more difficult. The EU's frustration with its mixed track record in rule of law and other governance reform led it to create, along with the OECD, the SIGMA think tank to support candidate countries, potential candidates, and other neighboring states in governance reform.

All of these multinational bodies are joined by individual countries that, like the United States, have decided that assisting the development of the rule of law in other countries is worth their taxpayer money. A bevy of European countries, from Sweden to Italy, are engaged in rule-of-law promotion, as is the United Kingdom, Australia, Canada, and Japan. Each of these countries brings its own experience, history, and legal system to the effort. Japan, for instance, started providing aid toward rule-of-law improvements in 1996 with a program in Vietnam and has since expanded that work throughout Asia, from Timor-Leste to Uzbekistan.[47] Japan has incorporated legal innovations from a number of mostly Western states since the Meiji Restoration of the late nineteenth century and sees its experience as providing useful lessons that can be exported to other countries undertaking similar transitions today. The United Kingdom does not break down its spending by "rule of law," but its "Governance and Civil Society" spending category has been either the largest or second largest area for foreign aid spending since 2005.[48] Like the United States, United Nations, World Bank, and other rule-of-law reformers, the United Kingdom engages in a wide range of rule-of-law activities in other countries. Yet insofar as these touch on laws or legal institutions, many UK practitioners will be unthinkingly drawing on their own common law system, which, like that of the United States, is best known in countries formerly colonized by the United Kingdom—and quite different from the systems of France and Germany, whose lawyers and aid practitioners are, similarly, carrying their own home experiences into the field. Moreover, each country—and some of the international entities such as the EU—share with the United States a broad range of methods for rule-of-law promotion beyond aid. The EU and OECD use membership requirements, as do NATO and the WTO. Individual countries may make diplomatic overtures to affect the rule of law. The World Bank and other development banks may use aid conditionality—their form of diplomacy. Meanwhile, each of these efforts may be contradictory. Many Eastern European countries spent part of the early 2000s caught between the World Bank's insistence that they reduce the size of their governments and the EU's requirements that their civil service reform beef up the number of government servants on the civil service, rather than political, payroll. Pity the poor country that is wracked by the well-meaning, uncoordinated, overlapping, overwhelming, contradictory efforts of many of these entities at once, as is most often the case.

A New Problem, and the Need for Tools that Work Together

One of the reasons that so many countries and international entities are having such difficulty organizing their rule-of-law strategy is that building the rule of law in other countries requires foreign policy practitioners and diplomats to work on an entirely new playing field. For most of the twentieth century, governments used carrots and sticks, rhetoric, and other elements of power to influence the decisionmakers of other countries. And for most of the twentieth century, influencing decisions was enough to ensure their implementation. When Ronald Reagan implored Mikhail Gorbachev to "tear down this wall," he felt no need to offer subsidized sledgehammers and cranes. John F. Kennedy didn't give Nikita Khrushchev technical assistance to help the Soviets remove their nuclear weapons from Cuba. Once other countries decided to act, their ability to do so was assumed.

But building the rule of law in weak states is one of a new set of foreign policy problems—such as fighting communicable disease, reducing climate change, or combating terrorism—where foreign policy must be used to affect domestic issues in other countries. In this new realm of activity, which some have taken to calling "formestic," the United States must get other governments not only to change their domestic policies, but also to implement those policies effectively. Unlike past issues of international relations, they require foreign countries to have the political willpower to change their policies and domestic structures with the capacity to implement that change. In weak states, getting a country to say it wants to do something, and making sure that it can, are two entirely separate endeavors.

The rule of law thus crosses typical boundaries between traditional diplomatic action to influence governmental decisionmakers, and development efforts to augment countries' infrastructure and technical capabilities. Yet while diplomacy and military relations have long been considered "high politics" in the United States, development and economic issues have been relegated to "low politics"—for do-gooding NGOs and aid agencies that fight for scraps of funding from Congress. Diplomats and politicians have looked at the long, slow, often unsuccessful work of development with indifference at best, disdain at worst. Meanwhile, foreign policy leaders viewed the rapid, but just as frequently unsuccessful, work of diplomacy as having greater importance.

Thus, in first-generation rule-of-law promotion, diplomatic pressure would work on one track, development assistance on another—with the two often uncoordinated, often speaking different languages, and certainly harboring different philosophies of change.[49] First-generation reformers treated the rule of law like a traditional development program to build a road or create a modern banking structure. Technocratic programs provided aid and technical assistance to create rule-of-law infrastructure. Development professionals and lawyers built courthouses, trained judges and lawyers, and printed laws, assuming that by making institutions of justice in other countries look like those in the United States, they could bring about the rule of law. Meanwhile, U.S. politicians and diplomats would exert pressure for particular human rights activists or make some rhetorical statements on the need to quell corruption. But for the most part, decisions of high politics—such as a presidential visit, a state dinner, U.S. military base placement, and other such diplomatic carrots—were made with no reference to a country's success in rule-of-law reform. Rather than harnessing the power each field could provide, early rule of law reforms disadvantaged both. If development and diplomacy were viewed as sound waves, they too often canceled each other out.

This tendency is one reason for the repeated setbacks in first-generation rule-of-law reform. Because unlike building a school or establishing a microfinance program, the rule of law is intimately connected with the power balance *within* states. Building the rule of law in countries emerging from autocratic, nepotistic, kleptocratic, and highly centralized political systems requires fundamental political change that interferes with the most intimate workings of power. Persuading other governments to improve their rule of law is no small request. It means asking heads of government to give up their control over the judiciary, to prosecute international criminals who may be quite popular at home, to convince parliamentarians to pass laws limiting cronyism that benefits themselves. Building the rule of law is in large part about limiting the power of the state, but, paradoxically, governments themselves must take the measures necessary for these major changes. Significant incentive shifts, shaped in part by outside pressure and by the creation of other pressure groups within another country, are essential if politicians are to relinquish this degree of personal power. To shape the contours of decisionmaking for those in other governments, diplomacy—the main tool to alter incentives within other states—may be required. Diplomacy may not always help achieve rule-of-law goals—the United States has many valid interests in other countries, and rule of law will not always be the priority—but it cannot undermine them. Certainly, diplomats cannot undermine rule-of-law reform and then blame development professionals for their lack of success. The United States can hardly improve the rule of law in other countries if its diplomats consider these issues too small-scale to bother with.

Meanwhile, U.S. development agencies must think far more politically to undertake successful rule-of-law reform. Rule-of-law reform affects the most macro levels of power. But even seemingly minor reforms, such as computerizing courts, reduce judges' abilities to collect bribes for various aspects of case management. Passing commercial bankruptcy laws may unwittingly favor some well-connected businesses over others. Development professionals must be trained to consider the political changes within countries and use external and internal means of pressure to bolster their own programs. Yet development professionals are not given the skills or tools to think and act like politicians. Instead, long-term planning, and multiyear funding cycles—as well as earmarks and extensive oversight from Congress—make it almost impossible for development aid to react to political windows of opportunity. Much of the new momentum toward political economy in donor agencies is rhetorical, with superficial generalities taking the place of real program change. For second-generation rule-of-law reform to succeed, aid agencies need to be empowered to make more decisions with less oversight, to have funds that can respond to windows of opportunity, and to think more like politicians and advocacy institutions than like apolitical technocrats.

The new Quadrennial Diplomacy and Development Review could be a significant step in the right direction for meeting these challenges head-on. To succeed, it will need to be implemented, requiring cultural change and power shifts within the United States and the 35 government entities now in charge of this work. The changes needed at home are almost as large as those being sought in other countries.

The Outsiders: Building the Rule of Law in Weak States

Efforts to stimulate rule-of-law improvements take place in nearly every country. These countries fall into two groups: fully sovereign states and a small group of post-conflict states in which the United States and other international actors have a significant degree of direct control alongside, or above, the local government, namely: Kosovo, Bosnia, East Timor, Afghanistan, and Iraq. Of the 184 countries in which the United

States has attempted rule-of-law reforms, all but about five are fully sovereign states. Moreover, the problems of the larger body of countries are formidable: Honduras, for instance, had a higher homicide rate in 2011 than Iraq or war-torn Afghanistan.[50] Therefore, this book focuses on activities within fully sovereign states, which constitute the vast majority of rule-of-law reform efforts.[51]

One difference between the two categories is the role of the United States and other outside reformers within the country. While in post-conflict states, outside actors may have some direct control over the levers of power and the agencies of government, in most countries where the United States and other outside reformers undertake rule-of-law reform, they are looking to facilitate significant change in a complex domestic system from outside that system.[52] Outsider status has two significant repercussions. First, at some point, the outsiders will leave, while locals will stay. Outside reformers have inevitably limited knowledge and short time horizons, while local stakeholders are, as the word implies, playing for high stakes that will affect their lives over the long term of their political, judicial, business, or activist careers. Second, because outsiders are not there for the long haul, if they wish to create sustainable or societal change, they must work through local actors. If they cannot persuade locals to take up the cause and make it their own, or create internal demand for the rule of law, they will not succeed. Even the most simple, supposedly technical reform is likely to create winners and losers—and while the winners from improved rule of law are fairly diffuse across society, the losers are often single individuals or small groups who are well aware of their potential loss.[53] Outsiders must marshal their own resources, both by locating supporters of reform and considering the best lever for change.

Rule-of-law reformers, whether from the United States or elsewhere, must be realistic, as well as humble, regarding their likelihood of significant impact. Helping individuals to reset cultural norms or assisting them in building a structure that places checks and balances on power is not simple work. Yet reformers should also not despair of ever having impact. Rule-of-law reformers may not be insiders, but they have leverage—money, media attention, diplomatic pressure, the ability to bring together like-minded reformers in different countries to share ideas.

Levers can wield immense power—Archimedes, their inventor, famously declared, "Give me a place to stand, and I will move the earth."[54] But to gain any lasting change, rule-of-law reformers must ensure that their lever is positioned in the right place and that they are prying the right rock. Second-generation reformers working at the political and cultural roots of reform must plan their strategy based on these realities. They must begin by considering what end they are trying to achieve, and they must then locate the parts of society where outside leverage is most likely to be able to affect change, given the political and social realities of the country in which reform is being attempted.

Throughout the book, I have woven in examples drawn from case studies. I particularly look at Indonesia, where the United States has its largest rule-of-law building program in any fully sovereign state (the two biggest overall are in Iraq and Afghanistan, both post-conflict states). Other cases draw on Albania, a relatively weak, aid-dependent Balkan country, and Romania, a relatively strong state that recently joined the European Union. These cases draw on my own research and interviews. I will also bring in shorter examples from Latin America and Africa as necessary to illustrate points, relying for these on the excellent fieldwork of colleagues, and occasional illuminating media.

The Book's Structure

This chapter has described the basic framework for rule-of-law reform: who is doing it within the United States, its significance to foreign policy, and the need for the U.S. development and diplomatic communities to work together more easily if they are going to start doing it better. The chapter has also described the fundamental differences between first- and second-generation rule-of-law reform. While first-generation reformers focused on changing laws and institutions to look like those of their Western counterparts, using an institution-focused definition of the rule of law and a limited set of tools, the growing group of second-generation reforms looks at the rule of law based on the ends it serves in society and recognizes that power structures and cultural norms must be affected if these ends are to be achieved. Second-generation reform thus focuses on different objects of change—and uses a broader palette of methods to leverage that change, recognizing that ultimately, outsiders must rely on and assist locals as they alter their own societies.

The second chapter looks at why the United States is engaging in rule-of-law reform at all. After all, if Americans are not very good at such reforms, and these reforms are costing taxpayers a billion dollars a year, why not cede the field to someone who has a better track record? The chapter describes the history of U.S. rule-of-law reform efforts, showing how the United States has repeatedly found new reasons to reform the rule of law in order to promote its own security, spread human rights, and assist with economic development in poor states. U.S. history, and the litany of reasons that keep being devised to engage in this work, suggest that the United States is going to keep doing it. It also shows some of the early hurdles for success: U.S. rule of law efforts are actually pointed at three different goals that are occasionally contradictory and are often in tension. Further complicating the picture, sometimes the United States is pursuing these goals for the good of the reforming country and conceiving of its own self-interest in broad terms—while at other times, the United States is actually altering rule-of-law institutions in other countries solely to meet its own needs and is not really engaged in rule-of-law reform at all.

The third chapter picks up on this skeptical note to pause for doubt. Is the United States really building the rule of law at all? Or is it actually engaged in a neocolonial enterprise in which it seeks to use its power to alter cultures and change institutions in order to benefit its own value sets, business enterprises, and security goals? Is rule-of-law reform really just a new kind of gunboat diplomacy? Only by conceding that these skeptical views are not only valid, but are also held by a good number of people in the countries the United States is attempting to reform, can Americans be honest about their own mixed motives for reform—and see how they are perceived in other countries. The chapter also looks at quite another type of doubt: concern that the United States simply cannot build the rule of law in other countries, and shouldn't try. It concludes by conceding that altering the rule of law is slow and difficult—but that the United States is going to keep trying and should endeavor to find ways to get better at it. Ultimately, working with locals to alter their own countries in ways that are desired by a significant portion of the population makes the U.S. efforts both more legitimate and more effective.

The fourth chapter is an in-depth look into the four objects of change already mentioned. It looks at the theories of change that lie behind efforts to alter laws, rebuild institutions, reform power structures, and affect cultural norms. It also shows how the neglected areas of power structure and cultural reform are crucial for the rule of law to take hold.

But how can the United States alter such delicate relationships within a country—particularly after acknowledging that the United States is always, and ultimately, an outsider who will leave? The fifth chapter describes the four main methods that can be used to bring about change within another country: top-down programs, bottom-up reform, diplomacy, and enmeshment—whether in its weak form of exchange programs, or a more robust form in which countries enter into international organizations with rule of law membership requirements and strong legal structures that reinforce the rule of law within the organization. The chapter describes the methods themselves and how they work, then looks at the pros and cons of each to see where they work, and where they are less likely to be effective.

But this is all somewhat abstract. The sixth chapter provides examples of each of the sixteen tactics reformers can use, and how these tactics look in the field, from building advocacy coalitions to leveraging NATO membership requirements. By deploying these tactics together, based on a strong theory of how to create change in a particular country, reformers can create strategy. In doing so, they should also keep in mind reality—even if they do not control all the U.S. government agencies active in a particular country, their plans can be scuttled by another agency acting in a way that appears to undermine the rule-of-law agenda. A well-planned strategy has to take into account these interaction effects, acknowledging that there may well be other U.S. interests at play that will not work in tandem with rule-of-law reform and planning strategy to accommodate, rather than ignore, this reality.

Second-generation rule-of-law reform differs so significantly from first-generation ways of thinking, planning, and implementing reforms that it can leave a practitioner breathless. How does a country desk officer take this new set of ideas into account to craft a better rule-of-law program for a country that clearly seems to need improvement? The seventh chapter offers a clear, practical methodology for instituting a second-generation rule-of-law reform program—starting with a country assessment, and continuing through the creation of metrics and sequencing. For practitioners in the field, this chapter provides a guide for creating second-generation reform programs.

The concluding chapter pulls together all of these ideas to offer ten concrete takeaways for implementing second-generation reform programs, and with a dose of humility, the hope that together, practitioners and researchers dedicated to improving the rule of law abroad can make a positive difference in the world.

CHAPTER TWO

GOALS: WHY ARE WE DOING THIS?

The United States is determined to deepen its cooperation with our partners in this region and beyond. This commitment is solid because it is solidly based on American interests. We have an abiding security interest in a region where almost any significant outbreak of international violence would threaten our well-being and that of our friends. We have an abiding economic interest in a region that is experiencing explosive growth. We have an abiding strategic interest in a region whose cooperation we need in responding to threats of proliferation, terrorism, narcotics, and damage to the environment. And we have an abiding political interest in supporting democracy and respect for human rights and the rule of law, including the Universal Declaration of Human Rights, because stability and prosperity ultimately depend on it.

– Secretary of State Madeleine K. Albright, Opening Statement to ASEAN Post-Ministerial Meeting, July 1997

What is the United States doing paying for anticorruption folk songs to be piped into Albanian villages, or videotaping Indonesian police to deepen their appreciation for community policing? Like Bilbo Baggins, the hobbit who was plucked from his contented shire life and found himself, after a host of adventures, trapped inside a mountain fighting a terrifying army of goblins, it might well occur to us to ask how the United States and other countries involved in rule-of-law assistance got to this juncture—and whether it makes sense for them to be here.[1]

Like the unwitting hobbit on his great adventure, the United States walked into rule-of-law promotion step-by-step, with little idea of where it would end up. Building the rule of law abroad did not burst forth full-grown from the head of a Zeus-like policymaker. It evolved organically from a set of diverse activities involving reforming laws and legal institutions in other countries that were pursued during the Cold War and post–Cold War era. The activities had various goals: Some were intended solely to improve U.S. national security, without reference to the effects they would have on the reforming country's domestic justice system. Others were crafted to spread values such as human rights and democracy. Yet others were focused on helping poor countries develop through market-based economic reforms. In the early 1990s, as policymakers recognized the interrelationships among reforms needed to pursue each of these goals, they began to coalesce into a single concept: the pursuit of the rule of law.

In many cases, self-interest catalyzed early U.S. efforts at reform. Not surprisingly, self-interest continues to play a role in programs that cost U.S. taxpayers billions of dollars a year. In many instances the United States pursues changes to rule-of-law institutions abroad not to help a given country build the rule of law but largely to help its own security, increase its own market access, or spread American values. Examples—such as pressuring other countries to pass strong antiterrorist legislation—are most clear in the security realm. For instance, in 1993, the U.S. GAO estimated that most foreign police training was directed at meeting U.S. law enforcement needs, such as sharing accurate evidence on international crimes, rather than directed at internal needs of the reforming state.[2] There is nothing inherently wrong with self-interest—after all, U.S. citizens are paying for government-financed rule-of-law reform efforts abroad, and they have a right to a government that serves their interests. Moreover, in many cases, U.S. needs and those of the reforming country coincide. However, in other instances, self-interested efforts may actually impede the rule of law that the United States claims to want to build—tarnishing the concept itself and casting suspicion on the efforts of U.S. rule-of-law reform practitioners in general. Simply retitling various activities that affect legal institutions in other countries as "rule of law building" does not "miraculously eliminate the hard choices between ideals and interests," in the words of Thomas Carothers.[3]

Understanding this history is important because of such mixed motives. They may appear subtle to Americans, but they loom large in the minds of many people in the countries the United States claims to be reforming—and they can trip up current reform programs, building roadblocks that stand in the way of U.S. efforts to improve the rule of law. Moreover, the three main foreign policy goals desired by rule of law reform abroad are shared by most other actors in the field—from the OECD to Japan. Equally important, U.S. history has shaped the tactics used today and has built the convoluted funding lines and alphabet soup of agencies that hamper many U.S. efforts to influence the rule of law abroad. Only by accepting the inherent flaws in current thinking and in U.S. structures for implementing rule-of-law reform can practitioners hope to understand just how hard it is to improve the rule of law in other countries successfully—and how much of this effectiveness rests not on changing other countries, but on changing ourselves.

Enhancing Security

Security concerns first drove the United States to pay attention to rule of law issues in other countries. Although it wasn't called rule-of-law building, the U.S. created constabularies—paramilitary police forces—throughout Latin America more than a century ago. In 1898, the United States found itself occupying Cuba after the Mexican-American War. Caught between a breakdown of order on the island and demands from the American public to bring the troops home, the U.S. Army hit upon an innovative solution: Help the island police itself. The U.S. Army created a force of 1,600 Cuban constables led by American officers, which became, for a time, a highly competent police force in Cuba. The success would not be repeated. In the next two decades, U.S. Marines would enter Panama, Nicaragua, the Dominican Republic, and Haiti, establish constabularies, withdraw, and then watch these forces descend into corruption or take over governments through military coups or both—time and time again.[4]

In a post-conflict environment, it makes sense that an outside power would find itself building the rule of law: When law and order have broken down as a result of a vacuum of power and the United States is the occupying force, there is little choice. Security, however, is also one of the main reasons the United States has become involved in rule-of-law building in fully sovereign countries—and it is the main reason that, despite a track record of minimal success, the United States continues to be pulled back into the same activities.

In the early Cold War mentality of the 1950s, communist agents were viewed as transnational threats bent on eroding American democracy through ideology and guerrilla warfare. European countries responded with traditional national security activities. They took part in alliances such as NATO to protect against Soviet military aggression and sponsored intelligence activities to halt domestic infiltration. The United States took these measures a step further. With friendly authoritarian countries to the south eager for assistance to prop up their regimes, the United States began training and equipping police in Latin America to eradicate the perceived communist threat. In the 1960s, the Kennedy administration established a U.S. Agency for International Development (USAID) program for foreign police training, and by 1968 the United States was spending $60 million a year training police in 34 countries in criminal investigation techniques, counterinsurgency, riot control, weapon use, and bomb disposal. The United States also equipped foreign police forces with arms, transportation, and communication equipment.[5] The focus of these early efforts was on enhancing law enforcement in these countries to help U.S. security. Building "the rule of law" was never mentioned as a goal. Interventions tended to strengthen authoritarian governments and may have weakened the rule of law in these states.[6]

In the first of many cases where the multiple goals that would fall under the rule-of-law umbrella came into conflict, the desire for security against the communist threat clashed with growing concerns about human rights abuses caused by the "death squads" trained by the United States. In 1973, as the communist scare receded and human rights gained prominence, Congress passed legislation prohibiting U.S. agencies from using economic aid or military assistance for foreign police training. In December 1974, Congress strengthened the prohibition, ending USAID's training program and amending the Foreign Assistance Act to ban any aid disseminated from that act from being used for any police, prison, or intelligence reforms abroad.[7]

Yet while development professionals in the United States could no longer work with police, the technique of training police in weak states kept bubbling up. The United States needed these countries to secure themselves—and it needed their security forces to be able to work with U.S. law enforcement. The need was too great to stop altogether out of human rights concerns. Congressional legislation applied to development aid but did not apply to funds used by other agencies, such as the Department of Justice, the Drug Enforcement Administration, or the Federal Bureau of Investigation (FBI), all of which soon began training foreign police to meet presumed security needs of the United States. As new security issues arose, Congress began granting exemptions for specific programs or countries, while attempting to ameliorate human rights worries in these new efforts.

This early conflict among goals would have far-reaching consequences for U.S. rule-of-law reform. Even as it became clear to development professionals that criminal violence and other law and order deficiencies prevented development efforts from taking hold, the funding prohibition and the disapprobation for working with police kept them from doing anything.[8] Instead, improving police and prisons to further rule-of-law reform would pass into the realm of other agencies—leading to stovepiped assistance (such as undertaking police reform through the Department of Justice rather than USAID) that increasingly separated security reforms from other rule-of-law goals. This separation is one of the primary reasons for the multiplicity of agencies and lack of strategic thought and coordination among U.S. rule-of-law goals that continues today.

Meanwhile, the United States kept seeing security needs that could be met only by policing the world itself or training foreign police to do their jobs better. By the mid-1970s, Middle Eastern terrorism had become a serious threat to the United States and Europe, and in 1981, the U.S. passed legislation to resume police investigative training for antiterrorism activities. In 1983, Congress authorized an antiterrorism program in which foreign police were brought to the United States to train in counterterrorism techniques.[9] By 1985, following the slaying of four U.S. Marines and two other U.S. citizens in El Salvador by urban "terrorists," Congress allowed the Department of Defense to provide antiterrorism training, police vehicles, weapons, and communications equipment to Honduran and Salvadoran police.[10] Drug trafficking, money laundering, and international criminal syndicates that smuggled people and goods across borders were also seen as threats whose solution required foreign police training. To stop illegal immigration, the United States undertook police training in Haiti.[11] By 1981, police in the Eastern Caribbean Regional Security System and in Panama were being provided with military training to guard against drug trafficking and to protect the Panama Canal. As America's War on Drugs picked up steam under President Ronald Reagan, successive amendments to the original ban began to draw the Defense Department into an ever-expanding role in providing training, equipment, weapons, and even ammunition to foreign police units that were specifically organized to fight drugs.[12]

Earlier human rights concerns affected these programs. For instance, Congress made Defense Department assistance to the police in Honduras and El Salvador contingent on these countries making significant improvements in human rights. When they failed to show progress, Congress eliminated Defense Department assistance.[13] Training programs for foreign police had to take place in the United States, under the belief that training performed on U.S. soil was subject to greater scrutiny and was less prone to teaching techniques that could lead to human rights abuses than training performed abroad. Training was limited to skill-building for specific police needs in classes of thirty days or less, so that trainings could not become generalized policing programs where torture could creep into the curricula.[14] The difficulty of conducting serious, sound security training in short stints of classroom learning divorced from the local context was not the foremost consideration: Congress was doing its best to meet U.S. security needs while balancing its concern for human rights.

The attempt by Congress to create this balance through blunt legislation would shape all U.S. police training efforts in ways quite different than those conducted by other entities, such as the European Union. For instance, while the EU conducts multiyear programs abroad by matching up European and local law enforcement for in-depth training on the ground in their home countries, Congress did not begin allowing foreign police to be trained outside of the United States until 1990. Even then, like the U.S.-based programs, trainings are limited to a month and must be tightly focused on skill-building tied to international crime and terrorism, such as handling of detector dogs, rather than broad efforts to reform police cultures.[15] Thus, while the United States might invest significant funding for a multiyear police training mission in a country, the actual products tend to be modular, technocratic, short-term classes that often lack interaction with the local context. The nature of the assistance also tends to prevent the United States from achieving the norm-diffusion and general rule-of-law goals that advocates of these programs had hoped for. Moreover, such trainings out of context rarely work; numerous studies have found that training that cannot be applied immediately in the field is lost.[16]

Some of these efforts helped to build the domestic rule of law in other states—but that was at best an intermediate goal or side effect. The ultimate end was to increase U.S. security; efforts were based on stopping unwanted people, ideologies, or substances from reaching U.S. shores.

Yet by the mid-1980s, U.S. foreign policy broadly began to shift to a framework that emphasized democracy and human rights—both as goals in themselves and as prerequisites for other countries that would be friendly and helpful to U.S. security interests. This wide-ranging change also began affecting the rule-of-law paradigm in ways that will be discussed broadly in the next section. In the security field, the change was felt first with police assistance, beginning in 1985 when Congress's latest Security and Development Assistance Act allowed broader training to police throughout Latin America—but specifically prohibited the Department of Defense from providing this training.[17] Instead, Congress mandated the creation of a civilian agency under the Department of Justice—the International Criminal Investigative Training Assistance Program (ICITAP)—to train foreign police in what would become known as "democratic policing." For the first time, an American agency had an explicit focus on helping foreign governments build professional law enforcement services based on democratic principles and respect for human rights, while combating crime, corruption, and terrorism.[18]

As the paradigm shift from security to rule-of-law reform was occurring, U.S. involvement in police training abroad was growing. By 1990, in addition to ICITAP, the United States was using the Department of State's Bureau of International Narcotics and Law Enforcement, the Antiterrorism Assistance unit, and the Department of Defense (in limited circumstances) to provide police training to 125 countries.[19]

The fall of the Berlin Wall and the ensuing democratic enthusiasm solidified this sea change in thinking. In 1990, when the United States set about rebuilding the police in Panama following the U.S. invasion of that country, the legislation that enabled police training was no longer titled "security and development" as had been the case for past legislation with similar goals, but was instead named the "Urgent Assistance for Democracy in Panama Act"—an early sign of the growing importance of democracy itself as a goal of police training. The law permitted police training in human rights, civil law, and civilian law enforcement technique. The Defense Department was allowed to provide some equipment to Panamanian law enforcement—but only equipment that was standard to civilian police agencies. Meanwhile, the training itself was to be conducted by ICITAP along "democratic policing" lines.[20] Rather than a pinprick focus on security that would help the United States, the goal was to develop a "professional, civilian national police force . . . fully integrated into Panamanian society, capable of protecting its people, and dedicated to supporting the Panamanian constitution, laws, and human rights."[21] Not coincidentally, this shift was taking place just as the new democracies of Eastern Europe were emerging. In the Assistance for Democracy in Panama Act, Congress added a final provision allowing up to $10 million to be spent assisting the transition to democracy in Eastern Europe and Yugoslavia.

The transition from pinprick security reforms to creating security through rule-of-law–based democracies started under the Carter administration, gained ground in the Reagan administration, and reached its full flower in the early 1990s under President Bill Clinton. Seeking a new foreign policy "grand strategy" in the aftermath of the Cold War, top officials repeatedly linked U.S. security to the growth of stable democratic countries, with interdependent market economies.[22] This popularization of liberal internationalism and democratic peace theory became a theme of the Clinton administration. The need to build the rule of law in other countries in order to secure Americans at home ran throughout President Clinton's policies, such as his International Crime Control Strategy:

> The threat to U.S. interests posed by international crime can be viewed in three broad, interrelated categories: threats to Americans and their communities, threats to American businesses and financial institutions, and threats to global security and stability . . .
>
> For those countries that lack resources and expertise to mount complex or sustained investigations against international criminals, the Strategy calls for expanding training and technical assistance programs to turn foreign police forces, prosecutors and judges into more effective crime fighters. For those countries where the basic institutions of justice are not adequate to the everyday challenges of common crime, let alone the new challenges posed by increasingly sophisticated international crime, the Strategy maintains a country-specific, flexible approach to fostering development of effective criminal justice institutions. Such institutions will provide not only the foundation for the rule of law and lasting democratic government, but also the essential framework for international law enforcement cooperation.[23]

Albania is a clear example of the type of problems that lay behind this new rule-of-law focus. The first postcommunist country to allow U.S. military basing, in 1993, Albania became crucial to the United States in 1998 when it granted NATO free use of the country for operations during the Balkan wars. But its weak government and lack of the rule of law threatened these military operations and the security of U.S. personnel. In 1997 after failed pyramid schemes robbed many Albanians of their life savings, riots destroyed most of the country's infrastructure. The nation's prisoners broke free, and looters emptied its arms depots. The U.S. Central Intelligence Agency believed that Osama bin Laden spent time in Albania in the mid-1990s and possibly stole 1,000 passports during the riots.[24] The next year, Americans were evacuated from the country after a bomb threat to the U.S. Embassy. Further credible threats led top U.S. officials to cancel trips in 1999 when Albania was serving as a key U.S. base for the Kosovo air war. Although the Albanian government granted the CIA free rein to arrest individual terrorists on its territory, it was clear that such a violation of sovereignty was not enough. Ultimately, protecting U.S. and NATO military personnel, defending Americans against terrorism, and reducing the power of organized crime would require Albania to control its own territory and fight crime internally.[25]

By the mid-1990s, security was well established as a goal of rule-of-law reform. Attempts to build the security within other states, and more self-serving reforms to simply curb criminal spillover, would sit side-by-side under the rule-of-law umbrella.

The United States would never abandon all pinpoint reforms targeted primarily at its own security. Instead, these would now operate parallel to efforts to build a domestic rule of law in other states, with little to distinguish the two types of activities.

Improving Human Rights and Democracy

In the 1960s, the security community was joined by an entirely different set of people interested in rule-of-law reform—human rights activists and development practitioners eager to spread democracy. As scores of countries broke free from colonial rule, these development-oriented communities wanted to lend a hand to the newly independent countries.[26] Funded by the Ford Foundation, universities, and USAID, American academics and lawyers began training lawyers and judges abroad in the socially progressive law being practiced in the United States at the time in an effort to improve civil rights, development, and democracy in the newly decolonized countries in Africa (and occasionally Latin America). Their effort became known as the law and development movement.[27] In a speech to galvanize participants in these programs, U.S. Supreme Court Justice William O. Douglas explained how law reform would affect democracy and human rights:

> These newly developing nations need our help—not only our money and machines and food, but also the great capital of knowledge accumulated by our professors. . . . Refrigerators and radios can be easily exported—but not the democratic system. Ideas of liberty and freedom travel fast and far and are contagious. Yet their adaptation to particular societies requires trained people, disciplined people, dedicated people. It requires lawyers.[28]

The law and development movement was short-lived. After just a decade, early assessments derided reformers for ignoring cultural differences and trying to simply implant U.S. law into African and other contexts where they were not supported by historical or cultural traditions.[29] Yet as with security, supporting human rights and democracy abroad was too important, too embedded in the U.S. self-image, not to resurface.

President Jimmy Carter made human rights a political goal of U.S. diplomacy in the 1970s. Primarily focused on diplomatic tools, rather than development assistance, Carter used the power of rhetoric, sanctions, U.S. State Department Human Rights Reports, and other diplomatic measures to put the weight of the United States on the side of human rights in countries around the world. The effort encountered some resistance within the U.S. government—and certainly surprised a world that had grown used to a greater degree of U.S. realpolitik. However, from his presidency onward, democracy and human rights would have a funded place in the U.S. State Department—and a growing role in the diplomatic tool kit. Carter's efforts also provided a home for a set of individuals who cared about the democracy and human rights agenda and would become savvy political players in Washington who would work to push their issue into pertinent conversations, regardless of where they sat at any given moment in the Washington landscape.

In the 1980s, Ronald Reagan made promoting democracy a hallmark of his presidency (in rhetoric, if not always in action).[30] The Reagan administration fought internally between helping friendly authoritarian countries and making good on Reagan's strong pro-democracy speeches. The U.S. State Department's human rights and democracy contingent put its thumb on the scales on multiple occasions—perhaps most crucially, in its behind-the-scenes efforts on the National Bipartisan

Commission of 1984. The Kissinger Commission, as it was known, had been charged with offering recommendations for U.S. policy toward war-torn Central America—and despite the publicized realism of its namesake, it took a clear side in these battles thanks in part to the internal politicking of the State Department. The report stated that the United States should support democracy in Latin America and that improving the administration of justice was one way to do so. For a brief moment, a Congress composed of a Republican Senate and Democratic House agreed on policies to support the human rights concerns traditionally held by the left and the democratization desires often seen as the bastion of the right. It authorized funds for USAID to engage in judicial and rule-of-law reform, first in El Salvador, then in a series of Latin American countries, in order to bring to justice those responsible for a series of slayings and human rights abuses.[31]

To further bolster Latin American democracies, USAID offered legislative assistance to enshrine human rights into their laws and constitutions and to rewrite criminal codes. It soon became clear that legislation alone would make little difference when the system of justice itself was so flawed. Development practitioners began to fund justice reform, pioneering techniques to make courts more efficient and fair, reduce corruption, and cut red tape.[32]

But human rights reform ultimately required addressing the tendency of law enforcement to abuse citizens—and USAID was, ironically, still banned from undertaking police training in most countries under Section 660 legislation. In 1988, Congress allowed USAID to train police in forensic and investigative skills—techniques that were essential if police were to catch lawbreakers without resorting to torture and human rights abuse. The legislation also allowed USAID to develop law enforcement training curricula and improve police management, although the ongoing legal sensitivities in this sector would prevent USAID from becoming too involved in police training again.

Using rule-of-law reform to promote human rights and democracy spread from El Salvador to Honduras and Guatemala—and from there to the rest of Latin America, Eastern Europe, Africa, and even China. In the 1990s, as part of a larger expansion of democratization efforts across the U.S. government and in the broader development community, USAID created a Center for Democracy and Governance and rule-of-law reform programs were placed within it. The role of the rule of law in ensuring democracy and human rights remained a rather small side project of the larger democracy and human rights agenda—but it was now enshrined in the organizational chart.

As the third wave of democracy spread after the Soviet Union's demise, American lawyers flooded into Eastern Europe to rewrite constitutions and enhance the rule of law. Yet despite all the effort, many countries began to waver—their formal democratic processes, elections, and markets were eaten from the inside by corruption, law and order problems, and, at times, continuing human rights abuses—often by organized crime or drug gangs rather than governments themselves. Rule-of-law practices suited to rein in strong states seemed ill-suited to deal with these "captured" and fragile, or corrupt states with strong non-state actors, which scholar Joel Migdal characterized as "strong societies and weak states."[33]

Until this period, theoretical paradigms to promote the rule of law had been built on limiting the state—which was still needed in countries that had recently been totalitarian. Yet as wars flared in the Balkans, secession movements grew in former corners of the Soviet Union, and criminal gangs expanded their power, it became clear that while governments needed to be limited, they also needed to be strong enough to protect their citizens from human rights abuses, violence, extortion, and other rule-of-law failures caused by other citizens and organized criminals.

Meanwhile, waves of reformist governments were beaten back in second and third elections by postcommunist parties. In parts of Eastern Europe and Latin America, polls showed skepticism about the democratic experiment—which many citizens had expected to bring prosperity and happiness, but which had, in reality, freed them from one set of tyrannies while delivering a new set of problems. Outsider efforts to catalyze rule-of-law reform in these transitioning countries became more and more important—as an end in itself, and to show that democracy could "deliver." Creating market-oriented economies became part of that effort.

Catalyzing Market Development

The most recent additions to the rule-of-law community have been economists and others looking to spur economic growth in developing countries. Since 1949, when the United States first gave development assistance under the Point Four program, the development field has leapt from one idea to another in search of a way to reliably help poor countries. Funding has shifted from building roads, dams, and electrical infrastructure, to funding primary education, population control measures, or the "green revolution" in agriculture.[34] Each trend brought with it unintended consequences, none was a silver bullet, and throughout the world, many developing countries stagnated.

By the late 1980s, development aid was increasingly embattled. The Reagan-Thatcher pro-market, anti-aid philosophy was ascendant. The "Asian Tigers," whose level of economic development in the 1960s had been comparable to poor African countries, had shot into the ranks of developed economies through export-oriented trade—not handouts and development aid. Their success fueled a prominent group of economists in the development field to move away from traditional aid and to look toward markets as the answer. This intellectual movement became codified in the Washington Consensus, a theory claiming that reorienting economies toward open trade, not aid itself, was the spur for development.[35] In fact, the Asian economies that had catalyzed these changes were hardly poster children for open markets—theirs had been managed economies in which the government played a strong role in directing markets, encouraging companies toward export-led growth to force industries to gain the benefits of competition, while often offering these companies tariffs to protect their markets at home. Despite the ahistorical origins, the move toward markets as the means to development had caught hold. Economists began to insert conditionality within aid programs, forcing countries to privatize businesses, reduce tariffs, and institute other market-oriented policies in exchange for aid. Many in the development community saw this growing conditionality as imperialistic. Others decried the Washington Consensus for not showing the hoped-for results. After billions of dollars spent, aid had few sustained successes to show at the country-wide level.[36] And a Republican-led Congress was demanding that if aid agencies wanted to keep their budgets, they needed to demonstrate impact, not coddle dependency.

Into this mix stepped Douglass North and a set of fellow economists who claimed that economic growth in the West was partially due to the existence of particularly useful social institutions.[37] While capital, human resources, and other traditional economic inputs were important, the "new institutional economics" saw regulatory bodies, non-corrupt civil services, and functioning legal systems as essential elements that enabled trade and the private market to function in favor of development.

The idea that commercial law, contracts, and fair arbitration are necessary for economic growth had roots that stretch back for centuries. A hundred years ago, Max Weber cited legal institutions as important to the development of capitalism in Western Europe. Far earlier, Shakespeare wrote *The Merchant of Venice*, whose plot turns on the idea that Venice must uphold its laws—and despite the court's abhorrence of Shylock's deadly contract, failing to honor such a document would skew legal precedent and create "no force in the decrees of Venice." The subtext is that Venice, a trading and financial center of the Middle Ages, could thrive only if its laws were trusted and contracts upheld.

In modern times, North's theory was given empirical support by Hernando de Soto, whose book *The Other Path* used a wealth of anecdotal and statistical data to demonstrate the difficulty of opening a business when laws and regulations were overly complex.[38] His work also showed how the lack of property rights kept poor individuals from expanding their homes and businesses, and thus from accumulating capital and developing. Anecdotal accounts in the development field (particularly from the World Bank's Africa section) had long claimed that cultural norms and corruption were harming Africa's ability to share in market-led growth; suddenly practitioners had theoretical grounding for these long-held and ignored claims. The new institutional economics also gave a conceptual foundation to studies that were shaking the foundations of the development profession. Foremost among these was Craig Burnside and David Dollar's study on aid effectiveness, which found that development aid was effective only in countries that had what came to be known as "good governance"—low corruption, functioning civil services and legal institutions, and non-onerous regulation.[39] The new institutional economics was embraced by

Robert Picciotto, head of evaluations at the World Bank, and soon by James Wolfensohn, the new World Bank president, who gave the ideas prominence in annual World Bank publications and conferences.[40] These fora set the tone for USAID and the rest of the aid community worldwide.

The new theories came onto the scene just as the countries of Eastern Europe were emerging from decades of communism. These countries actually wanted markets—but after fifty years of command-and-control economies, most lacked the most basic commercial laws. Their governments sent urgent calls to the U.S. State Department and the European Union asking for help drafting new laws and constitutions to create a basis for their new democracies. These organizations put calls out for lawyers and judges, and soon American lawyers found themselves stepping off airplanes in Poland, Hungary, and other newly liberated countries, redrafting laws and even constitutions alongside counterparts from the EU, OECD, Council of Europe, and a slew of nonprofit organizations. Their work quickly grew into broader efforts to create intellectual property rights, credit markets, land registration and other measures to codify private property, rules for foreign investment, specialized training in competition law, small-claims courts, arbitration, and other forms of alternative dispute resolution to enable contract enforcement. As early legal reforms alone bore little fruit, practitioners began to focus on the legal systems themselves. First, they published laws, which often weren't available to lawyers and judges in the new democracies. Soon, under the ambit of improving the rule of law to build a market economy, the United States and EU found themselves training magistrates and lawyers, rebuilding bar associations, and creating small claims courts and specialized arbitration mechanisms.[41]

By 2003, it was commonplace for Alan Greenspan, then chairman of the U.S. Federal Reserve, to begin a speech with the statement, "Market economies require a rule of law. A society without state protection of individual rights, especially the right to own property, would not build private long-term assets, a key ingredient of a growing modern economy."[42] USAID's rule of law website declared, "Long-term, sustainable economic and social development requires democratic governance rooted in the rule of law."[43] Efforts to reform commercial and civil law in order to build functioning modern markets became a regular aspect of USAID's reform efforts under its Economic Growth, Agriculture, and

Trade Bureau (a separate entity from the Bureau of Democracy, Conflict, and Humanitarian Assistance as the bureau that undertakes broader rule of law reforms for democracy and human rights was then called).[44] The Economic Growth Bureau began adding commercial law and commercial court reform to its portfolio from Europe to Africa, Latin America, and even in post-conflict countries like Iraq.

Despite this heady leap from academia to practice, the linkage between formal commercial aspects of the rule of law and economic development is mostly based on guesses and assumptions and remains largely unproven.[45] Clearly, economic growth has occurred in countries and in sectors of countries where the institutional environment was hardly satisfactory, such as China, while other countries have made great strides in institutional reform, but little growth has resulted.[46] In many countries with weak rule of law, international firms submit to international arbitration and simply sidestep, as best as possible, local legal institutions. In many ways, international firms try to function via a system reminiscent of the *lex mercatoria* of the Middle Ages—the specialized laws and self-created courts that cosmopolitan merchants used to do business internationally despite highly differentiated legal rules and practices in the various market towns through which they traveled. Meanwhile, local businesses may be held back as much by corruption, theft, and organized crime as by poor contract enforcement or a poor commercial court system. After all, most businesses try to operate without ever setting foot in a court, and many businesses even in countries with well-developed rule-of-law systems don't bother to go to court to enforce contracts because the cost and effort are not worth it. These law-and-order aspects of the rule of law tend to be ignored by those who enter the rule-of-law field to build market economies in developing countries—but could well be central to their goals.

The Scene in Europe

As mentioned in the first chapter, the United States is far from the only entity interested in establishing the rule of law in other countries. The EU and many European countries became active in promoting the rule-of-law in the 1990s. While they, like the United States, had used human rights sanctions on aid from the 1970s on, they entered the rule-of-law field as a whole just as the new paradigm was coming together—and thus, from the beginning, European countries and the EU conceptually linked security goals with market creation, human rights, and democratization. (Japan, Canada, and Australia became active in the rule of law at this point and also entered the field with the linkage among these three goals already established.) The EU also has a fourth aim in pursuing the rule of law: enabling successful integration of new member states. This integration process has been central to EU rule-of-law efforts. The EU created its rule-of-law reform model as a method for integrating new member states—and then decided that its entire model of integration was so positive that it would export it to its near abroad, and then try to bring it to farther-flung parts of the world such as Africa and Asia. Thus, understanding the integration process is essential to understanding European rule-of-law promotion strategies—and is an important addition for U.S. practitioners to see how the method of enmeshment can work at its strongest.

The EU's entry into the rule-of-law field—and the interest of many European countries in the effort—grew out of the specific history of the 1990s. As Eastern Europeans clamored to join their Western brethren, the then-European Commission wanted to make good on its long-term rhetorical commitment to ending the division of the continent. Yet it was in the midst of the Maastricht monetary union and was expanding to take in Scandinavian countries, as well as dealing with German reunification. Meanwhile, the growth of the Russian mafia, smuggling, and trafficking in drugs, arms, and people, had all emerged as serious problems in Eastern Europe since the Soviet Union's collapse, and much of Western Europe wanted to pull up its drawbridge against these threats.[47]

Germany, sharing a border and historic ties with many of the Eastern European countries, was the most threatened by the spillover of international crime and fears of nationalism and Russian expansion.[48] Germany began to argue for a wider view of security that encompassed not just military but also criminal and migration threats, following similar arguments made by thinkers in NATO and scholars in academia.[49] It then posed the need for integration as a security issue and argued that if the EU did not extend a hand, the newly independent countries might disintegrate, destabilize Western Europe, or turn toward the East once more.[50] Europe needed to reconstruct its viewpoint to see integration, rather than exclusion, as the best means of maintaining security in the new world order. Western academics concurred, as did Clinton administration officials, who catalyzed the Partnership for Peace program as an anteroom to NATO while calling on the EU to act similarly on integration.[51]

But security worries could be argued both ways. While failing to admit the newly independent states could have security implications, widening the EU would allow weak Eastern European countries into a community about to sign the Maastricht Treaty that would allow the free movement of capital, goods, people, and services within its borders. The EU had to be sure that the free movement of people and goods would not lead to more smuggling and illegal immigration.[52] Meanwhile, it wanted to promote democracy and human rights throughout Europe and desired its near abroad to be populated with market economies that would expand the European economy as a whole.

As the EU focused on completing its internal market reforms, it crafted a set of policies that would provide an ingenious, if inadvertent, solution to this rule-of-law dilemma. It would deepen justice and home affairs criteria within the EU, and then widen to include the new states so that the newly deepened commitments could legitimately be exported into the new candidate states—along with democracy, human rights, and working markets. At Maastricht in 1992, the European Union made justice and home affairs cooperation—which included police, border, customs, and judicial cooperation in criminal matters, as well as drug and organized crime issues—a third pillar of the EU for all member states.[53] In Copenhagen in 1993, the European Union drew up membership criteria for enlargement that required new countries wishing to enter the union to have achieved the stability of institutions guaranteeing human rights, the rule of law, and democracy; possess a functioning market economy; and have the ability to take on the obligations of membership, including the security requirements in the justice and home affairs realm, and the transposition of the entire body of European law known as the *acquis communautaire*. The first criterion on human rights, the rule of law, and democracy would become known as the "political criterion" that would form the non-negotiable hurdle states must pass before negotiations could open for candidate status.[54] Building state institutions, market economies, and justice and home affairs cooperation would become legitimate areas of diplomatic pressure and development assistance that the EU would provide to countries in the accession process.

By the dawn of the twenty-first century, the European Union was active in promoting the rule of law in countries throughout Eastern Europe, the former Soviet Union, and Africa—and was attempting work in Asia and Latin America. Its goals were largely the same as those in the United States—but its methods were often different. However, in both cases, similar issues create tension in the entire rule-of-law enterprise, as described below.

Conclusion

The United States, Europe, and other countries are pursuing rule-of-law reform abroad for their own security, their desire to spread human rights and democracy, and their belief that it will help economic development abroad. By 2003, the European Commission was summing up the multiple goals of rule-of-law reform in statements such as this one:

> The EC takes a holistic approach to its broadened policy agenda, acknowledging the inter-relationship of different issues and addressing them through integrated policies. Thus, terrorism, organised crime and illegal migration undermine the rule of law, discourage investment, and hinder development. Similarly economic and trade development can best flourish in countries that not only encourage economic freedom but also respect human rights and the rule of law, practice good governance and rule democratically.[55]

These reasons may be interdependent, but it's important to remember that three separate goals are being pursued. At times, conflating the three can be useful for diplomacy. For example, then-Secretary of State Madeleine Albright discussed the rule of law as a way to make China a good place to do business when talking to U.S. business representatives—then evoked it as a way of assisting political dissidents when answering a reporter's human rights question.[56] But such multiplicities of meaning do not do away with hard choices. There is no reason to believe that rule-of-law reform to help businesses will assist with human rights. The three goals ultimately support one another—for instance, lower crime rates can make police less apprehensive, and thus reduce police brutality and human rights abuse. Yet progress in one goal does not necessarily lead to progress in another—and, in some cases, they may undermine each other in the short run. In Somaliland, a United Nations Development Program (UNDP) undertaking to improve law and order—a huge problem in the initially anarchic state—ran up against another UNDP effort to improve the rights of prisoners, who were being forced into overcrowded, dangerous, crime-ridden prisons. If the first reform program were successful, it would lead to the arrest of greater numbers of people, increasing prison crowding.[57] While these goals were essential and compatible in the long term, implementing each program would have unintended side effects in the short term that could not lead to positive metrics for both.

In other cases, efforts that are intended to help build the rule of law in one area can backfire and reduce the rule of law in another. In Costa Rica, success in gaining workers the right to unionize improved human and labor rights—but it simultaneously discouraged business and reduced market-based economic development.[58] In the 1990s, the U.S. Justice Department and USAID helped Colombia create special judicial bodies with "faceless judges" to prosecute high-profile drug traffickers and leftist rebels without fear of retaliation—yet U.S. and other human rights activists criticized the anonymous judicial proceedings on the grounds that they violated due process.[59] Similar clashes are now occurring with antiterrorism reforms that the United States is pursuing globally, which may assist with security, but which human rights organizations claim are undermining hard-fought civil liberties protections. The unitary notion of "building the rule of law" obscures conflicts among the three goals.

Mixed goals are not the only problem with rule-of-law reasoning. Too often, aid agencies jumped from the goal to the most obvious institutions in that field—without real empirical work to show that the institution in question is the most relevant to the problem. As already discussed, the desire to build the rule of law to help economic growth has led to a set of reform efforts that work to modernize commercial laws, build small-claims courts, and train legal professionals in new commercial concepts. But it is plausible—in fact, likely—that businesses are just as stymied by corruption and organized crime as by problems that reside in commercial law. Similarly, those who work in the rule-of-law field in order to pursue human rights tend to focus on enacting human rights laws and supporting human rights NGOs. They often shun working with the police—in fact, human rights activists were the force that got Congress to bar development aid from being spent on police training. Yet law enforcement is the very institution most likely to need cultural reform and oversight if human rights are to improve. Leaping from the reason we are engaged in the field to the most obvious rule of law institution, rather than seeing the problem as part of an interdependent system, ensures that any efforts are less likely to be successful.

A final flaw in conceptualization leads countries to confuse altering rule-of-law institutions in other states in order to help themselves, with actual rule-of-law reform. As rule-of-law programs grew organically out of earlier security reforms, the United States began to use similar language to discuss efforts to train police, or pass commercial laws, that were in its own interests—and those programs meant to do these things because they were in the interests of reforming countries. The EU has an even more difficult problem separating self-interest from rule of law reform. Because its integration process requires countries joining the EU to integrate 80,000 pages of law (known as the *acquis communautaire*) into their books, what is required to improve the rule of law abroad, and what is needed to accede to the EU, have become merged and confused. The convoluted relationship among self-interest, true assistance, and paternalism is what we turn to in the next chapter.

CHAPTER THREE

PAUSING FOR DOUBT: ARE WE REALLY BUILDING THE RULE OF LAW?

It would not be very difficult to show that the phrase "the Rule of Law" has become meaningless thanks to ideological abuse and general over-use. It may well have become just another one of those self-congratulatory rhetorical devices that grace the public utterances of Anglo-American politicians. No intellectual effort need therefore be wasted on this bit of ruling-class chatter.

– Judith Shklar

By this point, a reader may have amassed quite a few concerns. If the rule of law is at heart about power, culture, and the relationship between a state and society, what right does the United States (or any other country or international body) have to poke around and affect the delicate workings of other governments? Is this really a form of neocolonialism, in which rule-of-law rhetoric just sugarcoats efforts to augment our power, create friendly governments, and help our companies? Even if the United States or European Union mean what they say about human rights, isn't promoting them in other countries simply a form of cultural imperialism? Or perhaps qualms about power politics aren't so bothersome—but the attempt to "nation-build" seems audacious and foolhardy. If the United States can't do this well, why do it at all? Shouldn't such countries be left to stew in their own juices, while the United States focuses its attention on more important players on the world stage? The questions are important—and this chapter addresses them head-on.

Legitimacy: We Should Quit Sticking Our Nose in Other Countries' Business

The problem of legitimacy when one country is acting upon another is relatively new. In centuries past, when confronted with threats that emanated from countries that lacked the ability or will to contain them, stronger states would violate sovereignty with impunity. Russia annexed Central Asia to provide a buffer zone against what it saw as threats to the motherland. The United Kingdom built its colonial empire in part to protect the shipping routes needed to supply the jewel in its crown, India. And the United States, as already discussed, intervened repeatedly in Latin America to ensure friendly governments, protect businesses, and prevent crises from spilling over onto our shores. Colonialism through direct rule, or quasi-colonialism through the export and imposition of laws and governing systems run by puppet governments, was past centuries' response to governance failures in other states. Separate sets of laws for colonizer and colonized, which invariably favored the former, were the norm for most colonial nations. These efforts were unabashedly intended to protect the conqueror, not to bring the rule of law to the conquered. And no one thought to apologize.

Yet good intentions often followed on the coattails of victory. For some, aspirations to build a better, more just system for the local population merely masked naked power—but for others, colonialist expansion really was seen as a way to do good for the disadvantaged in other nations. It is worth remembering that Rudyard Kipling's famous poem "The White Man's Burden" was not a lament but a call to action. Subtitled "The United States and the Philippine Islands," it was written as an appeal to the United States to take up the task of developing the archipelago it had recently won as part of the Spanish-American War. For some, colonial service fulfilled the same moral purpose that the Peace Corps would later serve. It is this tortured colonial history that lies beneath the surface of rule-of-law reform today.[1]

In modern times, blatant disregard for sovereignty is considered unseemly. Yet it is true that the effort to build the rule of law in other countries has led to a degree of intrusion into the domestic affairs of other states unparalleled except under colonialism. From one perspective, what developed countries are doing on the ground to build the rule of law in other states is a stunning breach of sovereignty. In Albania, the entire legal code has been rewritten by a host of foreign nationals. USAID is encouraging multiple Latin American countries to switch from written, accusatorial, French-style courts to oral, Anglo-style systems. Indonesia was forced to establish a court to prosecute its own generals under massive international duress following the violence in East Timor.

Moreover, such activities occur only in countries where the power imbalance between the "assistor" and the "assisted" is great.[2] The United States has no rule-of-law building programs in Japan, despite that country's suspiciously high 99 percent conviction rate.[3] Nor does the United States undertake anticorruption reforms in Italy, despite evidence such as a 2007 study by the Confesercenti business organization that the country's biggest business is organized crime.[4] The United Kingdom may be unhappy that the U.S. government has held some of its citizens in Guantánamo Bay without due process, but it responds through regular diplomatic channels and public statements, not by creating and funding new structures to rebuild the U.S. judicial system. This power imbalance is not lost on countries that the United States and other countries and international bodies are trying to reform: Albanian politicians claim in private conversations that their country has been unjustly singled out for criticism for its law-and-order problems, while the EU ignored similar issues in Italy and Greece.[5] Such perceptions of unfairness not only delegitimize rule-of-law work; they also harm development practitioners' ability to be effective.

If this is neocolonialism, however, it is far more complex than the existing theoretical models of core-periphery exploitation.[6] While it is true that the United States does not intervene in developed countries, no rule-of-law building efforts, even in weak states, can be undertaken without the permission—or even request—of the host country. Many development practitioners on the ground are aware that even with such explicit permission, the power imbalance is too great for the target country to have full agency and ownership over its decision. They also know the literature, which claims persuasively that without real country ownership, development aid fails.[7] Therefore, for pragmatic and normative reasons, many of the development organizations that implement rule-of-law building programs are immensely hesitant to impose upon the sovereignty of another country. While diplomats and officials at other government agencies, such as the U.S. Treasury Department, are often blunt, forceful, and unapologetic in asking host governments to change their policies, development programs are nearly desperate to find or create ownership of their programs on the part of those they are assisting.

The result appears Janus-faced and confusing to recipient countries. Institutions with economic interests (particularly the U.S. Treasury Department, IMF, and businesses themselves) often ride roughshod over concerns about sovereignty and legitimacy thanks to their institutional cultures and confidence in the technical absolutes of economic logic. Meanwhile, NGOs, private contractors, and development agencies that implement rule-of-law programs—which are arguably far more intrusive in their interference in the domestic politics of other countries—pretend to be technocratic and, well aware of their lack of mandate for political action, are extremely sensitive to sovereignty issues.[8] Thus, outsiders often seem to walk around their countries with one foot clomping about in a heavy boot, the other tiptoeing in a ballet slipper, extremely aware of and uncomfortable with intrusions on sovereignty, and constantly seeking local ownership. The mix of brazen power and deference can be mind-bending: It is as if a doctor, in the midst of performing open-heart surgery, kept asking the patient if she wanted to take the tools and do this herself.

But even more important to note is that despite the often significant power imbalances between the United States and the countries in which it is intervening, America gets its way only occasionally. One of the most interesting facts about outside attempts to build the rule of law is not what strong states have managed to make weaker states do—but what those weaker states have managed to resist. Albania has spent nearly two decades mired in ever-worsening corruption, despite expensive programs, carrots and sticks, and constant entreaties from the EU and the United States. Indonesia, despite a crippling, decade-long military embargo that eventually left the country without even the helicopters needed to rescue tsunami victims, did almost nothing in the 1990s to improve its human rights record to America's satisfaction.

This limited power, quite distinct from anything that can legitimately be called postcolonialism, is evident in the U.S. attempts since September 11 to get Indonesia to take terrorism seriously. In 2001, the United States invited President Megawati Sukarnoputri to visit Washington in an effort to reignite the rule-of-law reform process. When the long-scheduled visit occurred on September 12, 2001, all other rule of law issues had been supplanted by the problem of terrorism. According to any theory of neo-colonialism, the United States should have had a great deal of influence, as the second-largest Indonesian export market and its largest military supplier (before its human rights–related embargo). U.S. officials sought Megawati's help in rooting out terrorism and asked her to sign a bilateral statement on the topic. She agreed, but fearing domestic backlash if she was seen as being too friendly with the United States, she asked for—and received—concessions from the White House, including bilateral aid for economic development, so that she could prove to her people that she had not simply bowed to pressure.[9]

When Megawati returned home, instead of working with the United States on this joint security threat, her administration pandered to Islamic audiences. While she privately allowed the secret extradition of non-Indonesian al-Qaeda operatives to the United States, she did little else. Days after the September 11 attacks, Megawati's vice president claimed that the attack would "cleanse the sins of the United States" and then purportedly dined with militant Islamic leaders, including Abu Bakar Bashir, believed to be the spiritual head of Jemaah Islamiya, the organization accused in the subsequent Bali bombings. Megawati exerted intense diplomatic pressure on the Philippines to release two prominent Indonesian politicians who had been caught there with bomb-making ingredients in suitcases.[10] After U.S. intelligence uncovered a major attack planned by Jemaah Islamiya, the United States launched a campaign to persuade Indonesia to improve its security. In September 2002, U.S.

Embassy officials met with their Indonesian counterparts to demand the arrest of Abu Bakar Bashir. The United States warned that the bilateral relationship was in the balance and threatened to reduce the size of the U.S. Embassy if Indonesia did not act. Megawati and her vice president were unmoved. Having reached power with the support of Islamist political parties but without a strong public constituency, Megawati chose to favor domestic politics over U.S. pressure.[11] Deeper law-and-order reform occurred only after Jemaah Islamiya actually did attack Bali and Jakarta and a new president not beholden to an Islamist power base was elected.[12] Unlike the direct nature of colonialism or occupation, in most rule of law interventions, foreign countries remain outsiders. They can demand, fund, and manipulate incentive structures—but they do not control the governments, and ultimately they cannot force change.[13]

In thinking about legitimacy, program designers should consider multiple levels. First, are the ends that are being pursued legitimate? Then, are the means legitimate? And third, do the actors themselves have legitimacy to act?[14] These questions should give pause and then be answered satisfactorily before proceeding too far, not just because doing otherwise would risk moral illegitimacy, but also because reforms seen as illegitimate are less likely to be supported by society, and therefore are less sustainable. Regardless of one's feelings about the legitimacy of spreading cultural norms in other countries, from an effectiveness standpoint, it is better to begin with reforms that are supported locally—and to press for more controversial reforms only when a domestic constituency can be organized in their favor.

Cultural Imperialism: We Have No Right to Force Our Rights on Others

The charge of cultural imperialism is the sidekick of the legitimacy issue. The rule of law, like its bedfellows democracy and human rights, is often accused of being a Western concept, imposed on indigenous cultures and non-Western nations through cultural arrogance.

Again, there is reality behind this criticism. The legal field, not known for its anthropological analysis, has frequently ignored local customs such as the lack of liquidity in the land market because of cultural rules tying land to specific families, or refusal to use bankruptcy laws not out of a lack of such laws but out of a feeling that bankruptcy is shameful. The U.S. focus on intellectual property law is often baffling to countries for whom the concept of intellectual property is not commonly understood, or in which copying goods is considered a compliment—as in parts of Indonesia, where a Muslim saying suggests that people who share knowledge will go to heaven.[15]

The charge of "cultural imperialism" is a matter of personal morality; it is for each reader to decide. It is clear, however, that cultural differences exist in many areas of the rule of law—and that ignoring these differences can reduce the effectiveness of rule-of-law reforms. Many postcommunist countries see social and economic rights as more important than political and civil rights, and they resent outside efforts to legislate the latter—which are, by their nature, counter-majoritarian. If outsiders want to focus on human rights, many believe, they shouldn't focus on small, marginalized communities such as prisoners, the Roma, or homosexuals—they should focus instead on increasing economic welfare that helps the majority. The poll mentioned in chapter 1, in which Albanians wanted to punish a canny flower seller for "corruption" but saw students who pay off their teachers for good grades as legitimate, points to differences in a foundational rule-of-law concept, even among Western nations. In many African countries, the idea that government officeholders have a responsibility to faceless citizens to steward public funds is a far weaker notion than the norm of responsibility to take care of one's extended family, or client relationships with one's tribe or village. In a number of Islamic societies, Sharia law is opposed to giving women equal justice; their testimony is legally discounted compared with male claims. Meanwhile, in many Indian villages, equality under the law is held de jure, but de facto, the idea that a low-caste person should be treated as the equal of a high-caste community member strikes many as not only unjust, but also blasphemous. These cultural beliefs mean that efforts to work for equality under the law, or even anticorruption, can run smack into norms pointing in the other direction. Either reformers admit that the rule of law requires altering these cultural norms, or they will fail.

However, cultures are not immutable. There is nothing inherently sinister about cultural change; cultures are constantly altering themselves. One need only watch an English period drama or an episode of "Mad Men," a television show set in the world of Madison Avenue advertising in the 1960s, to see just how much Western culture has changed in a few decades, from vastly improving women's rights to legalizing gay marriage. In Germany, the notion of *rechtsstaat* originally meant only that the government had to rule *by* law to limit arbitrariness. The concept did not have substantive content. After the Nazi regime showed the limitations of this idea, Germany amended its own understanding of *rechtsstaat* so that rights are now inherent in the concept.[16]

Moreover, cultures are constantly taking in, and responding to, notions from afar. These ideas may be consciously pushed by reform-minded outsiders. Many countries, for instance, have signed on to the UN Declaration of Human Rights—accepting a set of norms that they can then, legitimately, be expected to uphold. Ideas may also be welcomed from within via Hollywood movies, Internet chat rooms, satellite television, and music. Outside of a few remote Amazonian rain forest tribes, most cultural ideas are a fusion. They are constantly changing as cultures rub against each other. Contests between different ideas of what is culturally acceptable are as likely to be fights within a country as debates between outsiders and citizens. In some cases, different cultures may coexist in the same country and lead to rule of law conflicts—such as the French decision to bar *hijab* and the reaction from some of its Muslim citizens. In other cases, a single culture may be undergoing change. For instance, Ethiopia criminalized marriage via kidnap and rape—a traditional practice not in keeping with the government's idea of a modern state. Some people there agreed that this was a desirable change. One of them was a young Ethiopian rape victim trying to bring suit against her aggressor. She was supported by her father, many of her townspeople, and a police officer who had seen her flee. These bystanders felt, in their hearts, that what had long been allowed to happen was wrong and believed that amending this particular cultural practice was appropriate. Others, including the judge of that particular case, didn't want such traditional practices to change. Marriage by rape was how it had traditionally been done, and if the girl simply married her abductor, community peace would be restored.[17] The issue, like many human rights questions emerging in traditional societies, is contested internally; the ideas are not solely the province of Western do-gooders.

In fact, looking at the most egregious case of undermining sovereignty for rule of law–based issues—whether the United Nations has the right to use military force to prevent severe human rights violations—the majority of citizens in every nation polled answered yes. In many cases where "sovereignty" is held up against rights, the battle is not really between the developed and developing worlds, but between elites and other citizens.[18] For instance, in the case of Ethiopia, elites such as powerful men use the notion of cultural tradition against less empowered individuals, such as young women.

Finally, much of the cultural alteration that needs to take place for rule of law reform resides in the realm of professional, not popular, culture. Judiciaries, police, and other rule of law professions must create norms of honesty, knowledge, and public service. Where professional cultures have become warped, so that legal professionals no longer serve the law, they must be altered. However, such professional norms are not what most mean when they accuse the West of cultural imperialism. It's useful to separate this sort of bread-and-butter rule of law reform from the more tricky issues of altering popular social norms with deep cultural meaning.

Success in rule of law reform cannot be achieved without acknowledging that altering social norms is part of the package. However, the United States and other countries and international bodies can be sensitive in their choice of tactics. Montesquieu, the French author of *The Spirit of the Laws*, considered this issue centuries ago and came to the conclusion that the proper realm to contest culture was with other norms and habits that fought it out among themselves in the cultural realm. Legislating changes in cultural norms was not only ineffective, but also led to despotism when it was enforced. More success with greater legitimacy would also be possible if the methods on such sensitive issues involved building domestic constituencies who shared those norms (bottom-up reform), rather than pursuing cultural change through strong-arm diplomacy or top-down efforts to rewrite laws.

While cultural imperialism may be less of a worry than it initially appears, very real differences in culture suggest that outsiders should also pick their issues carefully. While it hardly seems despotic to support women fleeing rapists, keep kleptocrats from stealing the wealth of their countries, or end "separate but equal" practices that relegated African Americans to second-class status in America, such positions can create cultural backlash. It makes sense for outsiders to begin with less contested concepts that are widely desired and gradually work toward more contested concepts in conjunction with locals who share their values.

Outsiders, whether American or from other countries, should also avoid forcing cultural changes that are on the cutting edge or are debated even within their own countries. These kinds of changes are not going to be the most essential for the rule of law, and where they are debated among rule-of-law reformers, they can cause real cynicism locally. For instance, in the 1990s, the EU pushed Eastern Europe hard for anti–death penalty legislation, while the United States, where the death penalty is legal, ignored the issue. Meanwhile, the U.S. Congress annually threatened to revoke Most Favored Nation trading status for China during the 1990s unless it curbed human rights abuses—while at the same time, Europe pushed for Chinese trade. Differences among programs across countries can certainly give the impression that reforming countries are being made to meet goals that simply fulfill great-power desires, rather than goals that are necessary for the rule of law itself.

Neocolonialism: Isn't This Just About Power?

Helping rape victims sounds very nice—but if you look at where the money is spent on the rule of law, it's largely in the field of security. It's reasonable to ask whether such concepts as equality and human rights are like, as in the colonial era, putting lipstick on a pig. "Rule-of-law" reforms are often seen by locals not as attempts to develop their countries but as thinly veiled efforts for the United States and Europe to protect their companies while opening foreign markets. In particularly anti-imperialist nations, locals may view rule-of-law reformers as little different than U.S. Commodore Matthew Perry, who used his gunboats to pry open Japanese markets previously closed to the United States.[19] For instance, the dean of a law school in Indonesia claimed that:

> USAID began sending lots of Indonesian lawyers to study in the U.S. so that the U.S. legal system would influence Indonesian law, and so more students would aspire to go to the U.S. That would further perpetuate the common law in a sort of self-feeding circle—this would all be good for U.S. business, since it is easier for U.S. business to operate in a common law environment. Really, the end goal behind all this push for understanding of the U.S. legal system and the common law is the U.S. trying to help its business interests.[20]

These suspicions may be conspiracy theories. They often underestimate goodwill and overestimate the importance of developing country markets to the United States—but they are not always unfounded. In the early years after the Cold War, the United States and the EU used legal reform as a way of fighting for influence over the newly independent states of Eastern Europe, and these maneuvers for primacy continue there and in other parts of the world.[21] The European Commission itself noted that:

> The priorities of the EU and other donors have however not always coincided with those of the NIS countries [newly independent states of the former Soviet Union]: while donors have been interested in strengthening the western borders of NIS countries in order to stem the flow of illegal migrants from moving further west, the priority of the NIS countries has been to reduce the flow of illegal migrants entering through their eastern borders. This clash of priorities is particularly evident in Russia, which is both an entry and exit point for illegal migrants.[22]

Is rule-of-law reform simply a nice cloak for getting what more powerful countries want? The only reasonable answer to this question is that, of course, the United States and European countries are promoting policies that are in their own interests—it would hardly suit a democratic government to spend taxpayer money pressing for policies that *weren't* in their interest. The more useful question is whether Americans and Europeans are promoting the rule of law in a way that helps powerful outside interests and harms locals. Here, the answer is more murky.

Some interventions appear to be pretty clearly win-win. Even if they may be disliked by entrenched constituencies who stand to lose as the rule of law improves in a country, they seem clearly in the country's overall interest. It is hard to argue against helping poor people gain greater access to efficient means for settling their disputes. And it would take a dyed-in-the-wool anti-imperialist to claim that passing sunshine laws that force politicians to disclose their contributors is a bad thing for a country's democratic system. Some values are simply fairly universal: After the Rwandan genocide, the United States dramatically increased support to reconstruct the justice sector in order to try the perpetrators, improve policing, build better prisons, and institute other reforms meant to enhance the general human rights environment.[23] Programs such as these are premised on the idea that it is in America's interest for other countries' governments to be serving their people, not fattening their own wallets, and for the poor in those countries to rely on their governments for justice rather than being forced to turn to insurgent groups such as the Taliban. Such a broad view of America's interests—like the view taken in President Clinton's International Crime Control Strategy quoted in the last chapter—allows for a great number of positive rule of law advances within other countries and hardly raises the stench of power politics.

Other activities may appear to be in the interests of the United States but are actually quite helpful locally, too. For instance, security reform in Latin America could be seen as nothing more than a program to help the United States, but when the World Bank surveyed the poor of that continent—as well as around the world—it found that they were as concerned about their personal safety as about unemployment and poverty.[24] Indonesia would have been better off if President Megawati had taken U.S. advice seriously and had prosecuted local terrorist groups before they bombed multiple sites in Jakarta and Bali, killing scores of people and sending the tourist trade into free fall.

Still other activities are clearly in U.S. interests and are largely neutral in terms of their effects on a country. For instance, a state moving out of a command-and-control economy that wants a more liquid market needs a modern bankruptcy law. It may adopt a European-style law that favors creditors, or an American-style law that favors debtors. The choice will have significant effects on the country's own market development.

American companies will clearly benefit if the local law is of a style with which they are familiar. But it's not clear that the country is worse off having an American-style law as opposed to a European-style law. Both involve trade-offs between dynamism and risk, and neither choice is bad. The best way to avoid appearances of power politics is for outsiders to consciously lay out the trade-offs and let the country choose for itself. Many American lawyers pushing for U.S.-style bankruptcy laws over other versions don't intend to engage in a values debate—they are simply ignorant of European systems. However, the appearance of their lobbying for laws that help American companies can make a population feel that it is being bullied. It is exactly the kind of appearance that the United States should take care to avoid, particularly when the payoff is, in fact, fairly low.

Human rights norms are another area where the effects of intervention are hard to measure. Does it help the United States if Latin American prisoners are better cared for and their prisons are less overcrowded? It probably does; given the flow of gang members from Central America to big cities in the United States and back, the less hardened these prisoners are, the better. Is it bad for the countries in question? Well, it is certainly better for the prisoners themselves—and for the guards who have to watch them. It might reduce recidivism, which would be positive for the country. On the other hand, when prisoners have better food and shelter than the working poor of a country, that can cause resentment.[25] Even harder to determine are U.S. programs in democratic policing. The United States frequently trains police in forensic investigative techniques that are essential to convincing law enforcement officials that they can abandon torture and coerced confessions and still have other forms of evidence to prosecute criminals. Such a switch in techniques clearly seems a net positive. But the police training can also have the side effect of strengthening the police, who often form an autocratic regime's power base. This has been the criticism of such work since the 1970s—and the U.S. attempts to ameliorate the worry have probably had the unintended consequence of simply making the resulting cookie-cutter programs less effective at achieving anything whatsoever.

Finally, some programs can have real, negative side effects—and the United States should be very careful before demanding them. Sometimes, these are obvious power plays—for instance, in 2005, NATO, the EU, and the United States forced through a whole series of antiterrorism measures in Albania, to the great anger of its elite, who felt that their civil liberties were being curtailed.[26] The United States had its reasons—as described in the last chapter, it believed that al-Qaeda was using the country as a base of operations, a particular problem for the U.S. and NATO troops stationed there. However, the sweeping nature of the laws were written for foreign audiences with little regard to local consequences and called for grounding all speedboats off the Albanian coast in an effort to curb smuggling. The laws may well have stopped some smugglers; they also caused legitimate commerce to grind to a halt.[27]

America should perhaps be the most careful when it comes to well-intentioned programs that are intended to help a given country but that can have negative side effects. Some of the most problematic interventions are value-neutral reforms that have the unintended consequence of tying up valuable resources. For instance, in the 1990s, Albania had approximately 300 lawyers. Of these, only a handful were English-speakers who could interact with foreigners, as well as highly trained—the profession had, after all, been banned under communism. So simply embarking on a rewrite of all of Albania's laws required the nearly full-time services of the nation's most educated legal professionals. This choice of activities involves opportunity costs; lawyers rewriting laws cannot be trying the thousands of property cases that filled courts (and stymied economic development) following the end of communism, or taking on other needed legal activities. The same can be said for the plethora of small rule-of-law grants that struggling Ministries of Justice have to report on—turning a Ministry of Justice into a grant-writing and responding office is not the best use of local human capital, though the same criticism can be made of nearly any development area, not just the rule of law. These opportunity costs are a real problem in many rule-of-law interventions, and one that the United States would do well to take more seriously. Intervening in any complex, interdependent system is bound to have unintended consequences. Often, these practical problems actually cause more trouble to reforming countries than the sexier, more obvious issues of morality and power politics.

Credibility: Can the United States Alter the Rule of Law in Other Countries?

The final concern follows an entirely different tack. Should the United States be attempting to build the rule of law in other countries when America itself still has so many rule-of-law failings at home, and when our work overseas has such a limited track record of success? Is it right to spend taxpayer dollars on solutions that would be great if they worked, but that rarely seem to succeed? After all, America has its own corruption issues—witness the fracas over Illinois Governor Rod Blagojevich, who put Barack Obama's former Senate seat up for sale, or former Louisiana Congressman William Jefferson, who hid $90,000 in bribes in his freezer. Law-and-order breakdowns occur regularly in cities from Washington, D.C., to New Orleans; police brutality remains an issue in Los Angeles; and problems with organized crime continue in New Jersey and Nevada. What gives Americans the slightest confidence that we can solve problems in other countries, when problems such as these can't be solved at home?

Like the other critiques, there is some solid sense in this one. The rule of law is complex, and it is never complete—even in the United States, the failures are legion. And yet, common sense suggests that in most of the United States, the rule of law is generally better than in a number of weak countries. There is a reason that most parents would worry more about their child spending a semester studying abroad in Somalia than in Savannah. More to the point, just because America has its own political and technical challenges with implementation doesn't mean problems can't be solved. Since the 1960s, the United States has made leaps and bounds in improving equality before the law, deepening human rights, and solving law-and-order problems in some of the nation's biggest cities. Empirically proven techniques are known to improve some rule-of-law goals—such as deploying police based on an analysis of crime statistics in various neighborhoods, or cracking down on small quality of life crimes to avoid larger criminal problems. In other words, occasionally failing to stick to one's diet doesn't mean someone doesn't know *how* to lose weight. In part, it is through learning domestically that the United States can learn how to create effective rule-of-law programs in other countries. For instance, in New York, it took a tough, controversial mayor to press through crime-fighting techniques despite a great deal of resistance. It would be wise for the United States to take such lessons about what success requires above and beyond technical knowledge, and to apply those lessons to programs abroad. In fact, one good way to improve the track record of success abroad is to mix teams of development specialists and diplomats with the police officers, anticorruption prosecutors, and other reformers who have succeeded in the United States and other countries that have overcome similar failures. Learning from success in America and elsewhere might mean the difference between success and failure in rule of law programs abroad.

But there is also a deeper, more holistic layer to this critique. Like those who claim that some cultures are inimical to democracy, there is both research and popular opinion that suggests some countries are such fallow ground for rule of law reform that reformers shouldn't waste their time. The task is impossible, the thinking goes—not because of reformers' own failures, but because the rule of law is ultimately a political and cultural phenomenon that has emerged in only a few countries as a result of unique confluences of social and historical conditions.[28] In countries where the soil has not already been prepared, skeptics say, there is no point in trying to plant seeds. The only way to improve the rule of law, they would have you believe, may be to "become a British colony and then wait 200 years."

There is serious academic research to back this idea. A body of scholarship suggests that legal and political history, demographics, education levels, and economic development determine which countries adopt the rule of law and which do not. Daniel Treisman's studies have found significant correlations between lower levels of corruption and countries with British colonial history and widespread Protestantism. Edward Banfield has suggested that there are strong links between corruption and societies with ethics based in "amoral familism"—basically, strong ties among families, and weak ties binding families to a larger community.[29]

The historical-cultural critique is often made implicitly. For instance, constitutional scholar A. E. Dick Howard explains why some Eastern European countries gravitated toward the rule of law more rapidly than others by claiming:

> Those lands that lay within the Hapsburg domain fell heir to Austrian traditions of a Rechtstaat [rule-of-law state]. The Austro-Hungarian Empire . . . developed a strong tradition favoring the rule of law in its successor states in Central Europe. Peoples under Ottoman rule were not so fortunate.[30]

According to this theory, the rule of law is not amenable to change catalyzed by outsiders, because "the distant past appears as important as—or more important than—current policy."[31] No supply of law, lawyers, or legal institutions, and no sudden change of regime can undo the damage done by centuries of authoritarian tradition or ingrained cultural attitudes. Reform can occur only through the slow passage of time and internal history. Obviously, few practitioners engaged in rule-of-law reform accept this hypothesis. Yet its fatalism looms over reformers in the field and agencies arguing for rule-of-law funding, and it has never been shaken.

However, history shows us that cultures and political dynamics change—and sometimes, they change quickly. A generation of realists was surprised by the fall of the Soviet Union—and surprised again when democratic protests broke out across the Middle East in 2011. Unique confluences of demographics and historical moments—in the case of the Arab Spring, the youth bulge across many developing countries, married to a lack of job opportunities, sclerotic and corrupt governments, and widespread media showing how other countries function—created conditions that were ripe for cultural upheaval demanding an end to corruption and human rights abuse—core tenets of the rule of law. Even without such cataclysmic changes, norms can alter. As discussed earlier in this chapter, witness America's own demographic shift toward gay rights over just three decades. And political culture can change, often as a result of organized movements led by unique individuals rather than the pure structural forces of history. The progressive movement in the United States at the turn of the last century took advantage of historical moments—but its organizers also deserve significant credit for bringing the rule of law to the United States, which at the time was awash in corruption, with shaky law and order, and compromised judges. As outsiders in other countries, Americans may not be able to bring about all of this change—but they can put a thumb on the scale, helping countries to build their own versions of the progressive movement, for instance, when windows of opportunity open and nascent desire exists.

The real lesson of this critique is to take culture, politics, and history seriously. There are moments when a country has a greater likelihood of adopting rule-of-law norms, and then there are eras when doing so will be a more uphill battle. Reformers should not take a generic approach to reform, and sequencing cannot be established *a priori*. It must grow out of an understanding of a unique country with unique circumstances. Reformers must pay attention to cultural and political windows of opportunity when there is fluidity in the system. It is easier to pass laws requiring government transparency soon after a major corruption scandal hits the press. It is simpler to gain equal rights for minority groups when they actually form majorities in certain voting districts. There is greater likelihood of ensuring equality under the law when a large segment of middle-class business owners will benefit from it and can be organized to fight for it. These moments do not occur in neat annual cycles that fit yearly reporting requirements. But nor is it necessary to wait two hundred years. The United States has been undertaking rule of law reform in many countries for two decades—plenty of time to seek these moments of opportunity and make the most of them when they arrived.

Conclusion

Those who see rule-of-law promotion as either overly imperialistic or hopelessly idealistic have arguments in their favor. But those who believe that such arguments will stop the United States and other reformers from engaging in rule-of-law promotion are, frankly, unrealistic. Even if Americans agreed that they are wrong to try, or unable to succeed, history suggests that they will attempt rule-of-law reforms again and again. In one way or another, strengthening the judiciaries, building the police forces, and otherwise reforming rule-of-law structures in other countries is a solution that the United States has returned to regularly, under both Republican and Democratic administrations, for more than a hundred years. Moreover, the United States is inadvertently altering the rule of law in other countries through its diplomacy, procurement, and other national activities—often in ways that are negative. Rule-of-law programs are at least a counterweight to this foreign policy reality. In any case, the United States is surely going to continue to engage in efforts to build the rule of law in other countries. And it is going to undertake activities to affect rule-of-law institutions in order to meet its own needs. The realistic choices are to try to do this better, or to do it worse. America is clearly unable, as a country, to remain outside the fray.

Instead of condemning the past, it is best to learn from it. A few takeaways are possible from this chapter, both for skeptics and for deeply committed rule-of-law reformers. First, it is worth keeping in mind that not everything called "rule-of-law reform" is geared toward building the rule of law. Changes to rule-of-law institutions may be intended to create a more friendly business climate for foreign investors or to press for certain human rights norms that are favored by the United States but that are not actually necessary to build a rule-of-law state. Where the United States can refrain from such pure self-interest, it should. And it should at least be aware of how such initiatives can sully other work that is focused on building the domestic rule of law.

Second, rule-of-law reform does depend on altering the social compact and affecting cultural norms. This change may not be illegitimate in the least, but it should be acknowledged: If all the subcultures and professional cultures of a country fully supported the rule of law, they probably would not need help from outsiders. A country's population or leadership may like the idea of the "rule of law" but be less keen on some of the specific reforms that outsiders deem necessary for its achievement—whether gender-neutral laws in highly traditional states, or anticorruption norms in a culture in which families seek not to end corruption but to benefit from it. Cultural disagreements can cause a demand gap that reduces reform success. It is easy to hide such clashes under a term to which everyone gives lip service. However, when the feel-good "rule of law" is boiled down to a specific goal, and that specific goal is undesirable to locals, successful reform is likely to be difficult no matter which reform strategy is chosen.

Finally, culture, history, and politics do matter. History should not deter the United States from trying to promote the rule of law in other countries—but it does suggest changes to the way the reform is carried out. Instead of following routine sequences or mix-and-match reforms, the United States needs to be much more attuned to power dynamics, cultural shifts, and moments of flux in other countries' social systems. Such an approach is a hallmark of second-generation reform and is the method that will flow through the following chapters.

CHAPTER FOUR

WHAT MUST CHANGE? THE FOUR OBJECTS OF REFORM

The Mafia enjoyed remarkable success for more than a century. . . . From the very beginning it concealed its fundamental aim; namely, to exercise power and become wealthy in illegal ways, behind the alluring mask of the "society of honor." This "society" was supposedly an association of just and wise men capable of ensuring the order, safety and justice that the State, distant, indifferent, perhaps even hostile, could not or would not guarantee. And as it gradually spread and embraced every possible source of profit—construction, food markets, public contracts, contraband of cigarettes, narcotrafficking—[it] employed every means possible—nepotism, corruption, threats, extreme violence—to increase the gap between citizens and the State and to prevent the development of a civic conscience. It was precisely this dominance over the mental attitude and spirit of the people that guaranteed the Mafia absolute control over the island.

– Enzo lo Dato, executive director of the Sicilian Renaissance Institute[1]

On Salt Spring Island in Vancouver, British Columbia, local vendors sell bunches of flowers, fresh vegetables, and homemade honey. Such roadside stands dot towns the world over—but on this little Canadian isle, there is a difference. No one bothers to man the stands. They work on the honor system. Cash boxes are simply left next to the offerings, with small signs proclaiming prices. Customers walk up, take what they want, and leave their money. When my incredulous boyfriend remarked to some locals that a customer could simply steal all the wares—or the cash box itself—the islanders laughed at him. "You Americans!" they said. "So little trust!"

What accounts for Salt Spring Island's apparently idyllic rule of law system? Does it have better laws than more crime-ridden cities in Canada or the United States—or stronger courts, jails, and lawyers? Such legal institutions hardly seem likely to be what is on the average person's mind when she decides not to steal strawberries. So what makes this society work?

In the first chapter, I mentioned the famous Archimedes quote—if he had a lever long enough, he could move the world. But what should that lever be prying up? One of the key differences between first- and second-generation rule-of-law reform is that first-generation reform focused on altering laws and institutions to make them look more like those in "rule-of-law countries." Too often, these laws and institutions became ends in themselves, altered toward no clear goal other than modernity. Second-generation reforms pay greater attention to power and cultural norms—using legal and institutional reforms largely to influence these more core challenges. If the rule of law is a relationship between state and society, then first-generation reformers are focused on the material elements of the bond: perfume, roses, a nice house—while second-generation reformers are working to ensure that the wedding vows are upheld.

The fact that first-generation reformers focused on laws and institutions makes a lot of sense at first glance. Consider a typical transitioning state. Many lawyers and even judges don't know what the laws actually are, because the laws are unpublished. If they did know, they would find many laws outdated and inappropriate, particularly for a modern commercial sector. The judiciary is riddled with corruption and unused to writing decisions; judges may not even be accustomed to thinking in terms of legal argument. Cabinet ministers try to interfere in judicial decisions when cases come too close to the top levels of power, while parliamentarians drive fancy cars and own vacation villas far outside their means, flouting their corruption and "above the law" status. Most of the population sees the government as an obstacle and feel little social opprobrium at violating laws, from bribing civil servants to taking justice into their own hands. Even accepted laws are difficult to enforce, due to a largely illiterate and overstretched police force, itself often in league with criminal gangs.

What must be changed for the rule of law to flourish? Is the core problem practical—a need for more modern laws? Does it call for technical help to create more efficient institutions? Is the issue at root political—a power structure that must be altered to establish new relationships among powerful sectors within a state and its society? Or is the core need a cultural, attitudinal change within the population or professional cultures of various legal and law enforcement professionals? If all of these areas require work, where should reform begin? Most rule-of-law scholarship involves debates over sub-issues within any one of these objects.[2] But first, it is clarifying to distinguish among these four major areas of rule-of-law reform. Let's take a look at each in turn.

The Laws: Get the Rules Right

Most first-generation rule-of-law reforms, particularly the aid programs enacted in Eastern Europe immediately after the fall of communism, started with legal change. Early reformers assumed that what countries needed in order to establish the rule of law was good laws.[3] Laws shape incentives, and by doing so, they affect the behavior of citizens, businesses, and government officials.[4] Many states reforming their rule-of-law structures are transitioning from communist, authoritarian, or outdated traditional legal structures. According to the legal theory of change, when new and improved laws are introduced, they change the rules of the game, creating new ways of acting that support a rule-of-law state. Ideally, the local legal system grafts onto these "legal transplants" and creates new local laws around the imported laws to further incentivize compliance. Just as digging a ditch channels water flow, and that flow further deepens the ditch, following these new laws and constitutional structures is expected to create habitual patterns of behavior that entrench the rule of law.

Based on this logic, rule-of-law reforms often begin by redrafting constitutions and rewriting individual laws or codes. Creating and rewriting constitutions has been part of the reform package from postwar efforts in Japan and Germany in the 1940s, to the spate of Western constitution-drafting in Africa after decolonization in the 1960s, to the constitutional conferences that took place throughout Central and Eastern Europe in the 1990s, and the constitutional efforts in Afghanistan, Iraq, and the post–Arab Spring countries in this decade.[5] As Giovanni Sartori notes, "Of the 170 or so written documents called constitutions in today's world, more than half have been written since 1974."[6] The well-developed subfield of constitutional theory has grown around questions of how to create the best constitution, leading to ongoing debates over presidential vs. parliamentary systems, whether constitutional courts or courts of cassation are needed to judge the constitutionality of new laws, and methods of constitutionally enshrining judicial independence.[7]

Having a well-crafted constitution seems to be a *sine qua non* for the rule of law. After all, constitutions delineate the structure of power among elements of government, and between government and society. If those are done right, the rule-of-law should follow. Prescribing canny constitutional structures that force officials to share power or check each other's actions will "disperse power and protect liberty by pitting ambition against ambition and power against power."[8] Isn't that the very bedrock of reforming the power structure?

In fact, it is probably too much to ask from mere words on paper. Constitutions are ignored or amended the world over. Most second-generation reformers would instead hold a weaker view: A good constitution can't ensure a rule of law state, but a bad constitution can make it far more difficult to develop the rule of law. Moreover, second-generation reformers would focus as much on the process of constitution drafting as on the content—a constitution that enjoys widespread buy-in from the citizenry and major spheres of power has a greater chance of being upheld than one drafted by a few constitutional lawyers and accepted by a rubber-stamp parliament. Why does the process matter so much? Constitutions depend on cultural norms, political habits, and common agreement. Only if these factors are added to the mere words on paper can constitutions succeed in becoming touchstones of moral legitimacy, garnering real power to shape the acceptable contours of a political system. As James Madison said, upon presenting what would become the Bill of Rights: "It may be thought that all paper barriers against the power of the community are too weak to be worthy of attention . . . . [Y]et, as they have [a] tendency to impress some degree of respect for them, to establish the public opinion in their favor, and rouse the attention of the whole community, it may be one means to control the majority from those acts to which they might otherwise be inclined."[9] Cultural acclimation and respect can transform "sheets of paper into hoops of steel," in the words of constitutionalist Walter Murphy.[10]

From constitution drafting, lawyers engaged in rule-of-law work slipped easily into rewriting laws themselves. Most of this work, then and now, focuses on ensuring that human rights are guaranteed, private property is legally enshrined and protected, and commercial codes are modern and comprehensive. Some hold that having modern Western laws on the books is useful but not sufficient to bring the rule of law. Others take a stronger view. Increased penalties for crime will improve law and order. Laws requiring transparency will reduce parliamentary corruption and bribery within the judiciary. Writing human rights laws and enshrining international covenants into national law will improve a state's support for human rights.[11]

The logic that private property leads teleologically toward a rule-of-law society, as an acorn contains the blueprint for an oak tree, has been a particularly strong motivator for some economists and lawyers. Once people have private property rights, they will seek ways to protect those rights and adjudicate between property claims, the theory goes, and will therefore demand just and efficient courts.[12] The "shock therapy" arguments made for Russia and some Eastern European states claimed that establishing private property would bring the rule of law. Once people owned things—and foreign businesses started to enter the country—they would demand the rule of law from the government and create it by adding laws onto the nascent private property regime.[13]

Similar logic led to the idea that a rule-of-law state could be created via commercial law, which would spill over to influence broader rule of law issues such as the power balance within the government and even human rights. This "Trojan horse" theory held particular appeal to international actors and aid agencies comfortable with technical commercial law reform but worried about their legitimacy in affecting change in more politically and culturally sensitive areas.[14] Moreover, commercial law reform was relatively cheap and fast, and it was assumed that it could be accomplished without a great deal of in-country knowledge—all factors that drew international actors toward a law-based theory of change in the early post–Cold War days.

Despite the obvious attractions of focusing on laws as the main object to leverage for rule-of-law reform, the problems associated with that approach have been known for years. In 1927, historian Guido de Ruggiero was already writing:

> The love of rationalistic simplification . . . leads people to think that in the mere technicalities of law they possess the means and the power to effect unlimited changes . . . [Such an illusion is] cherished by lawyers who imagine that, by drafting new constitutions and laws they can begin the work of history all over again, and know nothing of the force of traditions, habits, associations, and institutions.[15]

Fifty years later, the reform of the law–based law and development movement of the 1960s and 1970s was judged to have failed, largely because "a transfer [of laws] without theory cannot succeed, and a theory which does not take into account the pre-existing social and legal structures is worthless."[16] Similarly, the president of a major Russian academy commented at a conference of U.S. and European donors in 1996, "We cannot merely copy your laws, because we have our own history, traditions, and lawyers."[17] Westerners from throughout Europe and America rewrote nearly all the major legal codes in Albania, after the country's half century of extreme isolation. In the words of a practitioner who has spent much of his career in Eastern Europe, "Albanian lawyers today often speak proudly of the new system, noting, however, that the new laws are European, not Albanian, and that they are not actually being applied."[18] Charges of "legal imperialism" and general resentment of the imposition of an alien legal schema on an indigenous legal culture are frequently levied against rule-of-law reform through legal change—charges that work against country ownership of reform.[19]

Outsider-induced legal change ignores the supposition that constitutions and laws do not catalyze change but merely reflect change that has already taken place at a cultural level. Constitutions are "a *manifestation* of a people's determination to establish an entirely new basis for its polity"; they do not create that popular desire.[20] Foreign-created constitutions and laws, by definition, could never have the "expressive function of constitutional law," as legal scholar Cass Sunstein suggests.[21] Or as U.S. President John Adams poetically explained, "A constitution is a standard, a pillar, and a bond when it is understood, approved, and beloved. But without this intelligence and attachment, it might as well be a kite or balloon, flying in the air."[22] Constitutions, commercial law, and human rights laws enshrine cultural demands and norms; they do not create these. Constitutional reform can play a role in creating supportive power structures for a rule-of-law society and can garner popular support for rule of law norms when the citizenry is engaged in the legal or constitutional process. But in and of itself, a constitution is just a set of words strung together—particularly when drafted by foreign intervention.

Finally, rule of law promotion through law reform is posited on the idea of a strong state that enforces laws across the whole of its territory—a rarely accurate assumption. Countries undertaking rule-of-law reform are notorious for passing laws that they ignore, either by design (as occurred habitually in Romania from 2000 to 2004) or from lack of capacity to ensure enforcement. In many states, police may barely enforce the law, judiciaries may provide justice to the highest bidder, and local communities are "governed partly by their own customary practices and partly by the rules of the formal legal system," in the words of Julio Faundez, who describes such a mélange in Peru's highlands.[23] It is hard to imagine how law reform can change behavior if the laws are not enforced or even known in large parts of a country. Changing laws when enforcement and implementation are highly unlikely is, on its face, a rather ineffective way of changing behavior.

The theory that legal and constitutional reform could create the rule of law has eroded slowly and unevenly—but not totally. Some scholars drew a broad conclusion from the purported failures of legal change: Laws are rooted in and interpreted through cultures. Legal "transplants," as they came to be known, could not put down roots in culturally inhospitable soil, or they would be unrecognizably altered in the process of cultural adaptation.[24] Others in the development field decided that legal change was still necessary; it simply needed to be done using methods that more deeply anchored laws into the local society. In any case, the field as a whole recognized that legal change was not sufficient—laws, at the very least, needed strong implementing institutions to make a difference.[25]

Institutions: Ensure Proper Training, Equipment, and Funding

As law reform failed to deliver the hoped-for results, first-generation rule-of-law reformers turned to the institutions of justice, such as courts, police forces, law schools, magistrates' schools, and bar associations, among others.[26] Their logic was simple: Many societies have good laws but no rule of law because their institutions are poorly funded and malfunctioning. If institutions are created that look and function like those in rule-of-law states, they will achieve the rule of law. The theory grew from a visceral reaction to obvious problems reformers saw on the ground. The institutions of justice are so broken in many countries that bringing about the rule of law seems to require institutional repair, whatever else might be necessary. After the institutions of justice are reformed, it is assumed that they will function more competently.

A misreading of the scholarship of Douglass North and other "New Institutional Economists" added theoretical fuel to this common-sense supposition. These economists suggested that development rested on the success of a country's institutions. A close reading of the work would have made it clear that North defined "institutions" not as government agencies, law schools, bar associations, and the like, but as "the rules of the game in a society, or, more formally, the humanly devised constraints that shape human interaction."[27] These patterns of social behavior included intangibles such as cooperation and trust (factors that Robert Putnam cited as key to the development of northern Italy).[28] In North's conception, development economics needed to recognize the importance of political, social, and cultural structures, informal as well as formal. While he wrote about the importance of formal and informal laws and legal structures, he particularly distinguished between what he called institutions and the organizations such as the police or the court system that both influence institutions and are influenced by them. But as North's ideas electrified the rule-of-law field, funding agencies needed something more concrete than "political, social, and cultural structures" to fund. They began to use the new institutionalists' theories to support the belief that rule-of-law change was primarily achieved through the reform of concrete, material institutions—courts, police, law schools, and the like.

Thus, in country after country, U.S. efforts have attempted to support reforms that, when looked at in hindsight, make little sense as the best use of superpower money and time. For instance, after the collapse of the pyramid schemes in Albania, the country descended into anarchy. Rioters destroyed government institutions, including most courts and prisons. Prisoners ran free, raping and killing innocents. Looters overran military depots, stealing arms that soon spread throughout the country. The government lost control over large swaths of territory. Boatloads of refugees poured across the Adriatic into Italy. The chaos ended only when the Italian military intervened to restore order.[29] The rioting undid nearly all the development work of previous years, wasting billions of dollars in foreign aid.

The following year, USAID quite sensibly made building the rule of law its second strategic objective for the country. But the program was explicitly based on two stated hypotheses: "1) public actors in the legal system are generally not familiar with current Albanian law; 2) current actors do not behave according to international standards because they do not possess the necessary skills to perform their tasks."[30] In a country where parliamentarians ran smuggling rings and prominent criminals shared the podium with politicians during elections, these were odd assumptions.[31] They bypassed the political, cultural, and social structures that had allowed a complete breakdown of the Albanian state and instead led to technocratic programs. Over the next decade, USAID directed its small pool of funds (about $1 million a year) toward U.S.-based contractors charged with improving the magistrates' school, creating legal access for citizens, and training the judiciary in Albania's new laws. It later branched into case management reform and electronic distribution of cases. The latter programs could have been used to greater effect had they been seen as methods to curb corruption within the judiciary and prioritized. Instead, they were just one of the standard parts of the reform tool kit. Computers were given to older court presidents who often could not use them, and they gathered dust in back rooms. Case management software was tied up in donor disputes and still had not been fully implemented five years later.[32]

Because treating institutions as the focus of reform has been the main model of rule-of-law reform among practitioners, it has come in for a great deal of criticism, both theoretical and empirical. The problems with institution-based reform have long been recognized. More than fifteen years ago, in 1994, Harry Blair and Gary Hansen declared:

> Legal system strengthening was supported by USAID and other donors in all six countries. This strategy generally comprises the traditional institution building activities, including the introduction of new systems for court administration, recordkeeping, and budget and personnel management; the design and conduct of pre- and post-entry training programs for judges, court staff, and lawyers; and the acquisition of modern technology such as computers for case tracking. The most important lesson concerning legal system strengthening is that it is not necessarily the best place to begin an ROL [Rule of Law] development program.[33]

The World Bank noted that "there is a lack of any consensus on what a well-functioning system looks like, [and] uncertainties as to the extent of its impact on extra-sectoral goals."[34]

Perhaps the most damning criticism came out of programs that have achieved institutional success with little change to the rule of law. Scholar and practitioner Linn Hammergren describes how Latin America, after twenty years of reform, had tremendous institutional improvements within the court system, such as respectable courtrooms, judges who had access to continuing education and knew the law, and transparent case distribution systems, and yet it achieved very little improvement in the delivery of justice and the rule of law. Most Latin Americans still believed that courts "produce costly delays, render irrelevant, sometimes politicized or purchased judgments, and are increasingly removed from the interests and concerns of ordinary citizens," according to opinion polls, comments of national and international observers, and academic studies.[35] Institutions can be reformed in myriad ways, and those reforms can be successful—but still have little to no impact on the rule of law itself.[36]

In fact, there are many ways that well-functioning institutions can be organized in rule-of-law states. As David Bayley explains:

> Democratic countries may have decentralized police (the United States) or centralized ones (France), a single national police (Sweden) or multiple national police (Italy), close political supervision (United States) or remote political supervision (Japan), constitutional limits on police power (Canada) or statutory ones (Great Britain) and combined or separate police organizations for preventive as opposed to investigatory policing (United States/France).[37]

The same could be said about courts, prosecutors, law schools, and any other major rule-of-law institution. The particular organization seems to matter less than ensuring that oversight, checks and balances, and a professional culture that supports the rule of law are in place. As András Sajó says:

> The same legal and institutional arrangement may work in one post-communist state and turn out to be a total failure in the other. Perhaps the real difference is neither structural nor historical. Jurisprudential differences can be better understood if the requirements for carrying out the task of constitutional review are observed in the broader context of their government and political realities.[38]

These criticisms have led to a movement within the development community toward "best fit" institutions. Rather than creating institutions that look like their Western counterparts, cutting-edge practitioners are suggesting working more organically from what exists, paying more attention to local informal institutions, and incorporating alternative institutions—not just because institutional modeling is not realistic, but because it may not be the "best fit" for solving the problems inherent in the political and cultural structure of the reforming country.[39] Meanwhile, reforms that improve efficiency and the functioning of the police or courts but are technocratic and ignore deeper social and power issues can easily drift into helping authoritarian states rule *through* law—rather than helping the rule of law. Perversely, rule through law can actually entrench autocracy.

Instead of simply diving into technical reforms, second-generation reformers suggest looking at why institutions are so flawed and whose interests are served by maintaining poorly performing institutions. Thomas Carothers states, "The primary obstacles to [rule of law] reform are not technical or financial, but political and human. Rule-of-law reform will succeed only if it gets at the fundamental problem of leaders who refuse to be ruled by the law."[40] Malfunctioning institutions are not the cause of rule-of-law deficiencies—they are the symptom of a power structure that does not support the rule of law. We therefore turn to the third object of change: the power structure.

The Power Structure: Create Formal and Informal Checks and Balances on Power

In Nepal, the U.S. Institute of Peace decided to conduct a survey to determine how citizens viewed their police force. The results were eye-opening. Many Nepalis wanted to trust their police and wanted the police to control law enforcement in their villages—despite seeing the police as having a poor record at actually prosecuting infractions. Why the mixed messages? Because most people saw the problems with the police as being rooted not in the law enforcement institutions but in the political structure. The most common answer as to why the police did not provide satisfactory security was "political pressure." Citizens' perceptions appear to be backed up: nearly two-thirds of the police who were polled admitted witnessing political interference in the course of their duties. Meanwhile, more than half of the members of the legal profession and judiciary surveyed claimed that political connections played a role in access to justice and a fair trial.

But power structures played an even deeper role in insecurity in Nepal than obstructing justice and fair trials. The majority of respondents viewed political parties as directly responsible for serious crimes. Political parties were mentioned second only to criminals as responsible for murders, trafficking of women and children, weapons smuggling, vigilantism, and threats to members of civil society. Clearly, focusing on laws or technical police training will do little to improve the rule of law in Nepal if political parties and the power structure itself are the locus of crime.[41]

Nepal's need for a rule of law that can rein in its political parties is not new—it is a rediscovery of the central purpose of the rule of law. From the early Greeks who coined the idea of the rule of law to Enlightenment intellectuals shrugging away the chains of monarchy, the rule of law was primarily about power—forcing an absolute ruler to bend to the dictates of the law. The main obstacles to the rule of law were believed to be leaders who wished to remain above the law, to maintain their power to take property and abuse citizens. Take, for instance, England. The modern rule-of-law state is often seen as having its beginning at the moment that the English nobility forced the king to sign the Magna Carta, limiting absolute monarchical power, and endowing the citizens of England (or at least some of them) with rights. The core reform was not the drafting of the treaty, or the development of the judicial circuit—it was creating a force that amassed enough power to balance the power of the monarchy. This historical understanding was a driving force behind the idea of "checks and balances" in America's own power structure some five hundred years later.

The power structure is such an obvious starting point for the rule of law, and the rediscovery of its centrality has been repeated so many times since the modern field began that it is worth considering why it has been ignored so long by rule-of-law reforms.[42] In fact, worse than being ignored, early rule-of-law reform efforts were often designed to preserve problematic power structures—such as helping to train more efficient and effective police for authoritarian governments in Latin America. Part of the answer, clearly, is that outside powers may have ambiguous feelings toward a truly reformed power structure in other countries. Too many in the U.S. government felt that relations with autocrats, for instance, kept parts of the Middle East stable—or that partnering with the military over the civilian power structures in Pakistan was the only way to get things done. Such attitudes work against rule-of-law reforms that alter power structures. Another part of the answer is the fear among development practitioners that meddling in the power structures of other states is illegitimate—leading to a deliberate attempt to make such reform technocratic. As scholar Sue Unsworth has noted, powerful intellectual and institutional barriers prevent donors from recognizing the centrality of politics to development in general—and even more to governance reforms such as the rule of law.[43] The founding documents of the World Bank, for instance, preclude it from interfering in political matters. Despite reams of research from its own experts on the negative effects of corruption on development, the Bank could become involved in the field only when its legal vice presidency explicitly reconstrued rule of law reform as a technical issue of legal and institutional change.[44] With a vested interest in making the rule of law as technocratic as possible to meet its own legal mandate, the World Bank focused on technocratic issues such as predictability and efficiency of judicial institutions. Because so much of the rule-of-law field among development practitioners emanates from the World Bank, other development agencies followed this lead. Moreover, as Unsworth points out, the entire ethos of the aid community is that donor agencies will employ experts who will bring solutions. The human capital in such agencies tends to be technocratic, with few political scientists, anthropologists, or individuals who have worked in politics in their own countries. These technocratic experts have an entire vocabulary of ideas that encourages thinking in terms of analyzing "gaps" between current and ideal performance of institutions, rather than analyzing the political forces that might cause such gaps.

Yet simply declaring that rule-of-law reform is technical rather than political does not make it so. The choice to do so led the field in a direction that has made it less effective for twenty years and has obscured what second-generation reformers believe is the most important object for rule-of-law reform to change. Today, however, the importance of the power structure as the crucial object of change is back with a vengeance. As discussed in chapter 1, from Unsworth's own research at the UK aid agency Department for International Development, to the Problem-Driven Political Economy Analysis emanating out of the World Bank, to numerous Scandinavian methodologies, voices are emerging from important places to put politics back in its central position as a driver of change.[45]

Second-generation rule-of-law reformers hold that the rule of law is flawed, first and foremost, because powerful forces do not want it to exist. These forces may include the government or political parties, an oligarchic power structure based on nongovernmental power centers such as big businesses, or a "captured" political structure in which organized criminals wield significant state power. In each case, powerful individuals enjoy benefits from crime, corruption, nepotism, unlawful arrest of opponents, and simply having their desires carried out without obstacle.[46] While they may rail publicly against these "scourges," they will not, on their own, undertake changes that would allow their power to be checked. As an Albanian political commentator claimed:

> The Albanian political and business elite wants to keep pushing integration for the populist acclaim, but they don't actually want integration—they profit from having borders [to enable smuggling], from the lack of control—so they don't have a big incentive to actually do what is necessary to integrate, just to keep the process going. . . . But they need foreign support, so they pay lip service and make incremental changes.[47]

Only when the powerful accept limits on their power and submit to equality under the law will the rule of law begin to emerge. Laws and institutions are flawed because these powerful forces want them to be—and until that power can be checked with other power centers, all the new commercial laws, judicial restructuring, and computerization in the world will not affect the crux of the problem. Legal and institutional reform can always be overturned or ignored by those in control.[48] For instance, in Romania, a reformist government passed significant reforms of the criminal code, civil service laws, and a host of other measures. But when a new government that didn't share these norms took over, the reforms were simply overturned.

Nor does all power to block rule-of-law reform lie in the executive or parliament. Older judges may not believe in newer legal traditions—from new human rights norms to new capitalist structures in a formerly communist system—and may simply not act on such new rules.[49] Judges themselves may prefer opportunities for corruption, creating roadblocks to change within the judiciary. Power on a lesser scale may also reside in clerks who want to retain power over case assignment and management to gain the perks of potential kickbacks, or in notaries who want to limit access to their profession and ensure the need for multiple papers that require notarization in order to make their work more lucrative.

The centrality of power runs throughout the development literature, which cites over and over the importance of the "will to reform." Early writers on the rule of law within USAID decided that this "will to reform" was so important that there was no point in engaging in rule-of-law reform at all if it was not present.[50] Others thought that it was possible to construct "will" and built a set of tactics for such efforts, from picking "reformers" and helping them gain access to power to supporting citizen organizing and advocacy groups.[51] The new movement of second-generation thinking has deepened the development community's focus on power. Diplomats also tend to focus on power as key to achieving change in a state. Their own backgrounds and government-to-government interactions create a tendency to see powerful government leaders as the central actors who will spark or retard any country-wide change. Coming together around rule-of-law reform based on affecting power could thus be fruitful for healing the chasm that arises, all too commonly, between development experts and diplomats. These efforts, however, will succeed only if both diplomats and development practitioners switch their thinking from an interest in "power" based on individuals who happen to have "will" or not—to "power structures." In other words, they need to learn how to build the deeper, longer-lasting power blocs that can help individuals who start as reformers remain on the straight and narrow—and to push those who lack "will" toward at least a neutral stance.

What do reforms to a power structure look like, and how can the United States engage legitimately in such intimate workings of government? First, it is crucial to say what power structure is not: "picking a winner"—finding, and supporting, a reformer. Picking a winner is an unfortunate common tactic among diplomats and politicians, who identify "reformers" and seek to strengthen them with the additional power that can be bequeathed by outside legitimacy and plaudits.[52] It makes sense initially—a leader seems to really support the rule of law, so development practitioners should get behind that leader. Yet, sadly, this tactic constantly backfires—enshrining individuals whose beliefs in the rule of law were either not so strong to begin with, or supporting those whose honest beliefs in the rule of law deteriorate over time with the perks of power. For instance, international leaders were enamored of Albania's anticommunist President Sali Berisha in the early 1990s when he first came into office. His excellent English and habit of quoting America's Founding Fathers made them believe he shared their values. The initial years of his government were marked by significant economic growth—which blinded leaders of the international community to his growing authoritarianism and treatment of the judiciary as a tool of the executive.[53] Similar stories with even worse endings can be told about a host of countries where leaders who initially were reform-minded became captivated with their own power and importance and slowly switched sides without the awareness of their international cheering section. President Askar Akayev of Kyrgyzstan, for example, was a darling of international financial institutions and was lauded by U.S. diplomats for years as "the Thomas Jefferson of Central Asia"—but slowly accrued greater powers for himself and his family until he became just another autocrat, which led to his ouster by reformist forces in 2005.[54] In an example closer to home, the infamous William "Boss" Tweed became known in the nineteenth century for creating peace and order amid New York's Civil War draft riots, creating a workable and fair system for draft exemptions, and gaining home rule for New York City. In his early days, Tweed was considered a reformer and was regularly invited to speak to progressive clubs—until his Tammany ring was responsible for graft estimated at between $1 billion and $4 billion in today's dollars.[55]

Of course, it goes without saying that leadership matters. It is important that people in positions of power believe in the rule of law. Without a reformer at the helm, a country or institution is unlikely to undertake rule-of-law reform. Having a reform-minded leader in power can open the floodgates for change. Romania, for instance, took leaps and bounds toward the rule of law during Monica Macovei's short tenure as minister of justice. Macovei, a former president of the Helsinki Commission, was not perfect—her lack of bureaucratic savvy cost her allies, and her willingness to pursue corruption wherever she found it would cost her her job in 2007. Yet the reforms she enacted were essential. She initiated legislation to improve judicial performance, disbanded the Justice Ministry's secret service (which had been wiretapping judges), and implemented background checks to remove judges and prosecutors who had collaborated with the powerful security services that continued to spread fear fifteen years after the fall of communism.[56] She increased the salaries of judges and prosecutors to make them less susceptible to bribes and reinvigorated the National Anticorruption Directorate, which took aim at major corruption cases.[57]

Outsiders can certainly advance rule-of-law reform by helping reformers gain power and supporting them once they are in control. Macovei, for instance, would not have gained her position if the European Union had not put extreme pressure on Romania to meet membership requirements before its date to accede to the Union. But that support needs to include, first and foremost, working with those reformers to create the checks and balances on power that will curb their own potential excesses, as well as those of future leaders who may be less reform-minded. In other words, having a reformer in power does not substitute for deeper reforms that change the power structure.

As illustration, take the case of Valeriu Stoica, an earlier reformist minister of justice in Romania. Stoica took control in 1996 just as EU aid began to flow to the country, and EU officials were eager to support the dynamic reform-minded leader. Stoica removed many older judges with communist sympathies and appointed younger, forward-thinking judges as court presidents. He cut judicial vacancies in half and amended various laws to speed court cases, reducing backlogs from more than 480,000 civil cases at the beginning of 1997 to only 173,000 less than two years later. He improved human rights by restraining the prosecutorial excesses of the previous administration.[58] He raised judicial wages and increased the judicial authority's budget to cover wages and administration, reducing incentives for corruption. In 1999, he established an ombudsman with a functioning staff and budget, and he drafted a series of legal code reforms.[59] The National Institute of Magistrates—an institution he cherished and helped grow—was intended to train the next generation of judges to ensure that they were skilled and that they thought differently than their communist elders.[60]

Stoica was a reformer—but he was also a political party leader and was interested in amassing power. When one of his appointees mentioned granting more independence to a judicial body to protect it from future incursions, he grew angry and said, "You talk as if there will be future ministers."[61] Seeing only his reforms, and not his tendency toward power and control of the judiciary, international agencies working with him did not press him on the crucial issue of checking his own power. Instead of building other centers of power, outside reformers, thrilled by Stoica's flurry of activity, thought it was enough to pick a winner.

They were wrong. The next minister of justice, an extremely conservative former communist, used her powers over the court to reverse much of Stoica's work. She fired civil servants and replaced many of the newly appointed younger judges and court presidents with judges from the communist era. She reduced benefits and suspended judicial wage increases, making judges more dependent on the benefits the ministry could hand out at will (through the Supreme Council of Magistrates). She issued letters to court presidents suggesting that they "consider" the "social consequences" of implementing various property laws—thin code not to enforce property rights.[62] She then nominated her husband as the head of the Constitutional Court.[63]

Such can be the consequences of picking a winner, rather than focusing on the underlying structures of power. Power structure reform can include helping a real reformer attain power. But once that reformer gets into power, one of the most important ways the international community can work with such an individual is to create the structures of accountability that serve to check and balance different power sources.

Some of these checks and balances are "horizontal"—using one government structure to check another. For instance, the United States has a judiciary and a legislature that can each check the powers of the president—and each other. Active prosecutors (along with the end of Prohibition) also checked the growing power of organized crime that threatened the rule of law in the 1930s. But horizontal checks are only one means of creating other centers of power. In the late 1800s, when big, consolidated businesses started to increasingly ignore the human rights and property rights of the common man—and courts did little to prevent them—citizens' movements and muckraking journalists formed a critical check on this new source of power. These "vertical" checks and balances use the power of citizens, through the media, and cultural disapprobation to curb the powerful.[64] The next chapter will provide concrete examples of modern tactics.

Laws and institutions are often needed to create or legalize the activities of these checks and balances. For instance, countries need legislation that allows citizen movements to form, ensures freedom of the press, and mandates the role of different government sectors. But as discussed above, such laws, while necessary, are not sufficient. They are upheld because powerful forces—and often, cultural acclimation—can enforce them. In places and at times where these relationships get out of whack and powers do not balance other powers, presidents may pack courts, fire civil servants, refuse to leave office, and otherwise ignore their legally mandated boundaries. Reforming power structures is not simply about creating shells of laws or institutions, but about ensuring that real power exists in different parts of society to check other parts. By helping to create an internal balance of power among domestic institutions, reformers catalyze local power dynamics to function on their own to uphold the rule of law, removing themselves from the role of outsiders constantly pressuring the government for rule-of-law improvements.

Social Norms: Enhance Public and Professional Cultures That Support the Rule of Law

When I was 23, I had a job evaluating development programs in rural India. Corruption was commonplace. In one particular government program, however, the corruption went so far that 100 percent of the funds had been stolen. It was the last straw. "Why don't you go to the papers and expose this story?" I asked the NGO director who had uncovered the crime. He gave a sardonic chuckle. "Ah, Rachel," he began. "If I went to the newspapers, they would thank me for the information. Then they would call the government minister and demand a bribe to squash it. If the papers did decide to publish the story, people would simply sigh. They don't expect anything more from government. And there are so many openly corrupt ministers. This one would not lose his job. Nothing would happen."

Power structures alone are not enough to uphold the rule of law. Cultural norms play a crucial role.[65] As mentioned in the first chapter, federal judges in the United States, while well-compensated compared to much of the country, makes less than their law clerks can make a year or two after joining a big-city law firm. And yet corruption is rare; the loss of honor would be devastating to most judges, and it is likely that a dishonest judge's career would end. Most people in Holland wouldn't consider bribing a police officer who pulls them over for a speeding ticket—creating fewer temptations for (relatively) low-paid law enforcement officials than in Mexico, where such offers of bribes are common. When social norms work to support the rule of law, they buttress institutions, laws, and the power structure. When they undermine the rule of law, they make it harder for each element of the system to do its work. The rule of law is a relationship between state and society—and it requires social norms, in mass culture and in the professional cultures of politicians, the media, the judiciary, and legal and law enforcement professionals to also support a culture of lawfulness.[66] As the mayor of Palermo and a force behind curbing the Sicilian mob likes to say, the rule of law is like a cart with two wheels. Law enforcement and society must work together in a mutually supportive relationship, or else the wheels spin at different speeds and the cart can't move.

As mentioned in the last chapter, rule-of-law reform can seem imperialistic enough without actually admitting that outside reformers are trying to affect social norms. As a result, it is hardly politically correct for rule-of-law programs to admit that altering culture may be an object of reform. Moreover, lazy thinking and essentialism can lead people to cite cultural variables as causal when they are really post hoc rationalizations: Confucianism, for instance, has been described as a reason for Asia's economic success—and the driving force behind its failures.[67]

Yet the importance of cultural norms as a crucial leverage point to affect the rule of law is too widely cited throughout history to be ignored because some thinkers will use it sloppily.[68] In 1835, Alexis de Tocqueville wrote:

> Europeans exaggerate the influence of geography on the lasting powers of democratic institutions. Too much importance is attached

> to laws and too little to mores. . . . If in the course of this book I have not succeeded in making the reader feel the importance I attach to the practical experience of the Americans, to their habits, opinions, and, in a word, their mores, in maintaining their laws, I have failed in the main object of my work.[69]

Nearly a century earlier, Montesquieu's famous *Spirit of the Laws* was based on the idea that the legal order of a state rested on the spirit that underlies the legal structure—the norms of society. Both their thoughts are echoed in Paula Dobriansky's statements centuries later when she was U.S. Undersecretary of State for Global Affairs:

> Corruption is not just a government problem, it is also a social problem. . . . Government efforts to enforce the law are insufficient in and of themselves to establish the rule of law in a country. This is a result of the fact that lawlessness and corruption often stem from social norms and historic practices. Because corruption may in some cases be the only way that businesses or individuals can pursue otherwise legitimate activities, it can become widely accepted. Thus, to promote the rule of law, a country must also build a culture of lawfulness.[70]

Cultural habits can present an obstacle to the rule of law in three main ways. Citizens may disobey laws en masse, making it impossible for a non-despotic state to fully uphold the law (such as with marijuana prohibitions in the United States or genital mutilation in much of Africa). Second, as with my experience in India, citizens and institutions of society such as the media may fail to expect their governments or fellow citizens to obey the rule of law, weakening the "vertical accountability" that social pressure plays in enforcing the rule of law. Finally, the culture of politicians or rule of law professionals may work against rule of law norms, disabling them from exercising "horizontal accountability." Let's look at each element in turn.

A popular culture that does not support the rule of law can take many forms: In Indonesia, families decry government corruption but then celebrate when a family member receives a "wet" job with chances for kickbacks. In Albania, according to the International Crisis Group, much of society began to see criminality as "legitimate," because the ill-gotten wealth could be used as a source of funds for economic development. Even some leading officials used this logic to justify crime, which they saw as a form of patriotism.[71] In inner-city America, distrust of the police can cause entire communities to go silent, preventing officers from finding witnesses and arresting wrongdoers even for crimes committed in broad daylight with spectators present.[72] In each case, informal rules governing socially acceptable behavior undermine the rule of law regardless of the laws, institutions, or political will of the state.

If most citizens break laws regularly, then only a despotic state with immense policing powers will have the power to enforce the rule of law. For a government to enforce the laws without resorting to undue repression, most people must simply follow the laws regardless of policing, because they accept the legitimacy of the bulk of the laws and their moral codes generally align with the laws.[73] In regions characterized by what Joel Migdal calls "strong societies, weak states," this relationship often breaks down.[74] Citizens may ignore the laws because they feel the state is so ineffectual that they must take the law into their own hands (vigilante justice), or because traditional practice is so far from formal law on the books that the latter is not seen as legitimate (as with dowry killings in India, child marriage in Nepal, or blood feud in the Middle East).[75] It can also occur when citizens perceive the government itself as illegitimate. In many communist countries, evading the law was seen as honorable. Now that democratic government is in place, however, these old habits of circumventing the state remain to undermine the rule of law.[76] Legal reform imposed from outside is particularly vulnerable to cultural failure: Despite EU pressure to improve the legal status of Roma, for instance, many Romanians are still deeply prejudiced. According to a 2005 opinion poll, 42 percent of the population—and 45 percent of the younger population, who presumably have been more influenced by the new laws—believe that Romanians and Roma "will always be irreconcilable."[77]

In the second instance, habits of apathy or ambivalence can undermine the rule of law. Often, citizens of weak states expect little from their government. They do not actually believe their governments will uphold the rule of law, and therefore do not hold their leaders up to rule-of-law standards. They have a history of, and therefore expect, corruption, state overreach, and inequality between the powerful and the powerless. The lack of societal condemnation for wrongdoing changes the incentive structures of government leaders and those in rule-of-law professions. For instance, while in cultures with strong norms against corruption, most politicians are curbed from greed by the knowledge that it could end their political careers; in cultures that assume all politicians are corrupt, there is little incentive to maintain one's honesty. In a catch-22, by expecting their governments to be venal, their businesses to break the law, or their organized criminals to be violent, citizens give up the vertical accountability they could otherwise use to curb such overreach. Such an apathetic culture can arise out of fatalism following a history of bad government. It can also grow from ambivalent attitudes within the culture to such flaws. For instance, during the Great Depression, the Assistant Secretary of Agriculture, Rexford Tugwell, famously fined his own father for a legal infraction.[78] Such behavior is seen as upholding the rule of law in the West. Yet scholar Robert Scalapino argues that concepts such as "applying rules without fear or favor" or "considering office holding to be a public trust" are foreign in many traditional Asian societies, where loyalty to friends, families, and co-workers trumps loyalty to some abstract notion of the rule of law or the state.[79]

Finally, professional norms in the rule-of-law professions, journalism, and politics may impede the rule of law. When professional cultures fail to support the rule of law, they cannot police themselves, and structures that are intended to serve as horizontal forms of accountability fail. In Indonesia, I walked into the home of a former minister of privatization, past a garage containing a Lexus and a BMW, and into a room-sized wine cellar decorated with medieval Chinese armor—hardly the usual trappings of someone on a government salary, but flaunted with no fear of social opprobrium. Nearly every country in the world has corruption, some level of government sloth, and some public employees who are less than skilled. Professional culture becomes an issue when these are the norm rather than the exception. Helping oneself to the perks that arise from government service is behavior that tends to break out quickly when social disdain and the fear of job loss no longer serve their policing function.

Once a tipping point is reached and breaking the law within a profession becomes the norm, "bucking the system" becomes difficult. For instance, in Indonesia I was told of a very honest judge who tried to live on his small public salary. He had to house his family far from Jakarta, wore old suits that were all he could afford, and carried a tattered old briefcase. Other members of the legal community saw him as idealistic, but ineffective—and did not think he appeared "proper" as a judge.[80] Instead of being seen as a hero standing up for spending taxpayer dollars wisely, he stood so far outside acceptable cultural norms that he was viewed as someone to be slightly pitied. In other cases where professional norms have "tipped," upholding the rule of law is not just out of step with one's colleagues, but can actually endanger one's career or life. In parts of Indonesia, low-level beat cops were expected to pass a certain amount of money up to their superior officers. The only way to amass such funds was through bribes—and failing to pass on the money could lead to beatings, or worse.[81]

A cultural theory of change claims that the rule of law ultimately exists only when it is upheld as an ideal in the mind of each citizen, and particularly in the professional norms of rule-of-law professionals.[82] For a culture of lawfulness to become the norm, reformers must target "the set of deeply rooted, historically conditioned attitudes about the nature of law, about the role of law in a society and the polity, about the proper organization and operation of the legal system, and about the way law is or should be made, applied, studied, perfected, and taught."[83] How can an outside reform effort do this, legitimately? Chapter 6 discusses a number of tactics. But one of the central insights is the importance of changing culture with culture, rather than trying to legislate cultural change, as first-generation reformers often unwittingly did. Even power structure reform can do little in the face of cultural disapprobation. Legal institutions and governmental powers, for instance, can insist on equal rights for all sectors of society—but a culture that does not support such rights can find ingenious ways to deny them, as the southern states in the United States did for years through Jim Crow laws. Laws and political reforms may be necessary, but they are not sufficient. In fact, some would argue that reforms that require cultural changes must start in the cultural dimension and then move to enshrinement in laws and power structures, rather than the other way around. As Montesquieu noted:

> We have said that the laws were the particular and precise institutions of the legislator [while] the mores and manners [were] the

> institutions of the nation in general. From this it follows that when one wants to change the mores and manners, one must not change them by the laws, as this would appear too tyrannical: it would be better to change them by other mores and manners.[84]

Or, as commercial legal practitioners Kathryn Hendley and Cheryl Gray argue, there is a need to "generate legal norms from actual practice and acceptance below."[85] The 2004 Arab Human Development Report stresses the need for civic education in human rights and political liberalism to "foster broader respect for legal tools and ideas among Arab citizens."[86] For particularly culturally based reforms, change may need to begin in the cultural dimension, and from there will spread to laws, institutions, and government.[87]

Just as legal and institutional reforms can at times be directed toward changing power structures, they can occasionally be used to alter social norms. For instance, a "culture" of vigilante justice may have its roots in a government that does not adequately enforce laws, rather than an inherently violent populace. In the United States, the West certainly has a culture of self-sufficiency, independence, and firearm ownership. However, vigilantism and unlawful violence diminished immensely as Texas Rangers and other forms of law enforcement gradually provided law and order.[88] While the cultural norms that spurred vigilante justice still exist, the unlawful behavior now rears its head as the rare crime, rather than a common zeitgeist. However, when one carries out institutional or legal reforms, it is crucial to remember that the institution is being changed to alter certain social norms—not as an end in itself. The goal is not to create an institution or law that looks like its counterpart in the United States—the goal is to change a behavior that is inimical to the rule of law. Meanwhile, because causation between institutions and norms often works in both directions, it can be hard to know whether structural change is enough to affect a more deeply embedded culture. As the World Bank writes:

> How much do people's attitudes, beliefs, and assumptions determine their social environment, and how much does the social environment determine their attitudes, beliefs, and assumptions? . . . Is the

> introduction of a new contract law unlikely to have an effect because the business culture prefers informal deals with family and friends, or does the preference for informal dealing exist only because no one has yet passed an efficient contract law?[89]

Truly cultural variables (as opposed to habits that grow around dysfunctional systems) are going to be difficult to alter. The correlation between Catholic countries and corruption is statistically strong, but what change does it suggest, since government funding for missionary activity to convert Catholic countries to other faiths hardly seems legitimate?[90] Lawrence Harrison, seeking to isolate cultural attributes that retard development, claims, "In progressive cultures, the radius of identification and trust extends beyond the family to the broader society. In static cultures, the family circumscribes community. Societies with a narrow radius of identification and trust are more prone to corruption, tax evasion, and nepotism."[91] His point echoes findings by Robert Putnam about southern Italy. But what can outsiders do to facilitate ties of trust and identification outside of the extended family? These are not rhetorical questions; they are research questions that must be answered for the cultural variable to receive its due.

Even deep social norms, however, are not impossible to change. In fact, societies can sometimes change quite rapidly. Witness how Teach for America has made teaching the number one job for elite college graduates for their first few years out of school—unthinkable when it began twenty years ago.[92] The sociologist Alex Inkeles suggests ways in which social institutions (such as the switch from farming to office and industrial work environments) can move people from traditional to modern societies, even altering people's concepts of time and space. Thus, new forms of work can create new roles for the individual that can "induce new attitudes and values." Some of his findings could be extrapolated to determine how to move people away from family-centric, community-denying societies that are especially prone to corruption.[93]

However, most top-down efforts at cultural reform skim much closer to the surface, resulting in television programs emphasizing the ills of corruption, or the funding of folk songs on clean government to be played throughout rural Albania.[94] While cultural change that is amenable to marketing-campaign style advertising may be possible (the "don't trash Texas" ad campaign did curb public littering there, and anti-AIDS campaigns in Botswana and Uganda have had significant effects on behavior), little research has been done on activating deeper changes. We still need to answer basic questions about tactics: for instance, can culture be changed in the heart of only one person at a time? Or, to reach a tipping point, must culture be changed at a group or national level?

One of the most potent, and most overlooked, vehicles for creating cultural change is honor and shame. The power of honor for animating action has been known for millennia: Thucydides listed it as one of the three reasons people go to war. Honor has motivated duels for centuries, and even the slightest sense of being dishonored—or "dissed"—is a frequent reason for crime and retribution in inner-city America. Militaries worldwide know the motivating force of bits of ribbon and metals that convey honor on their bearers. And parents worldwide know the power of role models in shaping the behavior of children. Professional honor, respect, and the role models that members of a profession look up to can be equally strong factors in motivating behavior among members of a rule of law profession. In crafting reform methods, looking at ways to augment honor among those who support the rule of law could be a particularly valuable effort.

The flip side of honor, of course, is shame. One of the most innovative, effective, and intentional efforts to alter social norms has come from development professionals using shame to change long-standing habits of cleanliness in traditional villages. In the field of sanitation, decades of efforts to change "institutions" (in this case, to build toilets) had failed to alter behavior. People continued to defecate openly and ignored newly built, donor-funded toilets, or used the new bathrooms for storage. Fed-up development practitioners finally decided to use shame to change behavior. They had villagers create a "poop map" of their towns, showing the areas in which open defecation took place, and then mapping water sources. The controversy over the method was great—but so were the results. In village after village, locals' disgust at realizing the overlap between their defecation sites and water sources led them to both build their own bathroom areas—and use them.[95] Not only was shame a more useful motivator for behavior than delivering technology, but it also created local "ownership" and was far less expensive than having the toilets built by outside groups. Shame and honor are social norms that have vast power and are underused in altering behavior in the rule-of-law field.

Creating a set of methods to affect social norms is made more difficult by political and cultural sensitivities. Outside attempts to alter social habits smack of imperialism and missionary work and are difficult to discuss openly. (It is telling that the shaming method of sanitation originated with development workers who were themselves from developing countries and who may have therefore been free from some of the legitimacy concerns of Western practitioners.) Yet the lack of debate prevents reformers from admitting that they are trying to affect the social norms of another country, discussing different methods for doing so, and measuring the success of their interventions. Second-generation rule-of-law reformers take seriously the methods by which they might—legitimately—affect social norms. Many of these methods will require work with internal reformers and local groups to affect professional and public norms from within, rather than pushing cultural change from outside. We will look at a few examples in chapter 6—but, ultimately, to address this important object of change more effectively, more research needs to be done.

Conclusion

Distinguishing among these four objects of change—laws, institutions, power structure, and cultural norms—is important, not only because it allows rule-of-law reformers to know why they are carrying out their reform, but also because it clarifies what they are doing and why. In Albania, for instance, President Sali Berisha purged the courts and law school of communists, then filled the vacancies with appointees from a six-month crash course he held for 400 "former dissidents." (Almost all were members of his Democratic Party and clansmen from his home region.) Many had no previous legal education, and some were illiterate, but 100 soon made up nearly a third of the judiciary, while the rest filled prosecutorial and other legal positions.[96] In addition to impeding justice, these "six-month judges" were making a laughingstock of the judiciary.

But the World Bank and Council of Europe disagreed over what to do to address the problem. The World Bank wanted the government to hold a test and then fire all judges who didn't pass; the Council of Europe was adamantly opposed. Neither side had the language to discuss their debate clearly: The World Bank saw Albania's core problem as a lack of skilled, knowledgeable judges—a technical, institutional view of change; while the Council of Europe, following a power structure view of reform, believed that maintaining an independent judiciary was the most crucial consideration and that it would be undermined if the executive were given the power to test judges' skill level. Both sides had a point. But without a common language, they couldn't articulate that they were working from different hypotheses of the root cause of Albania's rule-of-law difficulties.

First-generation rule-of-law reformers tended to focus on laws and institutions, while second-generation rule-of-law reform gives the greatest weight to altering the power structure of a country and also takes seriously the need to affect public and professional cultures. In most actual programs, all four objects of change will need to be addressed. Second-generation reform uses institutional and legal changes to affect power structures and social norms, rather than simply altering institutions and laws to look like those in the West. In the next chapter, we'll explore the methods of intervention outside reformers can use to affect each of these objects of change.

CHAPTER FIVE

METHODS OF INTERVENTION FROM OUTSIDE

We don't know yet how best to promote democracy in the Arab Middle East. . . . I think there are times when you throw spaghetti against the wall and see if it sticks.

– J. Scott Carpenter, former deputy assistant secretary of state in charge of the Middle East Partnership Initiative[1]

How can the United States, Europe, or another outside entity affect the laws, institutions, power structure, or social norms of another country? When asked this way, the inadequacy of studying the field solely through the lens of development aid (as the vast majority of current studies do) is obvious. Dozens of tools, from political speeches to the power of example, are available to affect other countries. While these methods encompass more than just development assistance, they are not infinite. The tools at the disposal of rule-of-law reformers can be grouped into four buckets, which constitute the main methods outsiders can use to influence change: top-down development aid and technical assistance to rule-of-law institutions; bottom-up funding and support for civil society, including

NGOs, businesses, membership organizations, and citizen movements; diplomacy using carrots and sticks to influence government decision-makers; and enmeshment into international institutions with rule-of-law norms and procedures, or, in a much weaker form, exchange programs.[2]

Each of these methods depends on actions taken by different sectors of society. By now, it should be clear that second-generation reform starts from the realization that outsiders can't create change in another country—locals are always going to be the conduit through which reform occurs. Archimedes' famous declaration on leverage was actually: "Give me a lever long enough, and a fulcrum strong enough, and I shall move the world." Local people and institutions form the fulcrum of this equation—they are the ones outsiders must "leverage" to create change. Each of the four methods relies on a different local "fulcrum," the strength of which will affect the suitability of different methods in different countries. Countries with tightly controlled civil societies, for example, may be less suited to reforms that depend on citizen action to catalyze change.

Each of the four methods can work on any object of reform (laws, institutions, power structures, and social norms), though some are better than others. Let's say, for instance, that the United States wishes for another government to be less corrupt, in order to be more certain that development funds were being used well and that international organized criminals would be caught and prosecuted. Taking a top-down reform approach, the United States could pay an American contractor to draft a transparency law and work with the local parliament to pass it. Under a bottom-up method, USAID could fund a civil society group to advocate within the country for anticorruption reform, training local activists in organizing and lobbying, and helping them to draft such a law for their own country. Another alternative is for the United States to take a diplomatic approach by making sure that when its top officials met with their counterparts in the country, their talking points include requests for greater transparency in government spending and campaign contributions. The United States could use a strong enmeshment method, pressing to make anticorruption measures a precondition of NATO membership under its rule-of-law criteria and creating a road map of reforms for local leaders to implement. Or the U.S. Embassy could use a weak enmeshment method by bringing elite members of the local government to Washington, D.C., on an exchange program to show them how the American system works, with the hope that the socialization would lead them to create a more transparent system in their own country.[3] For the best possible chance of success, the United States could even undertake all of these methods simultaneously.

A second-generation rule-of-law reform program should consider all four methods and should particularly look at how to use multiple methods in tandem to achieve reform. The four methods are depicted in table 5.1.

In robust rule-of-law reform programs, each of these methods may come into play at different times. None is inherently better or worse; each has unique attributes that make it more or less suited for pushing on a specific object of change and for catalyzing change in particular countries. This chapter looks at each in turn, describing first the method, then its pros and cons, and the conditions under which each is most likely to be used successfully.

The Top-Down Method (Funding and Technical Assistance to Institutions)

Someone was murdered in Mexico City on a fateful afternoon in 2005—that much was known. But Antonio Zúñiga, the mild-mannered computer repairman who was arrested for the crime, appears to have had nothing to do with the killing. The best-selling documentary in Mexico's history tracks the case of an innocent man jailed for years for a murder he did not commit. The film, *Presumed Guilty*, shows justice perverted at every step, from a jail so overcrowded that the accused must sleep on the floor beneath a bunk bed, to attorneys who ignore a negative forensic test. When it turns out that Zúñiga's attorney forged his documents, the finding earns the defendant a retrial. But elation turns to disappointment as the audience realizes that Zúñiga must face the same yawning judge, who hands down an identical sentence of twenty years in prison. Mexico's court banned the movie, but they could not keep people away. More than a million Mexicans have bought tickets to watch their justice system itself, finally, in the dock.

TABLE 5.1	FOUR METHODS OF RULE-OF-LAW REFORM	
LEVEL OF REMOVE	OUTSIDERS DEPLOY	
	Funding/Technical Assistance	Social/Political Pressure
Direct (Working with those who have it in their power to make rule-of-law change)	**Top-Down** Aid and technical assistance provided to government to affect laws and rule-of-law institutions in another country. **Fulcrum:** Laws and rule-of-law institutions	**Diplomacy** Carrots and sticks deployed with the announced intent of forcing the targeted government to change a specific rule-of-law issue (such as judicial independence). **Fulcrum:** Government decisionmakers
Indirect (Building a community that creates reform)	**Bottom-Up** Aid and technical assistance given to civil society (NGOs, business organizations, journalists, and individuals) to work for the rule of law, or spent in ways that enhance the ability of citizens or groups to work for rule-of-law reform. **Fulcrum:** Local NGOs, business associations, mass movements, the general public	**Enmeshment** Socialization into a community with rule-of-law norms and structures. In strongest form, membership in an international regime with rule-of-law membership requirements, legal structures, and arbitration mechanisms. **Fulcrum:** Culture of the government, bureaucracy, or citizenry, occasionally laws and institutions for some enmeshing regimes

The top-down method is the most straightforward means of addressing failures such as these that are presumed to reside in poorly educated judges, ill-trained lawyers, and cockroach-ridden jails. It is also the most commonly studied means for reforming the rule of law in other countries—and it was the only way most first-generation reformers conceived of rule-of-law reform. Top-down reforms occur when U.S. government agencies, working directly or through contractors and NGOs, provide funding and technical assistance to foreign governments and their rule-of-law agencies to improve institutions such as courts and prisons. Funding might pay for equipment (such as guns for police, or computers for court personnel), infrastructure (rebuilding a prison or courthouse), drafting laws, or holding educational workshops. As mentioned earlier, top-down reform should not be confused with reforming institutions as ends in themselves. Top-down aid and technical assistance to another government can be used to affect power structures, culture, laws, or institutions—or all of the above, as shown in a number of case studies in the next chapter.

Conditions for Success

Under what conditions is the top-down method likely to be most effective? Top-down reforms have traditionally provided funds and technical assistance to build basic rule-of-law abilities. For instance, in 1992, after a half-century under the communist system, many businesspeople in Eastern Europe had never seen a contract and basic commercial laws did not exist. Top-down reforms were used to draft laws and train the legal profession in the new commercial infrastructure. While some technocratic reform such as this might eventually be necessary, it has proven to be one of the least effective ways to use this method. Instead, top-down reforms are likely to have the greatest impact when they leave the details of technical institutional reform to the end of a reform process, and instead begin with reforming the power structure through the creation of competing horizontal institutions whose cultures bolster the rule of law. Supporting law schools, judicial schools, and bar associations that build ethical codes, professionalism, esprit de corps, and a sense of independence among alternative power centers such as the judiciary or lawyers can be an effective way for the United States to instill rule-of-law values.

Top-down methods can also be useful to spotlight an area of reform or create prestige, using culture to spur change. Funneling money to specific rule-of-law areas can serve as a useful signal that an outside agency regards an activity or an individual as important, thereby protecting reformers imperiled from within their institutions or helping them gain prestige in their agencies. This was an explicit goal of ICITAP in working to alter incentives within the Indonesian police academy. Since the program (described in depth in the next chapter) began, its leader explained:

> There is a great deal of added political value within the institution if you play the reform card—the insiders who play that card are the winners—so now those people are given more space within the institution. The game of reform is really all about helping different groups WITHIN the institution jockey for more weight and control of that institution.[4]

Top-down reform can be powerful, but the method has some inherent weaknesses. First, as already mentioned, top-down reform can fall into the trap of technocratic change and institution modeling (simply making local institutions look like their Western counterparts). Second, top-down reforms can be undertaken only in states that invite and allow foreigners to operate internally. That makes the reforms extremely dependent on political will at the top, since they can be shut down at the whim of the government. Yemen, for instance, stopped a $300,000 U.S. conflict-resolution program aimed at improving law and order in tribal areas, fearing external influence in sensitive domestic areas and accusing those running the program of being spies for the U.S. Central Intelligence Agency.[5] The method also cannot be used in countries where donor country aid restrictions prevent U.S. and EU programs from taking place. In fact, it should not be used in such dictatorships, since top-down reform gives money directly to governments, and thereby treats all governing entities as if, in the words of rule-of-law reformer Wade Channell, they had "the same basic underlying logic of protecting the general welfare, even though many governments have no intention of expanding the benefits of rule beyond their own clique, clan, or communities."[6] The assumption of government goodwill is particularly problematic for rule-of-law reform, when the very entity receiving the funds may be the obstacle.

A special problem of the top-down method is the unintended consequences such a method tends to engender. Top-down reforms, for instance, can easily spur corruption because of large influxes of money given to the government—particularly if it is spent on courthouses, jails, and other construction projects. Another common unintended consequence is overwhelming small or weak legal systems with an overcrowded agenda of reforms. In small states such as Rwanda, with only a few dozen staff in the Ministry of Justice, and small numbers of judges and lawyers with English language ability, even a handful of top-down reforms can overwhelm the actual work of the system. While not an inherent problem of top-down reform, when many agencies engage in this method in a single country, the outside projects can reduce governing officials' time and ability to engage in the actual legal work of the country.[7]

Finally, it is a truism in development literature that these outside inputs can do little good if they are not "owned" by reformers inside the country and backed by political will.[8] The external financing and assistance will eventually end, and locals will always have more staying power and more stake in the system than any outsider. Consequently, top-down reform may only work in agencies or arenas where locals can be found who are true believers and who have the personal ability to move their fellow citizens toward a rule-of-law goal.

The Bottom-Up Method (Indirect Funding and Assistance to Civil Society)

In Indonesia, some of the most creative work in the rule-of-law field has been undertaken by the Partnership for Governance Reform. The NGO's slogan, "pressure from without, capacity from within," sums up its strategy—and the core method of bottom-up reform. The Partnership uses the international organizations on its governing board (such as the World Bank and United Nations) to provide funding, keep a spotlight on the government, and press for reform, while the Indonesian Partnership staff and implementation partners use their local knowledge, personal relationships, and staying power to create the structures needed to make reform happen. As a staff member explained:

> The leadership of the Partnership from the beginning was Indonesian, and part of the idea in its founding is to capitalize on Indonesian

> ownership. To change a country, the process is quite political. It is very hard for foreigners to promote change because they cannot "read" the political process so well, they can't tell whether politicians are bluffing or not, and so on. So having Indonesians running the Partnership allows them to participate in a more savvy way in the political process.[9]

H. S. Dillon, the Partnership's charismatic executive director, structured the organization to have three decisionmaking bodies: a governing board that draws one-third of its members from outside donor agencies and two-thirds of its membership from Indonesians at the highest levels of business, government, parliament, and civil society; an executive board composed of just the Indonesian members of the governing board; and a policy committee made up of representatives from the donor agencies, two major government agencies, and the executive director. The European Union delegation's political officer explained:

> The Partnership isn't just a civil service organization—it's a different animal, because it can pick up the phone and talk to really important people, the movers and shakers here—the strength of the Partnership is that it can pull in these big players. . . . They have privileged access on an informal basis to the leading actors in Indonesian society—across all sectors, politics, media, activists, religious leaders—and that gives them tremendous ability to get things done.[10]

The current president of Indonesia was previously on the Partnership's governing board, as was the minister of justice, providing unprecedented access. The Partnership uses its personal relationships to the elite to organize and implement reforms. And vice versa. In 2003, when Bagir Manan, the minister of justice, wanted to reduce court corruption by having outside lawyers serve as temporary judges,[11] he called the Partnership for support in finding suitable lawyers. As locals, Partnership members are also willing to involve themselves deeply in the politics of their own country. One of their plans, for instance, has been to develop a database in which they would list corrupt politicians and their activities.

The Partnership has a particularly large amount of clout for a civil society organization, but that shows the power of this method of reform.

Bottom-up methods place outsiders at one remove. Rather than directly infusing funds and technical know-how into rule-of-law institutions, outside reformers fund locals to work on their own government, rule-of-law institutions, and culture, to create change. Outsiders may just give money, or they may also provide tools to the local reformers—such as training in organizing, polling, conducting surveys, and marshaling other data to rally domestic constituencies for change.[12] Bottom-up reform need not entail supporting NGOs, which are often seen as a foreign import and are not the only way for people to organize for social action. This reform method can also be undertaken through local structures such as religious organizations, as with the Polish Catholic Church's support for human rights under communism; self-help organizations, such as the microcredit groups of women that cover many developing countries; schools; or the local business community. Any of these could be a voice for the rule of law, and, indeed, they have played that role in places from Sicily to the Philippines.[13]

The bottom-up method is premised on the idea that the best way to create sustainable change in a foreign country is to build local constituencies for reform. These local constituencies share external reformers' values and promote their cause within the country; their local knowledge and legitimacy as citizens mean that they are able to engage in far more intrusive action in their own state than outsiders could rightfully undertake. They will also stay in their own countries to act as a sustained force for change, while outsiders will, inevitably, go. The bottom-up method has the potential to create a long-term multiplier effect by building local experts who, in addition to remaining in the country, are often more creative and flexible than outsiders can be and can pull into the cause friends, family, and others from their social and professional worlds.

Since the young Alexis de Tocqueville praised America's unique citizen groups and popular organizations more than two hundred years ago, U.S. leaders have recognized that civil society is part of what makes American democracy work.[14] The importance of building strong civil society organizations in other countries received a big boost after the fall of the Soviet Union, when development scholars working in the newly liberated countries of Eastern Europe went back to the roots of the democratic theory to see what made it tick. In some cases, USAID and other agencies now write terms of reference for contractors that call for incorporating top-down technical assistance for rule-of-law institutions with projects that create pressure and demand for reform from below. At other times, bottom-up reform is conducted as a parallel but uncoordinated method alongside other rule-of-law efforts.

The development community has embraced bottom-up reform. However, too often it conflates "civil society" with NGOs. Many NGOs are elite organizations, run by professionals in capital cities, without much connection to the actual citizenry of a country. Bottom-up methods work better when they engage not only NGOs that share their goals, but also member-based organizations—among them religious groups, businesses, professional associations, NGOs with broad membership throughout the country, and so on—that have the capacity to mobilize citizens. Since the method of change that bottom-up reform uses requires changing the relationship between the state and society, it works best when groups that broadly represent society are engaged.

Unfortunately, for years there has been disagreement between the development and diplomatic communities on the usefulness of bottom-up reform. Diplomats and the professional foreign policy establishment, when they acknowledged such reforms at all, showed little understanding of this method of change and tended to dismiss such reforms out of hand as affecting the edges of problems, not the crux. As individuals who chose to go into government, some had an innate bias that governments, not citizen groups, businesses, or religious organizations, were the most important actors in society. At times, diplomats' lack of support for the bottom-up method has resulted in a dangerous flaw: When civil society reforms are threatened by foreign governments, U.S. diplomats or foreign policy leaders sometimes failed to protect them—even when U.S. taxpayers were funding the reforms. At other times, the State Department has seen the worth of bottom-up work and has attempted to co-opt or coordinate these programs. That degree of government interest, however, can cause danger to individuals on the ground, making foreign governments view the program as a tool of U.S. national interest, rather than as helping them build their own rule of law.[15]

Luckily, this is changing. When civil society as a whole is threatened, the U.S. State Department generally speaks out—and more and more, the importance of civil society is being recognized by reformers within the State Department. In 2009, Secretary of State Hillary Clinton launched Civil Society 2.0, a program to assist civil society organizations in using digital tools to increase their reach and impact. The United States simultaneously promised to maintain the openness of the digital realm where, as the Arab Spring demonstrated, much civil society organizing now takes place. The following year, the State Department instituted a position, Senior Adviser for Civil Society and Emerging Democracies, to develop, coordinate, and operationalize civil society reforms. In 2011, the State Department created a Civil Society Advisory Committee to better integrate civil society in other countries into U.S. foreign policy and to improve the U.S. role in promoting the freedom of civil society abroad. These reforms at the top must now percolate through the bureaucracy to have maximum impact.

America's change of heart stands in sharp contrast to international organizations such as the United Nations and the EU, which frequently continue to dismiss the entire sector. When I interviewed European Commission staff in Albania, Romania, and Indonesia, all expressed reservations and distrust for bottom-up reform, concern about its effectiveness as well as its legitimacy, and uncertainty over their own abilities to choose partners wisely.[16] In Albania, the EU Justice and Home Affairs Minister stated that it was her job "to work with the government, not the population," while an Austrian judge sent to work with Albania's rule-of-law institutions mentioned that he tried to work with NGO organizations once, but that it just wasn't his style, so he stopped.[17] In Indonesia, the EU political officer described a large effort to work with the powerful Partnership for Governance Reform as simply a "grand gesture" of magnanimity, rather than a strategy.[18]

Conditions for Success

The lack of respect for bottom-up reform is a particular handicap, because this method is one of the most effective means of promoting the rule of law. It has four advantages over top-down reform that make it particularly impactful. First, as the Partnership staff member pointed out, local actors tend to understand the pressure points of their own systems better than foreigners. Scholar Stephen Golub notes that locals can "identify government agencies and personnel who manifest dedication" far better than donors and can work with them "around their reform-resistant colleagues. In this way, civil society acts as a supportive force for cooperative elements in the state and as a countervailing force against anti-reform elements."[19] Locals are not hampered by language barriers, nor are they going to gravitate toward English speakers or individuals with Western habits—Achilles' heels for top-down reform efforts. They also have a stronger feel for local reputations, making them better at finding leaders who can rally others, rather than reformers whose interpersonal styles may be fine for Western donors but can drive local people away.

Second, local groups, once started, can react more quickly than outsiders to political changes on the ground and can be far more flexible in taking advantage of windows of opportunity. Particularly for second-generation reformers who understand the importance of power structures and windows of opportunity, the local knowledge of political moments and the ability to react quickly make bottom-up reform invaluable.

Third, local actors have a greater stake than outsiders in achieving reform and also greater legitimacy in pursuing political and cultural reform. They are, after all, working for the betterment of their own country. They are likely to fight harder and with more creativity than outsiders who are there today and gone tomorrow. Moreover, their staying power makes them a political force within the country. Simply by helping to catalyze a pressure group, outsiders are creating a vertical check on government. A local power center is more difficult for recalcitrant governments or other groups to evade or wait out than outsiders who fly in for a few weeks or remain for only a few years.

Finally, reform-minded constituencies are simply more likely to exist among citizen groups than within many government agencies needing reform.[20] For second-generation reforms that consider support and opposition in building a reform program, this fact alone will lead many reformers toward bottom-up methods.

The strengths of bottom-up reform are heightened when the United States places itself at a second level of remove by providing grants to local organizations—not just NGOs, but businesses, religious organizations, and other membership groups—or to international NGOs with a strong local presence so that these organizations may pass along grant funds to local business groups, religious organizations, NGOs, and other reformers. By taking itself completely out of the equation, the U.S. government localizes reforms still further. In some cases, the United States can provide funding through NGOs created or catalyzed by the U.S. government, such as the Asia Foundation, National Democratic Institute, or International Republican Institute, which have staff on the ground in the country who speak the local language and know the local politics. These organizations can act with less taint of U.S. national interest than direct government aid, though such accusations can still dog their programming.

The United States can also help to support the establishment of local foundations, such as Indonesia's Partnership for Governance Reform, that share U.S. goals and values but are otherwise independent. Locals tend to appear far more legitimate—and can be, if the U.S. government relinquishes control and allows these organizations to determine their own fates and affect their own systems after the U.S. grants initial funds. Local funding agencies almost always have much-reduced paperwork than the U.S. government, allowing them to make smaller grants with fewer onerous reporting requirements. Moreover, reports to them do not necessarily need to be in English—meaning that they can sustain groups far smaller and more local than the U.S. government can support directly. Most of these local institutions can also provide funds far more rapidly to take advantage of windows of opportunity. Meanwhile, they have all the advantages of local sustainability, buy-in, and long time horizons that characterize bottom-up reform.

Bottom-up methods, particularly those that operate at a level of one remove, relinquish greater U.S. control for more flexibility. Unfortunately, the same reasons that this method can be so effective abroad can be a disadvantage in the highly political world of U.S. development aid. A number of the problems with bottom-up reform reside in the U.S. system—not in the method itself. Bottom-up reform can be uncomfortable for politicians wanting greater control and oversight over their programs and taxpayers' money: For bottom-up reform to leverage its strengths, money must be given to local groups without unduly tying their hands. Sometimes, those funds may be given to an extraordinarily effective and honest group, but they can also be wasted by self-serving locals. Bottom-up reform that genuinely creates local constituencies can also be slow to produce results, troubling politicians at home who want to be able to proclaim immediate returns on their investments, even at the expense of effective reform.[21]

The United States also compromises its own bottom-up work by a flavor-of-the-month capriciousness. In countries such as Albania, with no domestic funding for civil society, NGOs are dependent on international donors and those without a broad fundraising base must change their focus with donor money or go out of business.[22] As one NGO director recounted, "In 1999, donors provided a lot of psycho-social support to the [Kosovar] refugees, and so all the local NGOs moved into that area of work even if they had no special capacity to do it. A few years ago anticorruption work was the big deal, and all the local NGOs tweaked their programs to make them about corruption. Now trafficking is the big issue."[23] USAID tried to undertake a second-level-of-remove style reform by designating a U.S. nonprofit with local staff, known as Partners, to fund, train, and support the local nonprofit sector. But because it made its funding grants year to year and controlled the grant-making process, Partners lost its main added value in being able to take advantage of windows of opportunity and local knowledge. Instead, Partners was forced to make its grants to local NGOs based on the most recent fad in Washington, switching from "women and youth" programming in 2001–2004, to anticorruption, election monitoring, and advocacy in 2005–2007, with no real strategy based in local reality that would justify these changes. Thus, all the advantages of the bottom-up method were nullified, while its weaknesses were magnified.

Reformers using this method should also keep in mind a few other inherent weaknesses. First, bottom-up reform must be used with care against a powerful state inimical to civil society. It is possible to deploy bottom-up reform against closed states: The Helsinki Accords are an example of a bottom-up method that put significant pressure for reform on the Soviet Union. By drafting these accords, Western governments gave local citizens in the Soviet Union a set of rights, legitimated by their own government, that they could rally around and use to hold their own government to account, helping to delegitimize the Soviet Union from within. However, that work required a massive, multi-governmental outside effort at enmeshment that internal reformers seized upon. In contrast, modern-day Russia and much of Central Asia have closed local and U.S.-based NGOs and forced out foreign funders and technical assistants.[24] Such work can also be quite dangerous for locals on the ground and their supporters.

Second, governments—and even citizens themselves—may view bottom-up methods as somehow more "covert" than top-down assistance to government institutions.[25] They may fear the loss of government control, may deem such intrusions illegitimate offenses to their sovereignty, or may even claim CIA involvement. These claims are hard to eradicate, in part because they are based in historical reality. Early U.S. initiatives to fund civil society abroad often straddled the line between covert CIA funding and overt development funding.[26] The Asia Foundation, established as a private U.S. foundation in 1954 to operate throughout Asia, received initial funding from the Central Intelligence Agency in the 1950s and 1960s. CIA funding ended after public disclosure in 1967, but the rumors did not stop.[27] Accusations of such funding for these governance and human rights programs persisted—in fact, the National Endowment for Democracy was actually the Reagan administration's attempt to silence these whispering campaigns by doing overtly what the United States was accused of doing covertly.[28] Although the Asia Foundation still receives a portion of its funding from U.S. government contracts, it spent the 1990s diversifying in an attempt to distance itself not only from U.S. government funding but even from being seen as a U.S.-based organization, because such accusations harmed its efforts to work in other countries.[29] In Indonesia, where the Asia Foundation has operated for fifty years, its staff took great pleasure in the fact that when they were invited to attend a government event, they were listed as one of the "Indonesian associations" and not one of the "foreign" delegations.[30]

Third, the act of funding bottom-up reform can destroy some of its advantages, such as the legitimacy of local reformers, or their desire to stick with a project after external funding dries up. Bottom-up reform depends on finding locals who share at least some of the reform-minded desires of their outside funders.[31] Yet if locals identify too much with foreigners, they may be seen as elite, or even illegitimate, within their own countries. In 2001, for instance, an independent assessment of USAID's Democracy and Governance programs spoke scathingly of the "general failure of civic advocacy nongovernmental organizations (NGOs) to be genuinely representative of citizen concerns." Aligning local NGO work to the interests of foreign donors can lead even well-meaning NGOs to chase foreign funding, serving the interests of funders rather than any real local constituency or need.[32] By forcing locals to comply with outside agendas, the outsiders can destroy the locals' useful connections to their own society that give strength to the bottom-up method.[33]

Bottom-up funding can also attract locals looking to make money from foreign grants and contracts, rather than those genuinely interested in creating reform. Outright corruption among NGOs is not uncommon, particularly when foreign funding is flowing.[34] A 2001 study of Romanian NGOs, for instance, detailed the suspicion of Romanians toward most organizations and noted that their "tendency towards fraud and corruption, with double billing and dubious accounting further undermined the reputation of these groups."[35] In Nepal, a boy once asked me how to start an NGO. "What do you want to do?" I asked him. "I don't know," he replied—"but that's where the money is." His answer was frighteningly similar to the reply of Willie Sutton when asked why he robbed banks! When NGOs are simply businesses chasing funding, not reformers cobbling together resources to solve a burning problem, they do not create a committed local force that will work on a problem after outside funding and interest is gone. However, even in serious cases of NGO funding gone awry, some good can come of the few that are legitimate—as demonstrated in the next chapter.

There are, of course, ways to tell the difference between self-serving NGOs, those created to serve the needs of external masters, and strong, committed organizations with local support—particularly if one speaks the local language and spends time on the ground. The best way to tell the difference is by deploying the same means that any investor uses when determining good business investments—meeting with the leaders, talking to clients, learning whether they do good work, understanding how they are viewed by others in the country.[36] NGO leadership and reputation simply matter a great deal more for effectiveness than their ability to write a good grant proposal in English. Unfortunately, the highly structured grant-making system of USAID—created to avoid the appearance of favoritism and corruption—actually works against such real due diligence. While the bottom-up method may work well, the U.S. system can make it hard to give funds to a well-intentioned, effective local group that writes grant proposals in poor English, while favoring slick proposals by skilled writers who have little impact on their societies.

Finally, funding NGOs, religious institutions, business organizations, and citizen movements can be an effective way to avoid government corruption, lack of interest, or incompetence. In the meantime, however, it does not help governments build their capacities. Funding NGOs to change a dysfunctional government can do a lot of good; funding NGOs to replicate services to get around a dysfunctional government can create a para-state society working in parallel to a largely parasitical government, as seems to have occurred in Bangladesh. That may be a trade-off reformers are willing to make in, say, the delivery of humanitarian food aid. But because the rule of law depends on having a state strong enough to maintain a monopoly on violence and deliver justice, ultimately, rule-of-law reform does need to engage the state. Bottom-up reform can be useful for getting a more reform-minded group into power, or for creating vertical checks and balances on power that can force change from below—after which, top-down assistance has a window of opportunity for effectiveness that would not have been open otherwise.

The Diplomatic Method (Applying Direct Political Pressure on the Government)

When the Reagan administration took office, it unequivocally supported General Augusto Pinochet, the dictatorial leader of Chile. As late as the mid-1980s, after the death squads, "disappeared" students, torture, and destruction of the justice system, some U.S. government officials such as Jeane Kirkpatrick wanted to continue to support Chile's staunch anti-communist leader. But former secretary of state George Shultz wrote in his memoirs, "By the start of the second Reagan term . . . I was convinced that the U.S. approach was not working. We understood Pinochet; he was not changing. But he did not understand us; we wanted a more open government, rule of law, and a government headed by elected officials."[37] Shultz worked to win support for his views within the Reagan administration. He then forged a bipartisan alliance against Pinochet, unifying the government's message so that the Assistant Secretary of State for Latin America, Elliott Abrams, could legitimately say, "U.S. [g]overnment policy toward Chile is straightforward and unequivocal: we support a transition to democracy."[38] Shultz then prevailed on Reagan to send a new ambassador to Chile who worked to meet with representatives of opposition parties and promote free and fair elections. Pinochet fought against the unaccustomed U.S. pressure, claiming to be holding back the tide of communism. Eventually, miscalculating his own popularity, he agreed to hold a plebiscite. Abrams and Democratic senator Tom Harkin worked to unify the Chilean opposition, which came together as the Coalition of Parties for the No Vote. Pinochet lost the plebiscite, and the next year Chileans held a democratic election that returned the country to freedom and put it back on the course toward the rule of law.[39]

Diplomacy is the calibrated use of carrots, sticks, and rhetoric to affect the decisions of government leaders in other countries. A diplomatic method of change is based on the idea that government decisions are the key to the rule of law. Diplomacy assumes that if the rulers can be made to change their minds, reform will follow—whether that ultimately requires improved laws, better-funded institutions, cultural shifts, or leaders who themselves follow the law.

Diplomacy is the traditional method of international relations—state sovereignty is maintained geographically; one state is not directly working inside the borders of another. Instead, pressure is brought to bear to change government leaders' incentives. These leaders may never share foreigners' beliefs in the rule of law, but diplomacy assumes that if the incentive structure is properly calibrated, they will choose to do what is desired of them by outsiders in order to maintain their hold on power. Typical sticks include sanctions, trade embargoes, and aid conditionality.[40] Typical carrots include the provision of aid; trade privileges; and membership in coveted organizations such as the WTO or NATO, whose membership requirements include the rule of law.[41] Rhetoric might take place in public speeches, or in private conversations between government leaders that pressure countries toward improved adherence to the rule of law. Conditionality on aid is a form of diplomacy: The Millennium Challenge Account, for instance, is an assistance program intended to alter the incentive structures of foreign governments by providing aid only to countries that meet a series of good governance indicators, including the rule of law.[42] The United States can use its stature and that of government appointees to provide legitimacy to reformers and rule-of-law leaders by meeting with them, inviting them to Washington, and praising them in speeches.[43] Diplomacy can also take the form of laws passed within the United States that affect other countries. The 2010 Dodd-Frank Act, for instance, requires all oil, mining, and gas companies registered in the United States to report payments made to foreign governments. This means that even foreign companies such as PetroChina and BP, because they are registered in America, will have to make such disclosures if they make payments to, for instance, a government in Africa. While not directed at any one country, these business disclosures are a means of pressuring corrupt governments by creating a forum through which their theft can be discovered and publicized to their people.

The United States has used diplomacy to affect other countries' rule-of-law incentives from the time of Woodrow Wilson. The method increased in importance after 1974 when Congress inserted human rights conditionality into the Foreign Assistance Act and human rights took on a higher priority within U.S. diplomacy.[44] The Carter administration cut off military and economic aid to countries such as Uruguay and Argentina to protest human rights violations. President Reagan frequently pressured the Soviet Union on issues of human rights and political prisoners and changed his stance on countries from Chile to the Philippines to support greater rule of law. All subsequent presidents have used greater and lesser degrees of pressure to speak to other countries' leaders about improving their records on the rule of law, human rights, and democracy. However, such rhetoric has often been undermined by other diplomatic tools. By pressing rhetorically for the rule of law but increasing executive power in the United States and enabling torture and other rule-of-law breaches in other countries, President George W. Bush showed some of the problems of hypocrisy and lack of even-handedness inherent in pressing for the rule of law through diplomacy.

The United States, because of its power, has particular ability to use diplomacy—but it is not alone. The EU uses diplomacy when it chooses to enforce its membership conditionality, writes its trade practices, and determines its sanctions. Other countries use trade diplomacy to a far greater extent than the United States. In fact, diplomacy is in some ways harder for a hegemon to wield than for a country or entity with narrower interests.

Conditions for Success

Given U.S. power in the world, diplomacy has the potential to be a very strong tool to force change. And given second-generation reformers' focus on the power structure as the most crucial object of change, it might appear that diplomacy is the most useful method. After all, if the rule of law is weak because governments wish to keep their privileges, perks, and power, then having U.S. government leaders press local government leaders would appear to be the most direct route to change. However, using the diplomatic method to *bring about* change is not at all the same as focusing on power structures as the *object* of change. All four methods can focus on power structures. Diplomacy has the potential to be the most direct and can be useful if it can actually be deployed successfully. But it relies on two unreliable fulcrums: government decisionmakers in the United States and in other countries. Both have serious shortcomings that often prevent this method from reaching its potential.

It's worth starting with the problems within the United States (which are shared by many other countries and international entities) because diplomacy usually never really gets off the ground. Research shows that effective diplomacy—at least with regard to sanctions—requires a definite and discrete policy goal. A general goal such as "improved" rule of law does not make a useful diplomatic benchmark.[45] When diplomacy is too broad, countries can fulfill the letter but not the spirit, leaving external actors in a bind. For instance, if the United States presses a government to pass an antiterrorism law, and the law is enacted but then not enforced, what can the United States do? Yet formulating a discrete goal when using the cudgel of diplomacy can be tough. In its accession process, the EU is able to press hard for small rule-of-law issues through its progress reports. But the United States has no such micromanagement tool available. Diplomacy is also such a stong international statement that it cannot be used too often and is hard to use for smaller matters.

But the biggest challenge facing the United States in effectively deploying diplomacy as a method to affect the rule of law is the problem of mixed interests, and thus mixed messages. Considerable research shows that effective diplomacy requires the outside actor—whether that is the United States, or a coalition of countries—to be unified and strong in upholding conditionality. Mixed messages from different agencies of the U.S. government undermine effectiveness.[46] Diplomacy works only insofar as the United States is willing to hold its line, providing carrots or applying sticks as promised. Yet the reality is that short-term U.S. national interests do not always align with building the rule of law in other countries. As the United States balances its total relationship with another country, the rule of law jockeys with all sorts of other important national interests, from military basing rights, to trade deals, to desires to reward states that, for instance, side with the United States in unpopular fights in the UN Security Council. These realities are unlikely to change; the United States, after all, is a country with its own national interests—and at times, these are interpreted in narrow ways. While a tiny portion of U.S. aid goes through the rule of law screen within the Millennium Challenge Account, the vast majority of aid is directed at security needs that at times support authoritarian, rather than rule-of-law, norms.[47] Even when some in the U.S. government argue that overall national interest is served by supporting countries that abide by the rule of law, others can always be counted on to believe that more realist national interests are of a higher priority than using diplomacy to punish states that are not upholding the rule of law. As a result, U.S. diplomacy for the rule of law has been—and is likely to continue to be—consistently inconsistent.

Romania is a perfect example of the difficulty the United States has in using diplomacy to support rule-of-law efforts. In the 1990s as the Balkans descended into bloodshed, Romania acted as a stabilizing force in the Black Sea region.[48] It was also a strong ally during the war in Kosovo. In March 2000, a USAID report stated: "Romania took a bold stand supporting the NATO actions in the former Yugoslavia, a traditionally friendly neighbor, and has sustained its support under the Serbian embargo. This stance has cost significantly in economic and political terms."[49] After

September 11, 2001, Romania passed and implemented a steady stream of legislation requested by the United States to combat terrorism by curbing money laundering, criminalizing terrorist acts, and strengthening Romania's ability to cooperate with foreign intelligence agencies.[50] It also sent troops to Bosnia and Kosovo to augment NATO efforts there. These efforts earned accolades from the U.S. State Department, which declared Romania a "staunch ally of the United States in the global war against terrorism, providing full public and diplomatic support for U.S. goals."[51] Romania's assistance was also essential to the most controversial U.S. policies. The American invasion of Iraq was almost scuttled when Turkey's government refused, at the last minute, to allow U.S. troops to deploy from their country. Romania allowed the United States to use its base, saving U.S. war plans.[52] Romania also deployed troops to Iraq, giving the effort more of the desired aura of a multilateral initiative, and sent troops to Afghanistan as well.[53]

Romania's strong support for the United States was risky to its own interests: Its decision to help in the Iraq war and with CIA renditions risked alienating countries within the European Union while its accession was on the line. Thus, America's need to repay Romania for its stance as "a firm advocate of U.S. initiatives at the risk of alienating some of its neighbors" effectively neutered any use of diplomacy to press for the rule of law.[54] In fact, while the EU was faulting Romania's government for its corruption, and USAID was noting its venality, the Pentagon awarded the country military bases, which were seen as acts of thanks for tough diplomatic decisions. As Romania illustrates, it is simply reality that many countervailing pressures will neuter diplomacy's effectiveness at spurring rule-of-law reform.

Nor are such countervailing pressures always self-interested. In poor, weak states, the desire by outsiders to build the rule of law often conflicts with other goals such as humanitarian aid or keeping a fragile state from becoming a failed state. The Millennium Challenge Corporation has been criticized for not giving greater priority to poverty in its aid goals, since its governance indicators tended to benefit more mid-level countries rather than the poorest of the poor. In Afghanistan, hard-line fundamentalists gained control of the courts just a few years after the initial invasion. As the Taliban used these courts to assert control and legitimacy throughout the country, the United States withheld diplomatic pressure on the government, believing that President Hamid Karzai was attempting to balance a very delicate internal structure within the country.[55] Holding a strong diplomatic line in these cases is difficult.

Moreover, the U.S. government speaks with many voices. Frequently, Congress is more willing than the executive to press for "moral" criteria (as the rule of law is often described), a situation that has caused division across multiple administrations over issues such as China's Most Favored Nation trade status (delayed by Congress because of the Tiananmen Square human rights abuses, while advocated by both the George H.W. Bush and Bill Clinton administrations for business interests). The EU has a similar split between its more realpolitik-minded Commission, and the European Parliament, which tends to be a louder voice in human rights and democracy issues. These inconsistencies in the treatment of different countries, and among different portions of the government, reduce the ability of diplomacy to press for rule-of-law reforms. This reality is better acknowledged up front than lamented later. It usually means that where these mixed messages cannot be overcome, diplomacy, which could otherwise be quite potent, is not going to be the most effective strategy for building the rule of law.

Even if the U.S. government, the EU, or other countries are able to be perfectly consistent and willing to hold the line on rule-of-law criteria, different countries respond differently to diplomatic leverage. Stronger, more economically independent states with proud cultural legacies are less likely to be influenced by international rebuke or the suspension of aid.[56] It is difficult to imagine diplomacy working to alter Sharia law in Iran or Saudi Arabia, for instance. Because diplomacy is often a public, potentially shaming method (especially in the era of Wikileaks) it can also create cultural backlash and lead to a circling of the wagons—particularly in states bearing scars from colonialism.

In fact, in proud and self-sufficient states, diplomatic efforts to produce change can instead entrench the very attitudes that outsiders wish to change. A case in point is the U.S. government's failed effort to bring Indonesian perpetrators of human rights abuses to justice. As Indonesia's second-largest export market and its main military equipment supplier (in a country where the military served as a dual government for many years and remains a strong political presence), the United States should have had significant leverage in Indonesia. Yet diplomacy, the method most reliant on leverage, was almost completely unsuccessful. For fifteen years, Indonesia ignored significant U.S. diplomatic pressure, until finally the United States caved.

In 1992, the Indonesian military massacred hundreds of unarmed civilians in East Timor. Using diplomacy to enforce rule-of-law criteria, Congress cut off all military training assistance.[57] Congress lifted its training restrictions a little in 1995, but then bolstered them with an arms embargo in 1998 and 1999 following the violence around East Timor's vote for independence. A military embargo was the strongest diplomatic card the United States held. Indonesia's military relied on U.S. equipment, and spare parts were essential to maintenance. Ending the embargo became a key goal of Indonesia's foreign ministry.[58] Yet while Indonesia sent diplomatic missions and made requests, it did nearly nothing to meet the human rights demands of the United States. In fact, security forces were accused of killing two U.S. citizens in Papua in 2002.[59] The United States held strong in its conditionality for more than a decade, despite tactical disagreements between Congress, which favored hard diplomacy, and the Defense Department, which asserted that diplomacy wasn't working and called for enmeshment and socialization through military exchange programs as better methods to improve human rights.[60] Gradually, conditionality was reduced: For full military engagement, Indonesia needed to prosecute military personnel responsible for human rights violations, cooperate with international efforts to resolve these violations, and improve civilian control of the military. For training to resume, the U.S. secretary of state had to certify only that Indonesia's cooperation in prosecuting the 2002 Papua murders was improving.[61] Yet Indonesia made no effort to satisfy even this modest conditionality. Instead, it began purchasing arms from Russia, Germany, and South Korea.[62] As Indonesia put its own diplomatic leverage to work by tilting toward other suppliers, the U.S. desire to hold onto its conditionality after more than a decade of failure weakened. Finally, after the tsunami in 2004, when the Indonesian military showed itself so crippled from the U.S. embargo that it could not save its own people, the U.S. government gave up on its attempt to use diplomacy to push for human rights reforms.[63]

Last but far from least, even when diplomacy is successfully deployed by the United States and hits its mark in changing the attitudes of ruling party leaders, it can do little to affect problems that are outside the purview of these leaders. In a very weak state, many parts of the rule of law might lie outside government control—diplomacy, for instance, can hardly force the rump government of Somalia to clean up its law-and-order problem; the government does not have anything approaching a monoply on the use of violence. But even in stronger countries, the executive, which is the part of the government that diplomacy works on, may not have control of other branches of government. That can lead to awkward predicaments. The EU accession process, for instance, uses diplomacy to force foreign governments to pass laws all the time. But many of these laws are unpopular. So local governments, anxious to meet EU requirements, often pass the laws by executive order to sidestep the controversial legislative process. By forcing such action, the EU—and the United States, World Bank, or any outsider using diplomacy for legal reform—can actually undermine the rule-of-law processes it is trying to create.[64] Similarly, if a judiciary has been made independent, it undermines the rule of law for foreign governments to pressure the government to alter legal decisions—because doing so requires executive interference in the judiciary.[65] Diplomacy is also powerless to change cultural attitudes—norms that are usually beyond government's reach. Even if a country passes a law under duress from outside governments, to, for instance, protect minorities, that law may have no effect on culture. In fact, such a law might create a backlash effect against minorities. When culture is the most appropriate object of change, diplomacy is not going to be the most useful method.

Diplomacy, when it can be used successfully, is a very powerful tool. However, it must be used with sensitivity in the rule-of-law arena to avoid backlash. It is likely to be most successful when the United States can agree on a relatively discrete reform and can maintain its position. In some cases, the best that can be achieved should be the equivalent of the Hippocratic oath: It is essential that diplomacy does no harm and does not undermine other rule-of-law reforms. For this reason, it is often preferable that rule-of-law programs—especially bottom-up programs—*not* be coordinated diplomatically, but simply consulted. In other words, information can and should be shared, but such bottom-up programs should not be run through the diplomatic apparatus. Where possible, diplomacy can play a strong supporting role, though it may rarely lead the way in rule-of-law reform.

Enmeshment: (Indirect Socialization of Elites or Society)

For decades, the U.S. military has forged ties with counterparts in other countries. In Egypt, as democracy protesters took to the streets for weeks in early 2011, it was the Egyptian military that ultimately turned the tide by refusing to fire on its own people. Though the Egyptian military has hardly become a democratic force, did its deep ties with the U.S. armed forces help military leaders come to their historic conclusions? An Indonesian Army Major who had spent a year at the U.S. Army Command and General Staff College at Fort Leavenworth, Kansas, told his military sponsor that:

> The thing that most impressed him about the United States was that "everybody obeys the law." By that he meant such apparently trivial (to Americans) concepts as stopping at traffic signs, paying taxes voluntarily, accepting traffic tickets, and—most remarkable to Indonesians—that American military officers have no greater authority or power than ordinary civilian citizens.[66]

Enmeshment is perhaps the least commonly understood method of creating change in another country. But anyone who supports foreign exchange programs understands its logic—by socializing people into another culture, their norms and expectations can be changed—and they return to their own lives with newly opened eyes. In the rule-of-law context, the United States can either enmesh other countries into its own culture, through exchange programs for everyone from military leaders to parliamentarians and university students, or it can undertake a much stronger form of enmeshment by integrating other countries into international institutions—such as NATO or the WTO. Not only do these institutions build cultures of rule-of-law norms among their members, but they also have membership rules that "enmesh" other countries into legal structures that deepen the rule of law. While the EU looks at enmeshment as its main method of catalyzing change, both through integration into the EU itself, and through the creation of other regional groupings from South America to the Middle East, the United States only occasionally conceives of organizations like NATO or the WTO in this light.[67] Because American politicians, diplomats, and development professionals rarely think in quite these terms, it's important to take a deeper dive into understanding this method.

The most robust form of enmeshment ties a country into an international organization with binding rules. There is considerable evidence that this strong form of enmeshment has lasting effects, which seem to spring largely from the diplomacy phase, in which countries must reform to meet membership requirements—a process in which outsiders can legitimately assert real leverage. While arguing for the enlargement of the then-European Community in 1990 to consolidate democracy, Jack Snyder explained the theory of change well:

> The favorable political effect comes not just from interdependence, but from the institutional structures and changes in domestic interests that may or may not accompany high levels of interdependence. . . . The institutionalized, legal character of the relationship would make for predictability, irreversibility, and deeply penetrating effects on the domestic order of the state.[68]

For the United States and other non-EU countries, the WTO, NATO, or the Community of Democracies have the potential to harness some of the positive effects of enmeshment. To join the WTO, for instance, countries must agree to strict standards of transparency, consistency, and fairness, and must submit disputes to its legal decisionmaking mechanism. These strong forms of enmeshment are supplemented by weaker but still important forms of socialization: Complying with these membership requirements entails sending local lawyers and government bureaucrats to work with the international organization. These individuals build professional relationships with international colleagues who support rule-of-law norms. NATO membership requirements demand civilian control of the military and the rule of law. The Community of Democracies does not have deep and binding procedures that could keep countries, once members, on the straight and narrow. But it is constantly innovating, and the United States could support its movement in this direction.[69]

However, the United States rarely considers the strong form of enmeshment as a rule-of-law building tool when evaluating policies from trade deals to NATO membership. Unlike the EU, the United States has no history of an institutionally based enmeshment process of its own to draw on. Instead, the United States tends to give away membership in organizations as a diplomatic carrot, rather than using it as a method to create change.[70] This undermines enmeshment's strongest lever.

The lack of understanding of enmeshment as a method of spurring reform is changing, slightly, among some policymakers. In the early 1990s, some politicians and scholars urged using NATO as an enmeshment vehicle to solidify the new democracies in Eastern Europe. They specifically cited its membership requirement of the rule of law, as well as its ongoing military interaction stressing human rights values and civilian leadership, as means of affecting norms in those states.[71] The logic of enmeshment also fueled President Clinton's "engagement" method with China, though he was never able to explain it to skeptical Americans.[72] Paula Dobriansky, George W. Bush's Undersecretary of State for Global Affairs, who oversaw democratization and rule-of-law efforts in the State Department, also showed interest in enmeshment as a strategic method. She spoke, for instance, about using the Community of Democracies, the Organization of American States, and the EU as vehicles to support countries in legal activity and building a culture of lawfulness.[73] However, in general, the United States has chosen to stand apart from international institutions—and this political culture of "standing alone" makes it difficult to promote a widespread understanding of how strong, institutionally based enmeshment could be a useful tool. Unlike in Europe, enmeshment is not a method that is intuitive to the general public, and it is rarely on politicians' minds when they look for tools to push troubled countries toward the rule of law. Thus, the United States has difficulty pursuing enmeshment to its fullest.

Instead, the main way enmeshment is undertaken in the United States is by encouraging individuals in other countries to socialize themselves into the United States itself, through exchange programs, training, and similar activities. This less robust form of enmeshment is targeted only at individuals. For most American politicians who support it, the idea is simply that by seeing the United States, leaders from other countries will head home changed. Some scholars suggest that these programs function on a deeper level, by building transnational professional communities that share values, interests, and expertise. The social norms of these professional communities push individuals within them closer to rule-of-law ideals. After an exchange program, for instance, the local members of these shared communities then go back to reform their own states by tilting policy toward their common international agenda.[74] However, unlike strong enmeshment into international organizations, there is no scholarly proof that this weak form has any effect on actual government behavior.

The development community tends to deride this soft form of enmeshment. They see it as being no deeper than "bring foreigners to America to see how we do things here." Rather than supporting a process of interdependent cultural, structural, and institutional change, exchange program adherents seem to believe that rule-of-law failures are simply the result of a lack of knowledge—when people see how things are done in the United States, they will have an "aha" moment and return home to implement programs differently. But, skeptics say, even if simply being exposed to America succeeded in imparting American values, the political and cultural incentive structures faced at home are far too formidable for any single reformer to create much change. At its very best, such socialization might change the hearts and minds of a few—but these programs as they are currently designed are too small, diffuse, and unfocused. It would take far more planning on the part of the United States to bring together a group of reformers from a given country, socialize and train them as a unit, and then send them home to jointly create change.

Despite these difficulties, the weak form of enmeshment has planted deep roots in the minds of American members of Congress, diplomats, and the military. Ambassadors are often significant supporters of this weaker form of enmeshment. A multitude of programs exists to send foreign government officials on study tours and visits to the United States. The goal of these enmeshment programs is often simply to reward the leaders of other governments with a free trip as a diplomatic carrot, not as a socialization strategy. However, at times, they are aimed at changing the professional cultures and ideas of foreign leaders by introducing them to a new cultural and social milieu that is expected to influence their thinking when they return home. The Fulbright scholarship program has similar goals, as does the U.S. Visit program, which allows U.S. embassies to recommend individuals who "would benefit from time in the United States" to come to America for short tours and meet with counterparts in their professional community, in the belief that these tours will spread U.S. values.[75]

The Department of Defense views military exchanges and joint training exercises as enmeshment vehicles as well—and is, in fact, probably the strongest proponent of this weak form of enmeshment-based change. For instance, while the U.S. Congress tried to use strong negative diplomacy to force Indonesia to abide by human rights norms, the U.S. military and State Department backed enmeshment to achieve the same goal.[76] Both agencies sought to restore the International Military Education and Training (IMET) program to Indonesia's military, arguing that "we can think of no better means of encouraging better human rights performance by Indonesian military officers than giving them extensive exposure to U.S. military forces with our doctrines of respect for civilian authority and the rights of civilian populations."[77] Despite the claims of the Indonesian military leader at the beginning of this section, the effectiveness of such exchange programs depends on the degree to which these values are demonstrated and norms are spread among those in the trenches. A number of military leaders who later abused human rights were trained in U.S. programs.[78] While it may well be useful for the United States to have ties with other countries' militaries, it is not at all clear that such programs inculcate rule-of-law norms.

The World Bank and some other portions of the development community see business as a potential enmeshment vehicle. Foreign direct investment, particularly, is viewed as a method that can improve the local business culture by introducing foreign business practices—from keeping honest books, to fighting nepotism, or enforcing sexual harassment laws. There may be value to pursuing business as a means of changing culture. When the Organization for Economic Cooperation and Development brought European businesses to Indonesia for a conference, the business leaders' main feedback to their hosts was the need for greater transparency and reduced corruption if Indonesia wanted to attract more foreign capital and direct investment.[79] Such advice from a community the local government wishes to attract could spur change. However, in many countries, particularly those lacking a U.S.-style Foreign Corrupt Practices Act, foreign businesses accept and augment a culture of corruption, both by paying large bribes for contracts and by focusing on how to lock in benefits for themselves rather than working to create a level playing field. Many businesses lack an intrinsic interest in ensuring transparency and non-corruption so long as they are benefiting from the system. Nevertheless, the United States could do more to augment this form of enmeshment by promoting foreign direct investment, suggesting interesting partnerships between, for instance, USAID and the Department of Commerce.

Conditions for Success—Weak Enmeshment

While the United States prefers the weaker form of enmeshment through exchange, it is difficult to imagine this method having much effect. First, changing hearts and minds requires picking the right people who have the power to leverage change now or in the future. But often, embassies wish to use these programs as rewards or junkets, obviating this purpose. At other times, the United States does not even get to choose who participates. The U.S. government's IMET military training program, for instance, is supposed to inculcate American rule-of-law norms into overseas militaries. Romania was an active IMET participant, sending around 150 officers each year to the program and engaging in more than 40 joint programs.[80] However, a report on NATO enlargement found that Romania, which chose its own participants, used these trainings as patronage opportunities, undermining their worth for teaching rule-of-law norms.[81]

Even if the right people are chosen, and hearts and minds are changed, those individuals must amass power in an inimical system to make larger changes. The EU has repeatedly found that enmeshing local civil servants in its twinning programs failed because the bureaucrats it trained were swept aside when a new government entered power.[82] USAID and the State Department funded the Civitas program, which among other exchange trips, brought young Romanian politicians and civil servants to the United States on the assumption that "younger Romanian politicians and government employees need to benefit from exposure to the U.S. not only to learn new techniques but to generate closer ties with the American people."[83] Yet an independent evaluator of these programs cautioned against optimism:

> In the past years, it has been hoped that a new generation of political leaders would help to professionalize parties and politics in Romania. Many training programs were put in place and numerous young political leaders have benefited from overseas experiences. But hopes are dimming that this training of young political leaders will be able to surmount the rigid tendencies of the political system . . . the young comers [within one political party] soon got the reputation of being essentially clones of those who promoted them.[84]

The report claimed that without reform of the political "structures and rules that condition behavior," little change to Romania's political culture would occur.[85] U.S. diplomats and politicians may love the idea of foreign elites seeing the American system and returning with their eyes open and a set of new ideas in their pockets. But the reality is that a few newly socialized individuals acting alone are going to be fighting a considerable uphill path to change entrenched power dynamics. This weaker form of enmeshment through socialization has a place in the pantheon of tactics; it just cannot be considered a potent method to spur change on its own.

This is not to dismiss the idea of weak enmeshment altogether. Some wealthy philanthropists and organizations specialize in bringing together handpicked groups of reformers from within a country, socializing them with successful reformers in other countries, and giving them real training in how to create change within their own societies. While such reformers would still return to inimical institutions, they have a greater chance of altering the power structures and culture. With ongoing bottom-up aid and potentially top-down support, such a program has real ability to create change. But it is also far different from the scattershot tours of America that currently characterize many U.S. weak enmeshment programs.

Conditions for Success—Strong Enmeshment

While the integration process is far from perfect, the European Union has had immense success in using enmeshment to support rule-of-law reform. The lure of belonging to a desired community, combined with the conditionality of membership requirements, gives enmeshment significant power to create change.[86] In part, this is because politicians can use the desired membership to bind their government's hands in favor of reforms.[87] As then-EU President Romano Prodi proclaimed in 2002, discussing the EU's recent enlargement: "By holding up the goal of membership, we enabled these [central European] governments to implement the necessary reforms. Only this prospect sustained the reformers in their efforts to overcome nationalist and other resistance and fears of change and modernization."[88] Nor are such sentiments just EU self-congratulation: As Milan Rocen, Montenegro's Foreign Minister, said, thanks to the EU process, his country had "made more reforms in one year than it would have managed on its own in ten."[89]

If the United States began using the strong form of enmeshment as a method of change, it could become a particularly useful tool for countries reluctant to undertake rule-of-law reforms. Because strong enmeshment offers membership in a coveted group, it can be used to induce a reluctant country's compliance, while slowly changing norms in a way that diplomacy alone cannot achieve. Thus, enmeshment could be helpful for creating slow change in authoritarian states that may enter into an international organization with the intention of controlling the effects of enmeshment to their benefit (such as China's entry into the WTO) and may be surprised at the level of change brought about via socialization. For instance, China watchers claim that since joining the WTO, China has revised important laws and judicial decisions, dramatically transforming its regulatory environment. As former U.S. Ambassador Clark T. Randt Jr. explains, complying with the WTO's legal regulations and commercial law requirements has had "a profound effect on rule of law."[90]

However, the level of intellectual property theft and the rash of commercial scandals may belie this conclusion.[91] And even if the WTO is having such a "profound effect," there is no guarantee of spillover effects from one rule-of-law area (commercial law, in the case of the WTO, or civilian control of the military, in the case of NATO) to another. After all, many authoritarian governments, such as Spain under Franco, have had relatively sound commercial law without human rights; others had civilian control of the military while allowing immense corruption.[92]

Moreover, though there is little quantitative evidence yet on enmeshment's effects, anecdotal evidence suggests that strong enmeshment's greatest power for change lies in its membership conditionality—basically, a form of diplomacy. Once a country has been admitted to an international institution, the social and cultural aspects of reform can be quite slow at best, and extremely limited at worst. EU membership conditionality created a serious push for reform in Romania, for instance, as detailed in the next chapter. Under the guidelines for membership, Romania passed a spate of important laws that affected the power structure and appointed Monica Macovei, the nonpartisan, reform-minded minister of justice mentioned earlier. But the magic wore off once Romania entered the club: just three months later, amid a general Cabinet reshuffle, the government fired Macovei. She had crossed too many corrupt parliamentarians. Her replacement immediately forced out the prosecutor working on the biggest corruption cases and weakened other anticorruption reforms.[93]

If most of the work of enmeshment is done through membership conditionality, then regional coalitions with limited membership conditionality may have little to no enmeshment effects: ASEAN, for instance, inducted Burma (Myanmar) in the hope that "engagement" would lead to changes in the rule of law, but for a decade, no change emerged.[94] Yet even these weak coalitions may have an affect: Burma is in the process of opening, possibly because of leadership changes that were pushed by international forums and were originally believed to simply be window dressing, but which may be having real effect. Or the change may simply be resulting from fear of China; the history remains to be written. Other institutions with such conditionality may need to front-load their reform efforts, remaining aware that membership conditionality is their best chance to leverage reform.

The international community also needs to be able to apply such membership conditionality forcefully if it is going to have its desired effect. If we cannot do that—for the same reasons that we are hampered in our diplomacy—then we forgo the chance to use these enmeshment vehicles for real reform. Consider the cases of Albania versus Romania.

In Albania, NATO successfully used a strong form of enmeshment to excellent effect, and the United States supported NATO's efforts. Albania desperately wished to join the military alliance after the fall of its communist dictatorship. It applied for membership before NATO had even considered expanding and joined the Partnership for Peace, NATO's anteroom for Eastern Europe, as soon as membership opened in 1994. Its military engaged deeply with the Partnership for Peace trainings and joint exercises, and the country happily hosted NATO bases on its soil beginning with the Balkan wars. Yet its weak level of military and civilian development meant that NATO left it out of its first round of expansion in 1999.[95] Albania joined eight other NATO aspirants asking the Alliance to invite them all to join at the next NATO summit, but it was again bypassed in 2004, when seven other Eastern European nations joined.[96]

Instead of simply admitting Albania, NATO invited it (along with Macedonia and Croatia) to take part in a Membership Action Plan (MAP) program. Each country was asked to submit action plans each year for comment, forcing the countries to take seriously the ground rules for NATO membership and create plans to meet them. NATO's MAP for Albania asked the country for a number of rule-of-law measures, including:

- continuation of reforms that would enhance the development of a market economy and rule of law, while fighting against corruption;
- improving respect for human and minority rights, while supporting efforts for strengthening democratic institutions and increasing the efficiency of governance;
- strengthening of civilian control over military structures and command while continuing the military reforms that aim at the harmonization of legislation with that of the North Atlantic Alliance; and
- increasing compliance and participation in international efforts to fight terrorism and organized crime in relation to the participation of Albania in the antiterrorist coalition of states.[97]

By 1998, Albania had constitutionally enshrined NATO's requirement of civilian control of the military.[98] In 2005, the Albanian Armed Forces announced that 300 career military officers were "retiring"—possibly because they had gained positions through corruption or nepotism rather than merit.[99] While not a condition of NATO assistance, such dismissals would be necessary to help create the NATO military culture and rule-of-law values. Albania also complied with NATO requirements to release political documents on security and defense issues, which are no longer classified as state secrets and are now open to the public.[100] While Albania still has far to go, NATO's program of enmeshment with strong membership conditionality appears to have spurred real change in modernizing the military to meet NATO's requirements.[101] The United States supported Albania's bid for membership in 2008, while insisting on continued military professionalism, with a particular emphasis on improving the rule of law and reducing corruption.[102]

While the United States held back from using NATO as a political chit to give to Albania as an appreciative gesture, that is the exception, while Romania is closer to the rule. In Romania, NATO was clear that corruption and the continuing influence of the communist-era secret police in security agencies could undermine Romania's bid to join the alliance. Yet the United States was a steady supporter of Romania's candidacy because of Romania's significant assistance to the United States in the war on terrorism. President Bush invited Romania to join NATO in 2002, despite the country's corruption, revitalized secret police, and subservient judiciary.[103] U.S. hypocrisy was apparent in a USAID report claiming that the flurry of reform laws passed in 2003 (forced by the EU's membership conditionality) were "critical steps [that] have helped to lay the groundwork for an invitation to join NATO," despite the fact that the invitation was made before any of these laws had been passed.[104] If the United States treats membership organizations as simply a diplomatic reward, rather than a chance to engage, socialize, and change other countries, then it wastes a prime method—and opportunity—of reform.

Conclusion

While most studies to date have focused on promoting the rule of law via top-down methods, the most successful second-generation reform programs are likely to draw on all four methods at different times. Each way of leveraging change has its uses and drawbacks. Reformers can obtain maximum leverage when they deploy multiple methods to work toward the same objects of change.

Because no one method is best for all types of reform and in all situations, it makes sense to understand the types of change each is suited for, rather than to simply argue for one method and against another. Unfortunately, to date, debate has followed the latter course. Differences in culture between the development community, which tends to favor top-down and bottom-up approaches, and the diplomatic and political communities, which tend to prefer the diplomatic and enmeshment methods, preclude the United States from coordinating methods for greatest impact.[105] Thomas Carothers tells an illustrative anecdote about such culture clashes in his visits with two U.S. government officials involved in democracy promotion. In the first meeting, a USAID mission director describes the long-term efforts to improve democracy by bolstering independent media, encouraging NGOs, reforming the judiciary, and the like—efforts that used the top-down and bottom-up reform methods available to aid agencies, and largely functioned outside the capital city at the grassroots level. In the second meeting, a U.S. ambassador denigrated these programs and instead touted the importance of diplomacy and exchange programs that would target "key politicians with real influence." The embassy was to send them on tours to the United States and "keep the pressure on them at pivotal junctures to make sure they do the right things politically."[106] In U.S. embassies, even though USAID and political staff are housed in the same compound, development programs and political officers plan jointly only occasionally. Sometimes, consular officials are unaware of the development programs the United States is carrying out; at other times, they are aware but still do not coordinate political pressure with the needs of development programs. The new Quadrennial Diplomacy and Development Review tries to improve coordination through its idea of an ambassador as CEO of a complex, multi-agency enterprise. Some of the most cutting-edge diplomats and development professionals are realizing the need for their professional cultures to blend, particularly in the most problematic weak states. But whether the new State Department structures and these cultural shifts will catch on is yet to be seen.

The gap between the more traditional diplomatic and development cultures is unfortunate, because mixed messages and uncoordinated methods can undermine efforts to build the rule of law. If diplomacy is being used to push a government toward the rule of law, but development aid or military joint exercises continue, for instance, the diplomacy will not be taken seriously and the effects of the conditionality and sanctions will be undermined.[107] Scholars Adesnik and McFaul found that such mixed signals from different parts of the U.S. government undermined pro-democracy messages and allowed autocrats to believe they could remain in power.[108] Similarly, the slow, less glamorous top-down and bottom-up development methods can be overshadowed by the punch of high-profile diplomacy. Such were the findings of democracy assistance in Russia, in which premature claims by such groups as the Organization for Security and Cooperation in Europe that voting was free and fair provided leaders with cover that undermined the efforts of direct development practitioners to bring about democratic change.[109]

Understanding the four methods of change, their uses and drawbacks, and the contexts in which they are more and less likely to achieve their desired results is a first step toward building the mutual understanding needed to improve policy coherence and enable the methods of intervention to work together for greater impact. The final step is bringing together the methods of intervention and objects of reform, to understand the full array of tactics the United States might use, and how these can be deployed strategically. That is the topic of the next chapter.

CHAPTER SIX

STRATEGY AND IMPLEMENTATION: DEPLOYING TACTICS TOGETHER

There is nothing so useless as doing efficiently that which should not be done at all.

– Peter Drucker

International aid to the justice sector in Afghanistan has thus far been largely dysfunctional. The dysfunction was not for lack of a strategic vision—significant effort has been made to view the sector as a whole and to establish the coordinating bodies and mechanisms to implement that strategy. Rather, implementation has been piecemeal at best owing to rivalries, limited resources, and poor coordination of Afghan actors and donors.

– J. Alexander Thier[1]

In Romania, U.S. governance reformers launched a nuanced program to support local civil society groups bent on unseating their corrupt, communist-inspired leadership—just as the Pentagon decided to build military bases in poor parts of the country, providing an influx of jobs and money that bolstered the ruling government. In Albania, the EU spoke almost daily on the ills of corruption—while allowing the Ministry of Justice to steal EU development dollars with no repercussions. This is strategy gone awry. Instead of using multiple methods to bolster the rule of law, one hand destroys what the other hand is building. It is not good enough to protest that governments are complex and that the actions of one part are separate from those of another. Whether planned or serendipitous, the signals the United States—and other entities—send to a country are read as a whole by local leaders. The chances of success with rule-of-law reform are greater if we are more strategic in its planning and implementation as we deploy multiple methods together.

The United States may help or hurt its own rule-of-law programs through signals sent by different arms of the U.S. government that may not at all be connected with rule-of-law promotion. Some of these conflicting signals are inevitable, though no less detrimental. But if U.S. rule-of-law reformers recognize this reality and plan for it—while broadening their tool kits to consider all the methods of change at their disposal, they can use a larger set of tactics more strategically. By deploying clusters of tactics together, practitioners can deepen their impact, producing ever greater waves of change, rather than allowing unintended consequences to cancel out their efforts altogether. This chapter first describes each of the tactics that the United States (and other rule-of-law reforming entities) can employ to build the rule of law abroad, showing what each of these abstract methods and objects looks like in real life. It then shows how groups of tactics can be used strategically to maximize effectiveness. Table 6.1 gives a full sense of the tactics that can be used, and shades those that have the best chance of sustainable success. Darker shading shows tactics that can work, with caveats.

Much of first-generation reform was confined to the first two blocks in column one—or at best, a block of four tactics in columns one and two. These constraints make no sense when an entire array of tools is available. Yet nearly all rule-of-law writing focuses on these four tactics in the upper left of the chart. Some literature on aid conditionality shows the pros and cons of a few tactics in the third column, while the democratization literature covers row three: the power structure. Meanwhile, enmeshment tactics have barely been written about at all, and most tactics to affect culture are blank spots, where little is understood about what works or what has been tried.

These gaps in understanding the available tools and determining their effectiveness make the job of a practitioner on the ground, or a USAID staff member trying to write good terms of reference, needlessly difficult. If reformers believe that a law needs to be changed, what is the best tactic to change the law so it is accepted by the legal community, used, and upheld? If the goal is to foster judicial independence, what is the most sustainable way to do it, so independence does not simply allow a craven and unaccountable judiciary? If police are corrupt, what is the best way to change their actions? These questions don't have simple answers—but we can, at least, illuminate the available tactics and see which ones may or may not be better suited to a particular task. The rest of this chapter does just that, describing each tactic, how it might be used, and where it might work best. It is a first stab at a field that requires far more empirical research to help practitioners make more informed choices.

Reforming Laws: Four Tactics

Top-Down Reform to Change Laws: The simplest way for outsiders to change laws is to simply redraft laws and codes themselves or fund technical assistance programs that help local lawyers rewrite them. Usually, such work is done directly with government bodies alongside efforts to get such laws passed. Top-down legal reform has been one of the most commonly used tactics in rule-of-law reform.

The appeal of this tactic goes beyond theoretical logic—it is straightforward to accomplish and to measure: Aid agencies can claim to be writing a certain number of laws and can count how many, if any, of these laws pass. It is also cheap: As U.S. Court of Appeals Judge Richard Posner put it, "a modest investment in better rules" is easier than a "big investment in the judiciary."[2]

Top-down legal reform is a very useful method for getting a law on the books, if that is all that matters. Unfortunately, as described in chapter 4, it is less effective at getting society to accept a law, or the government

TABLE 6.1	TACTICS, WITH CONCRETE ILLUSTRATIONS OF INTERVENTIONS	
	METHODS	
OBJECTS FOR REFORM	Top-Down (Funding and technical assistance to rule-of-law institutions)	Bottom-Up (Funding and technical assistance to civil society)
Laws	**Tactical Examples** Foreign lawyers draft laws and provide them directly to ministries with the suggestion that they be passed	**Tactical Examples** Funding to civil society to advocate for new laws; referendums
Institutions	Judicial reform; police reform; building prisons; equipping police	Sponsoring poll on corruption in judiciary to spur civil society pressure; training journalists to improve legal reporting; funding civil society to work with courts
Power Structure	Strengthen alternative power structures (institutions of "horizontal accountability" such as courts, ombudsmen) to rein in government	Funding advocacy groups to shine light on government abuse, support advocacy groups organizing mass movements for political change, advocacy groups campaigning for anticorruption reforms
Culture	Funding for law schools, police academies, direct programs to affect popular culture	Funding for broad popular education on rule of law, local groups training schoolchildren or working with police or judges

to actually operate according to law. These problems with top-down legal reform do not condemn the tactic entirely: They simply set parameters that should be kept in mind when one considers whether a new law is needed, and how it should be brought into being.

Diplomacy (Pressure to force the government to institute change)	**Enmeshment** (Pressure and socialization via enmeshing a country in rule-of-law norms)
Tactical Examples Conditionality that requires a country to pass certain laws to receive aid	**Tactical Examples** Forcing a country to pass intellectual property laws to join WTO
Aid conditionality to create such things as ombudsmen and anti-corruption institutions (diplomacy other than aid conditionality is generally too blunt for institutional reform)	NATO training missions; U.S. police engagement
Rhetoric and pressure for judicial independence, fair trials, and so on	Strong enmeshment could force civilian control of military or demand independence of judiciary; weak enmeshment could socialize elites into rule-of-law norms through cultural enmeshment, and potentially create change of heart
Press government to allow free press, allow civil society groups, and other preconditions for cultural change	Cultural exchange programs, military training programs such as IMET

Bottom-Up Reform to Change Laws: To engage in legal reform that is more likely to create cultural acceptance or government enforcement, a bottom-up strategy is preferable. Under a bottom-up strategy, outside actors can fund civil society actors to lobby for certain laws or types of law—such as supporting local human rights organizations that advocate for human rights laws. Another means of such indirect legal action is to fund legal education that favors a certain normative agenda, in the hopes that the newly trained lawyers will themselves press for laws that would create social change. Such was the mechanism of change favored by the law and development movement.[3] Many modern rule-of-law projects fund NGOs that engage in class action, public interest, and test cases on behalf of groups or individuals suffering from an infringement of their rights, in the hope that these rights can be enshrined in law.[4] Bottom-up reform is often fruitfully combined with top-down reform—USAID, for instance, provided top-down assistance to draft Albania's constitution and also mobilized NGOs to advocate for constitutional provisions supporting human rights and the rule of law.[5]

By using bottom-up reform, the United States has the possibility of supporting a local group that cares about the law and will keep pressure on the government to enforce it. This method also provides a means to spread new norms throughout society. In Albania, USAID contractors decided to subcontract with a local Albanian NGO to turn a draft law against domestic violence into legislation. The Albanian NGO mustered 20,000 signatures for a petition. In doing so, it built cultural awareness of women's rights and the foreign concept of domestic violence.[6] Meanwhile, those who had worked on the project were committed to the concept and continued their efforts to spread women's rights even after the contract ended.[7]

In Romania, bottom-up reform to change laws was one step in creating an important shift in the power structure. Throughout the mid-1990s, USAID had funded Romanian civil society groups. Criticized by independent evaluators for funding many self-interested organizations, USAID nevertheless also managed to finance some serious entities that focused on advocating for laws crucial to altering the balance of power—such as legislation that allowed the NGO sector itself to operate, including tax incentives to support the sector, a simpler law on registering associations, and a Freedom of Information (FOI) law.[8] USAID had been extensively involved in the Freedom of Information initiative, through top-down efforts to help draft the law and then bottom-up support through contractors to assist the local NGO coalition in lobbying for the law and parrying government attempts to roll it back.[9]

The FOI law's success was a turning point in Romanian politics. The political opposition showed itself to be ineffectual, while the NGO coalition was effective and attracted media attention. The media treated NGOs as a serious political force, and they became the focus of major, ongoing coverage in the Romanian press. The coalition behind the FOI law's passage created a permanent Coalition for Transparency, which used the law to press for additional transparency and anticorruption reforms. Among the reforms was a rule that forced the government to allow public debate on draft laws, and a "sunshine" law demanded by EU conditionality that required greater government transparency.[10]

As is frequently the case when laws are used to change the power structure, the postcommunist government fought to undermine the spirit of these laws. It forbade most FOI requests and continued to manipulate judicial decisions.[11] Yet in combination with other reforms focused on the culture of the judiciary and discussed later in this chapter, these laws would prove crucial to forcing change. After 2003, the newly independent courts increasingly decided contested FOI requests in favor of openness, revealing a number of controversial government actions such as the prosecutor-general's illegal wiretapping of Romanian citizens.[12] Eventually, these FOI and sunshine laws would lead to a change of government in Romania. None of this would have occurred if the laws had not been embraced by local reformers who had an interest in their success. USAID may have paid contractors to draft the FOI law, but by using bottom-up rather than top-down reform, these laws were understood, desired, and used by the advocacy community to change their government structures toward openness and transparency—and to create a space for the nonprofit sector itself as an engine of vertical accountability.

Changing Laws through Diplomacy: Forcing a foreign government to change or pass laws through strong-arm diplomacy is a common tactic—and one that often results in the passage of the desired laws. The United States has used diplomacy to insist that countries around the world pass antiterrorist and anti–money laundering laws in the wake of September 11. The United States doesn't often place legal conditionality on its aid, but the World Bank frequently does—and as with the other diplomatic tactics, conditionality is effective in gaining legal passage.[13]

However, while diplomacy can force a government to put a law on the books, it is a dangerous tactic for reforming laws. Diplomacy suffers from the same problems of top-down reform: Laws may be passed and then ignored by the government and the citizenry, a problem that can reduce the weight of law more generally. An even greater danger is that governments will choose to enact laws demanded by the United States or other outside groups via executive orders that bypass legislatures. This is a frequent tactic of governments when they are forced to adopt unpopular laws. The overuse of executive orders to bypass parliament harms the rule of law itself by undermining the legislature's role as the state's lawmaking body. Such a situation occurred in Romania when laws demanded by outsiders did not have strong cultural or political support internally.[14]

Equally problematic, strong-arm tendencies can look imperialistic—and fail to win the cultural support necessary to instill meaning in the law. The European Commission, for instance, applied immense diplomatic pressure for Romania to change its law banning homosexuality. The intensity of the efforts surprised even Romania's negotiators.[15] The Ministry for European Integration lobbied the minister of justice for months until she finally agreed to submit the law. However, the change to the homosexuality law was widely unpopular in Romania's Orthodox and conservative society, and parliament was likely to reject it. Romania's EU negotiators took the nearly unprecedented step of arguing in parliament on behalf of the law, explaining that it was crucial for integration. With the point driven home, the law passed.[16] The legal change was certainly an important human rights step and may also have been useful to prevent future governments from using homosexuality against political opponents, a common communist tactic. But because the law was forced through with diplomatic pressure, rather than through bottom-up or cultural means, the EU achievement was limited. In 2005, 38 percent of Romanians still claimed that "homosexuals are hardly better than criminals"—not exactly a major cultural stride.[17] Forcing legal change by fiat can anger even those who would otherwise support cultural change. In Albania, the director of a women's rights NGO explained, "There have been lots of legal changes to enshrine gender equality and women's rights, but like most of the laws, the changes have resulted from international pressure, not from the government itself—just from the government kissing up to the EU without thinking through the consequences."[18] If a women's rights activist feels so dismissive toward laws to help women, imagine the attitude of someone who *didn't* support the law's substance.

Changing Laws through Enmeshment: Joining the WTO, the EU, NAFTA, and certain other international organizations forces a country to modify its laws to comply with the rules of these membership groups. At times, countries adopt required laws wholesale, without reference to the effects they will have internally. Yet unlike conditionality, enmeshment provides the space for the local community to adapt laws to some extent to fit the local context. It is also more mutual: The country wants to join a group, and the group has the right to set the rules for membership. While strong-arm diplomacy such as that employed by the European Union in the Romanian case may backfire, generally there is more room for a government to explain legal changes to its people when they occur as part of a membership process.

Like diplomacy and top-down reform, enmeshment is an effective way to ensure that laws are passed. Romania figured that out in 2003, the year before EU accession negotiations needed to close if the country wanted to take part in the "big bang" accession of 2004 and join the Union with eleven other countries.[19] After years of ignoring EU requests, suddenly Romania realized it really did need to act if it wanted to join the club. Romania's government undertook a spate of required reforms: It began screening all draft legislation for compatibility with the *acquis communautaire*, complied with the European Convention on Human Rights, and introduced a procedure to limit the use of executive orders that bypassed parliament. In a grand push of legal reform, Romania passed a civil servant statute to enshrine the civil service; laws against organized crime and money laundering; the "sunshine law" permitting public access to government information; and constitutional changes to enshrine the right to a fair trial, legal redress, and access to justice. Finally, in a move that would be decisive, the government passed a Judicial System Reform Strategy to legalize judicial independence.[20]

Instead of jubilation, however, international development professionals and local reformers barely commented on these seemingly historic legal changes. Most observers felt that the government, acting under duress, had no intention of implementing the new laws.[21] Their hunch was confirmed when the press gained access to leaked tapes of top executive officials openly discussing judicial manipulation, civil society manipulation, and corruption.[22] Enmeshment-based diplomacy could force legal passage—but it could not force implementation, cultural change, or real political commitment to reform.

Legal change achieved through means other than bottom-up reform will almost certainly lack an organized constituency backing reform, and the power to compel enforcement. Even laws as decisive as those passed in Romania may not be enough, in and of themselves, to have much effect on the rule of law. However, passage can still be useful. In combination with bottom-up strategies for power structure change and tactics to reform the professional culture of the judiciary, the laws passed by Romania through bottom-up tactics by the United States and enmeshment efforts of the EU would ultimately be decisive. Legal change *can* matter—as long as it is deployed in conjunction with other tactics and focused on the power structure. For the rest of the story, we must turn to other rule-of-law reform tactics.

Reforming Institutions: Four Tactics

Reforming Institutions through Top-Down Intervention: As mentioned previously, the billion-dollar rule-of-law reform industry is almost entirely based on using a top-down strategy toward institutional (and legal) reform. USAID, the World Bank, and other bilateral and multilateral development agencies computerize courts, create new magistrates' schools, build court buildings, buy printing presses to publish laws, create alternative venues to arbitrate disputes, and sponsor dozens of other programs all subsumed under this tactic.[23]

It is possible to engage in top-down reforms that work to alter institutions in order to affect the power structure or their professional cultures. Such reforms can be quite successful and are described under those tactical options. However, the majority of top-down institutional reforms follow the theory of change described by Thomas Carothers as "institutional modeling": Reformers alter institutions so that they look like U.S. organs of justice and believe that by doing so, they will cause these institutions to work and thereby bring about the rule of law.[24]

Institutional modeling, as discussed earlier, has come in for deservedly heavy criticism. As Javier Ciurlizza, the former Secretary General of the Andean Commission of Jurists, wrote:

> No amount of fancy computers and manuals describing methods of efficient management will disturb characteristics of the judiciary that have deep social, cultural and political roots. Five years' work and in excess of U.S. $400 million spent have not improved the credibility of judges. The entire bureaucratic culture will have to be changed somehow, if judicial reform projects are to deliver meaningful results.[25]

The problem is not confined to Latin America; it is part and parcel of the method. The EU, for example, commissioned an independent study of its rule-of-law programs in Albania from 1991 to 2004, which had cost European taxpayers around 275 million euros.[26] As the review states, the objectives of the justice sector program were to make:

> . . . justice efficient and effective, to pursue legal and institutional reform, to support the modernization of the judicial system, to strengthen the authority and effectiveness of the police, and to rebuild confidence in the internal security of the country. However, the actual outputs of this programme so far are that six courthouses have been rehabilitated, office furniture has been supplied, new minibuses and uniforms purchased, and training and expertise has been provided to the School of Magistrates.[27]

The report, and other independent sources, went on to condemn the program in ever more explicit terms. EU-purchased police vehicles were being used for joyriding around Tirana's streets rather than for fighting crime.[28] Training police in human rights could not overcome structural problems such as low wages and criminality among recruits.[29] Reports of police cooperation with organized criminals were matched by reports of police "death squads" targeting organized criminals.[30] While the EU succeeded in improving professionalism among civil servants, many of those trained were fired by the new government in 2002, despite their civil service status.

The problem with these reforms is not that they used top-down methods of change—the problem is focusing on institutions as ends in themselves and fixing the problems that seem "obvious" if one's point of reference is making them look like U.S. institutions. Top-down reform can be useful if it is focused on the institutional culture and the power structure in which these broken institutions function.

Reforming Institutions through Bottom-Up Intervention: Many practitioners saw these problems with top-down institutional change. But they couldn't ignore the very real problems within rule-of-law institutions that impeded justice. Instead, seeking better ways to alter institutions, they turned to bottom-up reform.[31] Rather than an outside funder paying a contractor to create a justice reform program, for instance, external agencies provide aid and technical assistance to local groups dedicated to reforming their own justice systems. At their best, bottom-up methods to improve institutions do not engage in technocratic reform but rely on the knowledge of local actors to identify real reformers and work with them to disarm countervailing forces.[32] The Asia Foundation's program in Indonesia demonstrates successful use of this tactic.

USAID began funding civil society in Indonesia in the early 1990s. On August 25, 1989, as the Soviet Union's foundations began to crack and Eastern Europeans poured through Hungary's newly opened border, USAID's Asia and Near East Bureau cabled all posts suggesting that they undertake new initiatives for promoting democratic pluralism, open markets, and open societies across all the Asian missions.[33] Although the Suharto regime was not amenable to rule-of-law reform, Eastern Europe had ignited Congress's and USAID's imagination of the possible.[34] Three weeks later, the USAID mission director in Indonesia approached the Asia Foundation to discuss cooperation.[35] USAID prepared a paper on democratic transition, making legal reform one of four focus areas, and then worked with the Asia Foundation to create a program.[36] By 1991, the Asia Foundation had received two grants totaling more than $700,000 for legal programming, funding that would increase throughout the decade as the Asia Foundation's IDEAL program became USAID's main rule-of-law effort.[37]

While the Asia Foundation was an international NGO, it had been in Indonesia for fifty years, and as such had deep local knowledge, and an Indonesian staff. In the early years of its programming, the Asia Foundation had supported a legal education program that had generated a group of pragmatic, reformist graduates who wanted to improve Indonesia's flawed legal institutions.[38] These students were mentored by some of the founders of Indonesia's most prominent legal reform NGO and other leading lawyers. In the months after Suharto's fall, these mentors provided the students with free space and initial funding to start their own NGO designed to press for legal reforms. Soon, that NGO had birthed two sister organizations that shared the same workspace, ideas, and savvy, to focus on different portions of their joint mission.

The Asia Foundation's local program managers saw a rare opportunity far earlier than an outside funder could have. Some exceptionally bright, reformist law graduates were willing to take significant salary cuts to begin pragmatic work on legal reform, and they had the backing of elder statesmen in the legal community. If USAID had been engaged in a top-down reform program, its operatives probably would not have even noticed these tiny new NGOs—and even if they had, delivering USAID funding would have taken years, not to mention the reams of paperwork the small organizations would have been obligated to fulfill. By pursuing a bottom-up strategy, USAID had already provided funds to the Asia Foundation. And the foundation's more flexible structure allowed it to move money quickly, in months rather than years. The Asia Foundation passed along grants to the small NGOs without the overwhelming reporting requirements required by USAID. They also offered financial and auditing assistance—just what these new NGOs needed to get started.

The reformist NGOs worked together. After publishing a 1999 book on judicial independence—still a new idea in Indonesia at the time—they brought together additional civil society organizations to form a Coalition for a New Constitution, through which they lobbied members of parliament and presented draft resolutions to forward ideas for a judicial commission and a bicameral parliament—ideas that were later written into the constitution. They built trust with enough experts on the constitutional drafting board to see drafts of revisions and submit counterproposals, making important constitutional changes that solidified greater judicial independence and internal oversight.[39] They thereby created an independent judiciary with support from below—and a vertical accountability system to keep the government from encroaching.

Unfortunately, an independent judiciary did not mean an honest judiciary. Corruption was, and continues to be, a significant problem that many outside reformers might otherwise have tried to address through top-down reform. While no reform has been very successful, the NGOs have had an impact. As one of the NGO leaders explained, they "decided we needed to have some friends in the judiciary if we were going to make a hole for reform there" and played a crucial role in selecting the Judicial Commission appointed to reduce judicial corruption from the inside.[40] To influence parliament's selection of judges, they published a book with each judge's track record, then lobbied members of parliament to select the better judges. Frustrated by the poor quality of candidates applying, they personally located reformists and promised them civil society backing and positive publicity if they applied for a seat on the commission. Through this intervention, the NGOs placed a few people known to them to be reformists on the crucial commission in charge of censoring judges.[41]

A window of opportunity opened when Bagir Manan, a distinguished legal scholar with deep ties to the legal reformers, was appointed Chief Justice of the Supreme Court.[42] With Manan in power and another friend, Abdul Rahmen Saleh, appointed to the Supreme Court, the NGOs had traction—as well as a chance to work with the highest levels of the court to root out the corruption in the judiciary. With Manan, the NGOs devised a series of blueprints for Supreme Court reform based on their earlier book analyzing judicial needs. Manan and his reformers were isolated at the top (he once told an outside reformer that he didn't even trust his secretary, and he asked foreign donors to send their money to the NGOs rather than to the court so that his corrupt staff wouldn't steal the money). Meanwhile, the NGOs worked to get buy-in across the initially reluctant court.[43]

Indonesia still has a long way to go on rule-of-law reform, and not all of these reforms have borne fruit. Nevertheless, as the Asia Foundation's Executive Director remarked in congressional testimony, "Indonesia is a country where the U.S. has gotten it right. In other words, through assistance to build democracy starting in the 1980s, a full decade before Suharto fell, the United States invested in organizations . . . and individuals who have since become the leaders of today's democratic Indonesia."[44] Five decades in country meant that the Asia Foundation was seen as more local and less colonial.[45] With Indonesians as program managers, they could spot opportunities and not fall into the trap of equating an NGO director's ability to speak English with competence. By buffering local NGOs from the whims of Washington, they could nurture NGOs undertaking the long, slow, work of rule-of-law reform.[46] And because the Asia Foundation was an independent NGO, it did not shy away from funding political work necessary to change power structures. Through bottom-up reform, the United States helped to create a group of Indonesians with the ability to push their own system toward reform in a way that blunted any overtones of neocolonialism and has a better chance than most methods of being successful.

The United States need not sponsor NGOs to engage in bottom-up reform. It can also provide data, surveys, and other fodder that can be seized upon by local citizens to mobilize for change. Alternatively, it can train people to serve as other paths of vertical accountability that press for institutional reform. Transparency International's corruption surveys, for instance, play a useful role in ranking countries based on perceptions of corruption and are used by NGOs internationally to press local governments. In Bangladesh, this survey was able to galvanize public outrage and harness the media against corrupt clerks and judges.[47] Such a program of data provision may not be enough to force change on its own—but in tandem with other methods of reform, it could yield results. USAID, for instance, used a top-down method to place contractors with the Albanian government to create an asset declaration process for politicians and to create a government anticorruption agency. Meanwhile, other USAID programs trained Albanian journalists in muckraking and spotting corruption. These programs have not been able to eliminate corruption in Albania, but they are at least pointing institutional reform in the right direction by focusing on the role of culture and power in punishing corruption, rather than simply modeling these institutions after their Western counterparts.

Reforming Institutions through Diplomacy: The most common form of diplomacy used to press for institutional reform is conditionality on aid. For instance, the IMF and World Bank often make aid conditional on a country's creating new institutions such as an ombudsman or an independent commercial court. In fact, the entire literature on aid conditionality is concerned with this single reform tactic. That literature tends to conclude that diplomacy cannot on its own bring about desired institutional reforms. As David Dollar states after presenting his ten case studies on aid and conditionality in Africa: "Reform really requires country ownership . . . conditionality cannot substitute for commitment. And when I say commitment, we mean really both the commitment of the government, the political leadership . . . [and] a much deeper commitment from the larger society."[48] Diplomacy that pressures government leaders cannot muster ownership from either the government or the populace. Therefore, it can be useful in a supporting role, to show that outside governments care about institutional reform, but it is rarely suited to achieving reform on its own.

Diplomacy is arguably too blunt an instrument to be used for the technical field of institutional reform. Diplomatic pressure is generally deployed only in the case of egregious institutional failures. For instance, Canada exerted strong diplomacy when Indonesian courts misused bankruptcy laws to declare a major, solvent Canadian insurance company bankrupt.[49] But such diplomacy can backfire, as mentioned in the last chapter, if the only solution is for the executive to interfere with judicial rulings.

Reforming Institutions through Enmeshment: The EU has had real success reforming institutions through enmeshment. NATO can help reform military institutions, as the Albania example in the last chapter illustrated, and the WTO process may reform financial institutions. But the United States has no comparable vehicle, no strong enmeshment process, that can focus on legal institutions.

Meanwhile, the weak forms of enmeshment now in use by the United States can do little other than change the hearts of institutional leaders. But even if those hearts really do change, it is rarely enough to affect institutions, as the case of the young Romanian leaders in the last chapter illustrates. Changing the hearts of a few is rarely going to be enough for these leaders to change their entire structures. Witness the Indonesian chief justice of the Supreme Court, Bagir Manan, who did not trust even his secretary or feel sufficiently powerful to change the court that he was ostensibly running. It takes a cohort of individuals, empowered together and imbued with a desire and the tools to work together to create change in most complex institutions. This is possible through well-designed exchange programs, but the scattershot way the United States chooses individuals for its exchange programs negates this possibility.

While bottom-up reform is the most effective method of reforming institutions of these four, even that method has limited success. The Indonesian case study is a best-case scenario—and yet the reformers could do little to really change the corruption endemic throughout the judiciary. The reality is that institutions are not the best object of change on which to focus a program of reform, because their problems are generally problems of power and culture. Institutional reform can play a crucial role in targeting the power structure or cultural changes—and ultimately, these are the objects that second-generation reformers must focus on for successful programs. We turn to these next.

Altering the Power Structure of Other Countries: Four Tactics

Altering the Power Structure through Top-Down Reform: In a top-down strategy to change power structures, development aid is often directed at building the reputation, independence, and ability of alternative power centers, so they may rein in the government to follow the law. Building alternative power centers may look awfully similar to top-down reform geared at institutional change—the United States, for instance, may help to create bar associations or judicial schools. But the goal is not to create technocratic fixes that make institutions in another country look like those in America: It is to create institutions that are empowered to affect the power dynamics within the country. Development projects to increase judicial independence, create or assist constitutional courts, and build independent anticorruption agencies or ombudsmen are all means of using top-down reform to place checks on other centers of power.

Because these reforms can look like institution modeling, it's important for reformers to constantly keep in mind that simply building modern institutions of justice does not lead to government accountability. Creating an electronic case-management system in a country that has electricity for only a few hours each day or giving computers to court leaders who have never used such a machine does nothing to empower the courts as an alternative power structure. Similarly, supporting the independence of extremely corrupt judiciaries is not going to create a useful force for horizontal accountability. Top-down reform will generally not be an effective method unless tactics are clearly formulated and directed toward changing the power structure.

At the same time, well-executed top-down reform focused on the power structure can have a significant effect. In the early 1990s, as Romania drifted under its largely unreformed postcommunist government, the program managers in USAID's Democracy and Growth section decided to focus their efforts on changing the power structure. They explicitly realized that Romania's leaders were uninterested in reform and so decided to focus most of their programming on bottom-up interventions. The top-down reforms they chose to undertake worked not through the government, but instead through institutions that were separate from government agencies and explicitly geared at enhancing independent spheres of power. In addition to creating a bar association—a standard reform across Eastern Europe—USAID funded the American Bar Association's Central European and Eurasian Law Initiative, ABA-CEELI, to create a "magistrates' association" to form a union of judges with the stated goal of building trust, self-awareness, and eventually independence. USAID also supported the drafting of laws for stronger judicial institutions and assisted in building the National Institute of Magistracy—the new magistrates' school that, in addition to teaching new judges, was intended to create a sense of pride and separation from the executive among judges and prosecutors. USAID felt that while the government was not interested in reform, it could organize the judiciary to deepen its clout and voice and, at some point, begin to fight for judicial independence.[50] The intentionality behind these reforms imbued these programs with a different focus than standard institutional modeling.

In 1996, when the new coalition government of civil society reformers came into office, a euphoric Democracy and Governance section undertook a five-month, top-to-bottom reassessment of its strategy. With reformers in power, it was felt that there was a "quantum increase in the political will to implement key reforms" and a new opportunity to "work at the top or through mechanisms which almost immediately lead to widespread replication." USAID decided to shift from top-down methods that could affect the power structure through horizontal accountability to a top-down strategy of institutional change. The new program would emphasize "laws, policies, and regulation along with the increased capacity to implement these."[51] USAID would be sorely disappointed by its switch to this more traditional tactic. While many such institutional reforms did pass under the reformist coalition, the coalition itself was short-lived. The new laws and institutions, unsupported by a strong foundation in structures of power that provided checks and balances, were overturned by the postcommunist government that followed. The limits of top-down technocratic institutional and legal reform were clear. Eventually, years later, the reforms of the power structure that USAID had begun would bear fruit as an empowered judiciary began to exercise real independence.

Altering the Power Structure through Bottom-Up Reform: From the "people power" of the Philippines, to the recent democratic movements across the Middle East, it is obvious that citizens of even the most authoritarian countries have a vast ability to achieve changes in the structures of power. But bottom-up reform doesn't require a once-in-a-generation mass mobilization of a fed-up citizenry. Building vertical accountability—constituencies at the citizen level that pressure the government to abide by the rule of law—can create change on a more day-to-day level.[52]

Scholars around the world have documented the power of bottom-up pressure on power structures to support rule-of-law reforms. In Jennifer Widner's comparative study of the creation of African constitutional courts, she found that international support for bottom-up pressure was crucial. By helping local civil society groups advocate for human rights and assisting businesses that desired clear commercial law enforcement, outside groups played a useful role in enshrining these changes to the power structure.[53] The scholar Stephen Golub has described the importance of citizen-led change to power structures in improving the rule of law in Asia, while a prescient David Mednicoff wrote in 2005 that a series of bottom-up efforts, from media reform to funding human rights advocacy groups, would be the best way to "chip away at state authoritarianism" in the Arab world.[54]

Romania provides an excellent case study of how bottom-up methods focused on the power structure can yield serious results. In 1995, USAID contracted with World Learning to create the Democracy Network, a program that would provide sub-grants to local NGOs to build their advocacy skills while enhancing the sector as a whole by altering the laws that impeded NGO development. The NGOs were to focus on a few issue areas, including the rule of law.[55] As mentioned earlier, USAID was not just rolling out the standard reform package. It decided that "retail activities with the private sector and NGOs made sense when the national government was less receptive to change." Instead of beating their heads against a wall working with a recalcitrant government, USAID program directors would deal "directly with a wide array of partners, mostly in the private and NGO sectors."[56] "Because there was less political will on the part of the former government to undertake fundamental structural reform," they consciously turned to a bottom-up strategy focused on building a strong NGO sector that could create vertical accountability. Practitioners at USAID had a clear conception of the role of NGOs in promoting the rule of law. They were building capacity to turn NGOs into a force that could change the power structure and culture, forming a domestic constituency for reform over the long term.

Westerners working with Romanian NGOs introduced the concept of advocacy, a word previously absent from the Romanian language.[57] USAID funding, funneled through contractors on the ground, enabled local NGOs to form themselves into national coalitions to advocate for changes mentioned earlier in this chapter that would help the sector as a whole. Finally, they lobbied for a Bureau of Public Information and Relations with Civil Society and for press coverage of parliamentary committee hearings so that NGOs would have access to needed information.

At first, this strategy looked like a losing bet. By the end of the 1990s, popular anger at the ineffective coalition government, which was composed of many civil society leaders, spilled into disdain for civil society itself. Romanians viewed the NGO sector with suspicion, seeing it as full of self-serving, overpaid entrepreneurs who created organizations solely to benefit themselves, rather than public-minded individuals working to help society.[58] Other donors had reduced or discontinued support to civil society, leaving USAID the lead donor financing this strategy.[59] A 2001 independent assessment of Romania's NGOs denounced the venality endemic to the sector (though singling out USAID-supported Pro Democracy as an exception). It also called the entire tactic into question, describing the political system as so closed to outside influence that advocacy NGOs could not change the government. The report largely recommended ending bottom-up tactics.

USAID's strategic plan, written at this time, repeats that "most NGO initiatives . . . proved ineffective."[60] However, it was not willing to give up on the tactic. While outside funding had created many dubious, ineffective organizations, it had also fertilized a few highly effective initiatives. Most importantly, it had created the civil society coalition that pushed for the Freedom of Information and sunshine laws that would play a critical role in reform.

In 2004, the Coalition for a Clean Parliament brought together civil society groups (most of which had become used to working together, thanks to the Coalition for Transparency) to establish a set of open, commonsense criteria for what constituted a "clean" member of parliament. They persuaded each of the three major parties to accept the criteria. The coalition then used the Freedom of Information law that the Coalition for Transparency had helped to pass to gather information on candidates. It determined who met the criteria, then sent these lists to the parties, allowing them to contest individual cases or withdraw the candidate from running. The parties decided to withdraw about a quarter of their original candidates. The coalition then released flyers nationwide with the final lists of corrupt candidates still running. These "blacklists" contained more candidates from the ruling party than any opposition party. The process was sophisticated, transparent, and reflected years of foreign support and technical assistance.

The coalition's power was clear from the government's reaction. The ruling party denounced the blacklist, encouraged candidates to sue coalition members, and accused coalition members of "conspiracy," calling them a "bunch of criminals." The party asked judges to stop the distribution of flyers, but partially as a result of the canny top-down funding and diplomacy to alter the power structure, the judges, with their newly granted legal independence, refused. After years of "telephone justice"—making decisions on cases based on telephoned directives from the executive—the judges felt strong and independent enough to fight for a cleaner system.

The government then met in secret sessions to create a countermovement, with party activists setting up parallel "civil society" organizations to dispute the flyers' claims. They even drew up fake lists, with opposition parliamentarian names blacklisted instead of their own, and distributed them to confuse the electorate. On the eve of elections, the Romanian press received leaked transcripts of government ministers describing their illegal activities and attempts to skew court cases and abet corruption. After civil society denounced attempts to stuff the ballot boxes, the government was forced into a runoff, which it lost.[61]

Many Romanians saw this 2005 election as their "Orange Revolution." It arguably would not have occurred without outside assistance targeted explicitly at changing the power structure through bottom-up reform. Yet it bore few marks of neocolonialism. Pressure on the government that would be illegitimate for another country to engage in, is a positive step for democracy when outsiders can help citizens take the reins and find their own voice, enabling them to emerge as a power center in their own countries. These findings are repeated worldwide, making it clear that bottom-up reform is a crucial method for changing a country's power structure. No other method can build the vertical accountability that is necessary for citizens to take ownership and hold their governments to account.

Altering the Power Structure through Diplomacy: Diplomacy is such a common method for the U.S. government to use to affect other countries' power structures that it is often forgotten. When Mubarak wavered in his decision to step down and give in to citizen demands for an accountable government that followed the rule of law, the Pentagon engaged in deep talks with Egyptian generals, while President Obama and Secretary of State Clinton spoke frequently about precisely where the United States stood on the issue on that particular day. Diplomacy eschews the idea that "political will" or "changes of heart" need to be internal and deeply felt. Instead, it uses carrots and sticks to affect the incentive structure of government leaders so that they see it as in their best interests to uphold the rule of law if they wish to keep U.S. trade, enter a coveted organization, or bestow the aid on their people that keeps them in power.[62]

Diplomacy can be very important to altering power structures. Many political prisoners undoubtedly owe their lives to U.S. diplomats asking after their well-being. Diplomacy can also curb government abuses by shining international light on an area a government would rather cover up. Diplomats can provide important stature or even security to an opposition movement by meeting with leaders or mentioning them in speeches. However, it is easy to overstate the role of diplomacy. Governments, even authoritarian governments, ultimately care more about domestic politics than international pressure. Indonesia's Prime Minister Megawati ignored steady U.S. pressure to act against Islamist extremists because she owed her power base in part to Islamist forces. Russia has ignored U.S. attempts to support civil society there. Nor is it only major powers that can ignore diplomacy—tiny Albania has withstood years of diplomatic pressure without making any significant changes to the cozy connections its government leaders enjoy with organized criminals. Diplomacy has an important role to play in supporting rule-of-law reforms, and it can certainly help political prisoners and clarify choices and consequences for government leaders. But it is rarely going to be enough in itself to force leaders to alter power structures. Only domestic pressure can do that—which is why top-down and bottom-up reforms to building horizontal and vertical accountability are so necessary

Altering the Power Structure through Enmeshment: Strong enmeshment clearly has the power to alter power structures—NATO membership, for instance, demands that civilians lead the military, and the WTO requires that commercial decisions be made by independent adjudicating bodies. Moreover, the fact that membership in international organizations is not a one-off case of diplomacy but enmeshes the country in an ongoing structure makes backsliding less likely.

It is unclear, though, whether the weaker form of enmeshment through exchanges and socialization can have a similar effect on the power structure. Liberal institutionalists believe that enmeshment has a unique capacity to change powerful actors' hearts, minds, and actions. By enmeshing leaders in international professional communities with "rule-of-law norms," they create a form of social pressure from peers that they believe will cause government leaders to alter their actions, and gradually their values, for peer approval. Through such alterations leaders will change their own power structures. That is asking a lot from loose peer networks.

This theory of change is interesting and worth exploring through more empirical study. Certainly, military leaders and police officers who have engaged in joint programs with international counterparts claim that they feel such a transnational community.[63] Yet one of the differences between the military programs and exchanges for parliamentarians is that the former are iterated: The same people meet over and over again, allowing for real relationships to be built with the potential for altering norms. However, it's hard to imagine that most short exchange programs can build a strong enough international culture to affect major changes to a country's power structure.

Building Cultures of Lawfulness: Four Tactics

It is almost unthinkable that modern American politicians, diplomats, or development professionals would suggest that they are trying to change the social norms of another country. Yet where corruption is expected behavior for a judge, or politicians believe they are above the law, cultural norms clearly must change for the rule of law to take hold. Thus, it is imperative to look at the available means for legitimately affecting cultural factors.

Using Top-Down Reform to Affect Culture: The top-down method can be an effective way to alter the professional cultures of legal and political institutions. The United States (as well as the EU and other donors) supported the magistrates' school in Romania in large part to encourage a more independent judiciary in which judges saw themselves as professionals, with professional ethics. The U.S. Department of State has supported "Culture of Lawfulness" programs in multiple countries to create democratic rule-of-law cultures among police. Working with police academies in countries such as Colombia, the contractor helps to develop a curriculum that becomes part of every new cadet's training. It introduces the concept of a culture of lawfulness in which both the police and the citizens play mutually supporting roles in building a rule-of-law society, and it reinforces the concepts through field activities.[64] The American Bar Association frequently works to create bar associations and professional codes of ethics for the legal profession of other countries.

In Indonesia, ICITAP fundamentally altered its normal police training program to try to change the culture of the Indonesian police. Law enforcement in Indonesia had long been the purview of a police force that was connected to the military. The brutality the police inflicted on citizens reflected cruelty within the force—officers would beat underlings physically and demand bribes from them, creating a circle of viciousness that the lower-level police would then inflict on the population. In 1999, when Indonesia's military faced international condemnation for its use of force against East Timor, the new president, Abdurrahman Wahid, a prominent human rights campaigner, seized on the armed forces' momentary weakness and stripped the military of its internal policing function.[65] By May of 2000, ICITAP was on the ground working to train the new force in democratic policing.

ICITAP generally runs technocratic, standardized trainings of less than three weeks that provide skills but don't address cultural issues or underlying causes for police incapacity.[66] These trainings fit the tight guidelines imposed by Congress, but in the eyes of the Indonesians working for ICITAP, they had very little impact.[67] In Indonesia, ICITAP offered a number of these prepackaged programs. The ambassador would ask for a human rights training, and ICITAP program officers would, as they described the process, trot out their three-week course. They also, however, began blazing an entirely new trail. ICITAP hired highly able and creative Indonesians and launched a unique program of "institutional transformation" geared to strategically consider "the driving forces of the reform process" to "change the whole structure of behavior, methods, and ethics of the police."[68] There were no guidelines or terms of reference, "the only present thing was the goal—to help the police improve themselves."[69] That improvement was about more than security: They aimed to build a professional, ethical, non-corrupt, and competent police force. And the object of change was explicitly cultural, not institutional, reform. As one ICITAP trainer explained: "It's all about cultural change. . . . It's not about how many students you put through the course, it's about changing the culture of the police."[70] The police academy rearranged its entire curriculum to fit ICITAP's five-month field officer training program and revamped its officer career path to make training at the academy respected, rather than a career dead end. ICITAP launched a program to help the Indonesian police collect and analyze crime statistics, then allocate funding and personnel based on these objectives. These statistical reforms made a real difference in American policing, but they are not intended to be technocratic. ICITAP hopes that the success of the new methods will move Indonesian police away from using beatings to extract confessions. ICITAP also realizes that changing a professional culture is highly political—it consciously works to elevate reformers and provide a platform to those on the force who are on board—whether these internal change agents actually believe in reform or just see which way the wind is blowing. It is too early to judge the effectiveness of this new approach, but it seems to be moving in a promising direction.

While hard to imagine how top-down reform alone could change an entire popular culture, it is clearly the most direct method for altering culture within any institution—which, once changed, can have an impact on mass culture. For instance, in Indonesia, many police really want the public involved in their reform efforts. As Santiago, an ICITAP program designer, explained:

> The police know that they have to win in the public sphere, because it is the only way that they can stand up to the military and stay independent. They need to make it so that the public can't argue that they can't do their work. So they care a lot about public opinion, they really want to show all their problems and ask how others—outsiders and in Indonesian society—can help them.[71]

That is the kind of institutional cultural change that could percolate over into mass culture.

Affecting Culture through Bottom-Up Reform: Bottom-up reform that supports civil society is perhaps the most obvious and legitimate means for outsiders to affect the mass, popular culture of another country without being seen as meddling in other people's affairs. In Indonesia, USAID began funding local human rights NGOs to strengthen the voice of local activists fighting the Suharto regime's attempt to frame human rights as a Western import. Other bottom-up efforts work with schoolchildren and textbooks to try to build a rule-of-law culture from the ground up. In post–World War II Japan, the United States rewrote textbooks to include an emphasis on the rule of law, human rights, and the role of the citizen in a democracy. They tried to do the same in Iraq half a century later.[72] The Culture of Lawfulness Project mentioned earlier also creates a rule-of-law curriculum for school districts, which is intended to build the sense among schoolchildren that they have a role in ensuring a rule-of-law culture. USAID funded civic education in Romania by sponsoring television programs aimed at increasing democratic and rule-of-law sentiment.[73]

In Indonesia, the world's biggest Muslim country, one of the most likely routes for cultural change is through religion. And Indonesia happens to have two very powerful Muslim organizations—known as NU and Muhammadiyah—that are the largest and most salient grassroots organizations across the archipelago.[74] The organizations have old and bitter rivalries, and nearly all Indonesians are associated with one or the other. The Partnership for Governance Reform was able to bring the two organizations together in a religiously focused, grassroots anticorruption campaign that enlisted the power of religion to change ambivalent cultural norms, in which people decried corruption in public while welcoming personal opportunities for self-enrichment.[75] Unlike the vast majority of rule-of-law activities worldwide, which focus on elites, this effort had deep reach into the grassroots. The Partnership made the leaders of these organizations change their internal systems before they began their campaigns, so that they could claim to be practicing what they preached. NU has agreed to reform its internal governance and to work against corruption in two of its religious education schools, while Muhammadiyah is undertaking governance reform in two of its hospitals and universities in Yogyakarta.[76]

Bottom-up efforts to affect mass culture can clearly have an impact. They are also likely to be more effective than direct U.S. efforts to reach the masses in other countries. Efforts such as the early days of the U.S.-backed Alhurra television station in Iraq appear heavy-handed and propagandistic in the twenty-first century and lack the local knowledge that civil society can bring to bear. The bottom-up method can also work to affect the professional culture of rule-of-law institutions—whether through shaming surveys on perceptions of corruption that are released to the public, or through supporting local civic groups to, say, engage in advocacy against police brutality. Bottom-up methods also have the potential for sustainability—a quality that is particularly necessary for long-term cultural shifts.

Affecting Culture through Diplomacy: The blunt arm of diplomacy, focused on pushing government decisionmakers, is not a method suited to altering social norms. It may, however, be used to open up the space for culture to amend itself—in an authoritarian country, for instance, diplomatic interventions may be essential to force the government to allow some freedom of speech or association necessary for new cultural ideas to take root. Diplomatic intervention can also be helpful to free human rights activists or provide some security for other civic actors advocating ideas that support the rule of law. But diplomacy works by creating incentives that force a government to act differently. Many years ago, such a method could have been used to force cultures to change through government decree: Ataturk, the father of modern Turkey, outlawed beards and forced his people to adopt Western dress; Franco forced Spain to maintain a traditional culture as the rest of Europe modernized. It is conceivable that outside diplomacy could effect similar change—but it would be considered colonialist and unacceptable in today's world.

It's equally important to note that strong diplomacy geared toward other goals can actually create cultural backlash. The Albanian women's rights activist who did not appreciate the EU's strong-arm tactics for passing women's rights laws is not alone. For years, Suharto used the fact that Western countries wanted Indonesia to improve its human rights record to argue that the concept of human rights was a Western import and that it was patriotic to eschew such norms. After the massacres during East Timor's vote for independence, the international community demanded that Indonesia punish the generals responsible. Prickling at the assault on its sovereignty represented by an internationalized tribunal, Indonesia insisted on conducting the trials itself. Eighteen individuals were eventually charged in the ad hoc Human Rights Court that Indonesia created; of those, three were convicted, and the sentences of all but one were overturned on appeal.[77] The court's decisions were condemned internationally, but they were popular in Indonesia. Many felt that the United States had been repeatedly hypocritical about human rights. As for the EU, one government minister mentioned to me a general feeling that the EU's human rights issues were simply a power play, since it had no such major human rights qualms when negotiating with China over trade agreements.[78] Even a human rights activist told me that the international pressure had actually reduced his sympathy for the East Timorese cause. Diplomacy is not only too heavy-handed to affect culture, but unless carefully applied, it can backfire in ways that solidify negative cultural tropes even when focused on other objects of change.

Affecting Culture through Enmeshment: Enmeshment, meanwhile, is a tool that is intended to work through culture. By socializing local leaders into a new peer group or institutional environment, enmeshment is designed to affect social norms. Most of this socialization takes place at the elite level, though some efforts, such as U.S. programs that admit college students to study in the United States, affect a slightly broader slice of the population. Exchange programs are the most common way in which the United States uses enmeshment to promote cultural change. During its decades of existence, the U.S. Information Agency organized visits for foreign judges and lawyers, placed "professionals in residence" for up to six months to help establish judicial systems, trained Eastern European journalists, sponsored American rule-of-law experts to give speaking tours throughout other countries, and provided educational and civic organizations in Eastern Europe with books on the theory and practice of democracy.[79]

There is clear anecdotal evidence that individual beliefs can be affected through enmeshment. For instance, in Albania, the local program director in charge of the EU's prison reform program talked openly about how much he liked taking part in the social norms of a European organization that worked hard, kept serious working hours, and focused on clear goals. He was proud not to be "sitting around drinking tea every day" as he summed up the life of various other public servants.[80] In Indonesia, the Dean of the University of Indonesia Law School described a State Department exchange trip that put him in touch with other law faculty, legal institutions, and the Supreme Court in the United States.

> It was very valuable . . . I got new ideas. For instance, I saw the offices the professors had in America—here, we are all together, we just have desks all together in one room. And I thought—we say we are a world-class university, but how can my professors do research when they must all share one room? So I learned about fundraising, too, from these university leaders in the States, who said they spent 70 percent of their time fundraising, and now I am determined to build a new building for offices.[81]

Such cultural change can have real ripple effects—making professors, for instance, feel like members of a respected profession. While enmeshment may be less useful for changing power dynamics, by putting new ideas in the heads of elites that ripple throughout their professions, it has the possibility of creating much deeper cultural reform over time.

Strategy: Deploying Tactics Together

When tactics are coordinated to work together, they create a strategy. This can be done unintentionally but with good effects, as the case studies of Romania throughout this chapter have shown. But second-generation rule-of-law professionals will have the greatest impact when they think not about which single tactic will work well, but about how to put together a series of tactics to create an effective strategy.

Indonesia's independent but corrupt judiciary, for instance, undermines its rule of law. Decisions are not regularized but are subject to the whims of individual judges, who too frequently provide "justice" to the highest bidder. The problem affects more than just Indonesians: Well-financed Canadian and British insurance firms have been declared insolvent thanks to unscrupulous judges willing to misinterpret bankruptcy laws. What could an outside country do to improve the situation?

First, it would rule out using diplomacy, since that would force the executive to assert control over an independent judiciary. Instead, it could create a strategy focused on changing the power structure and culture of the judiciary with an array of reinforcing tactics. Clearly, establishing a professional culture of honesty would be crucial. The strategy could begin with institutional reform directed at cultural change by establishing a single pathway into the judiciary—an elite school that is difficult to enter, tough in its training, and clear in its ethics, which raises the prestige of young people entering the profession. The school curriculum could socialize students into the responsibility that an honest, independent judiciary plays as a cornerstone of a democratic state. An enmeshment program focused on cultural change could help these new young judges gain allies in their profession. For instance, powerful sitting judges could be enmeshed in judicial training programs in the United States, where they would see the respect accorded to the judiciary, the honesty expected of judges, and the methods of legal reasoning used. Some hearts and minds might be opened. These trips could also be used to augment power structure reform, if they were offered only to sitting judges who were reformers or who did not oppose reform. By giving those on the reform bandwagon—or at least those not opposing reform—an all-expense-paid trip to the United States with their spouses, enmeshment could provide an incentive to reduce opposition.

Meanwhile, other tactics could augment changes to the power structure. A bottom-up reform could support a local NGO to build a judicial association for new judges—providing an alumni network and voice to the younger judges acculturated into a new system and giving them some collective power vis-à-vis the established, corrupt judiciary. As these judges gained power, a combined top-down and bottom-up reform focused on the power structure could create randomized case assignment and take promotion power away from older, more corrupt chief judges, reducing their control over the careers of the new generation of entering judges, giving the latter the ability to be honest, if they so choose. While there is no telling whether such reforms would work, the positive feedback created when one reform builds on another has the best possibility of success.

That said, strategy is not everything. Implementation matters just as much. A 1999 national survey funded jointly by USAID and the Soros Foundation found that more than 50 percent of private firms and nearly half of all citizens in Albania admitted to bribing public officials; more than half of all customs inspectors claimed to have purchased their positions; and the justice sector was viewed as the most corrupt sector of the country.[82] The United States then began using multiple methods to try to alter the country's power structure and culture. The U.S. Embassy started a bottom-up effort targeted at cultural change by funding anticorruption folk songs in rural villages (though these were derided by urban elites in Tirana) and supported bottom-up efforts to build nationwide civil society coalitions to raise awareness about corruption. A top-down effort at cultural reform paid contractors to augment the capacity and prestige of the inspectorate within the judiciary in order to reduce judicial corruption. A top-down tactic targeted at the power structure yielded a landmark law forcing public officials to declare their assets, and created and equipped an agency in charge of this declaration program to build horizontal accountability. Another top-down reform targeted at the power structure advised prosecutors on how to conduct anticorruption investigations and assisted with legislation.

In this case, strategy was savvy but implementation foundered. Because USAID and the State Department are so reliant on contractors, many simply repackaged their existing programs to fit the new "flavor-of-the-month" as they saw it—anticorruption reform. Rather than gaining the benefits of a savvy new strategy, this push ended up as policy disconnected from implementation. It is a worthy lesson that both strategy and implementation are crucial to success.[83]

While deploying tactics together can augment effectiveness, lack of strategy can also diminish impact. The United States is particularly vulnerable to contradictory programs and mixed messages because so many different government agencies tend to interact with any given country. More often than not, their efforts are uncoordinated and frequently undermine one another. A USAID contractor implementing an anticorruption program can hardly stop the Department of Defense from throwing money into a local economy and fueling graft and probably lacks the clout to persuade a State Department diplomat not to give undue honor to a particularly corrupt local politician by inviting him to an office visit. Yet while such tactical pitfalls may be unintentional, they are felt as a strategic whole by the country undergoing reform. Such signals are scanned for the seriousness with which the United States views its entire rule-of-law building project.

Unintentional contradictions in the signals the United States is sending can breed cynicism and call into question U.S. motives. In Albania, for instance, the largest local NGO and pressure group in the country, Mjaft! ("Enough!" in Albanian), did not want to engage in American anticorruption programs, even though it had a significant, mobilized base of the population organized against corruption. The organization's CEO distrusted the United States because of its efforts to pass antiterrorism laws in Albania while experiencing its own internal rule-of-law failings at Guantánamo and Abu Ghraib. This cynicism was compounded by activities outside U.S. government control: Tom Ridge, who had recently retired from leading the U.S. Department of Homeland Security and become a private citizen, repeatedly visited Albania to lobby the government to award contracts to various companies for which he was working. While the U.S. government had no control over Ridge, and many in the U.S. State Department had equal objections to heavy-handed antiterrorism laws, the most influential force in Albanian civil society pieced together a picture of U.S. motives based on the totality of their interactions, and that picture did not portray America's primary concern as promoting the rule of law in Albania.

How can programs be drafted that have the greatest strategic chance of success, are well-implemented, and avoid these unintended consequences? It's not easy. The next chapter provides a road map to begin the process.

CHAPTER SEVEN

CRAFTING A SECOND-GENERATION REFORM STRATEGY

The law embodies the story of a nation's development through many centuries, and it cannot be dealt with as if it contained only the axioms and corollaries of a book of mathematics.

– Oliver Wendell Holmes Jr., The Common Law

When Angola ended its civil war in 2002 after over twenty-five years of fighting, more than half a million people had been killed. Millions of refugees had abandoned their villages and fled to the cities, trying to save their children from kidnapping and conscription into the rebel armies, or gang rape and life as a rebel "wife." Rival militias cut off the noses and ears of public servants, looters ransacked and destroyed public buildings, and civic institutions from the courts to churches lay in ruins. In the aftermath of this devastation, USAID sponsored a program run by the U.S. Department of Commerce but clearly designed by people living on another planet. The effort would "provide technical assistance to the justice sector under a commercial law development program focusing on judicial case management, commercial code reform, and technical assistance to improve Angola's investment climate."[1] To be fair, other parts of the U.S. government were engaged in more relevant work: USAID's Democracy and Governance section began a child-soldier reintegration and civil society rebuilding program, while a separate contractor ran a program to spot conflict at the local level and attempt to address it before it got out of hand. I am sure that at some point in its development, judicial case management would be relevant to the business sector. But the notion that investment in Angola was lagging primarily because of poor judicial case management, rather than the haunting images of government officials without ears, an illiterate workforce that had known only war, and a quarter-century of economic disruption, is ludicrous—and precisely the kind of cookie-cutter program that second-generation rule-of-law reform seeks to end.[2]

Second-generation rule-of-law reform starts with the actual problems of a country and then looks at which parts of the rule of law must be improved in order to address those problems. Reformers consider a society's sociology to determine reform efforts that locals would support and to locate the best fulcrum for reform. Before settling on their programming, reformers choose metrics to measure success. This ensures that they are measuring a decline in the problem, not simply the outputs of their chosen solution. Only then do reformers begin formulating their strategy, focusing on power and culture as the primary objects of reform and seeking multiple methods to alter these characteristics, based on the social realities of the actual country. This method is such a departure from current practice that, before describing it in depth, we should quickly survey the status quo of first-generation reform. An overview of how today's programs work in practice is the best way to understand the flaws in what is being done now and demonstrate how different a second-generation approach could be.

The Status Quo

Today, a rule-of-law program might begin when a program officer or diplomat decides that the rule of law is a problem in country X.

The reason that the "rule of law" has become an area of concern could vary—perhaps there is a great deal of crime, or setting up a new business is deemed to take too long, or the democratic system is thought to be weak. At that point, a consultant is often flown into the country for two weeks to make a quick assessment of the country's court system and legal community. Immediately, the problem has switched from thinking about how to solve the original need (crime, or a poor business environment), to determining how to achieve legal institutional reform.

Depending on the problem, INL, USAID, or another agency might then be tasked with writing "terms of reference" describing the parameters of a program for contractors to bid on. The program officer—who may never have spent more than a few weeks in the country in question and may never have set foot outside its capital city—will read the consultant's report and then choose reform components from the standard menu of options that has been employed elsewhere. The Economic Growth section of USAID might choose to undertake some commercial law reform and train judges in intellectual property laws. If court efficiency is deemed a problem, computerization or case management may become part of the program. The World Bank might suggest an alternative dispute resolution process or an access-to-justice effort to aid those who are too poor or too intimidated to use the regular court system. If corruption is an issue, the local embassy might fund some exchange programs for jurists. The terms of reference might include other common program elements, such as constructing and repairing courthouses, buying furniture and other equipment, drafting laws, training legal personnel, and starting bar associations.[3] In other words, the standard first-generation program will employ a set of top-down activities focused on affecting institutions and laws, with perhaps a soft enmeshment option for legal professionals, and a bottom-up cultural change program, again for legal professionals—with little clarity on what they are trying to do or why. At its worst, a flavor-of-the-month set of goals will be overlaid on these standard programs. One year the United States will focus on "women and gender issues"; another year alternative dispute resolution will be all the rage. NGOs and contractors will retrofit old programs with the new buzzwords and continue to do basically the same things.[4]

Operating under the assumption that the rule of law is primarily a legal and technical issue, rather than a relationship between the state and its society, these first-generation programs all define rule-of-law problems as residing within courts, cops, and codes of law—the bastion of legal professionals, not political scientists. Their initial fact-finding mission will look at rule-of-law institutions, not at a country's power structure or cultural attitudes toward dispute resolution. The program will generally be implemented by lawyers, not anthropologists or sociologists.

The programming process will require planning and budgeting years in advance. The preliminary planning visits raise expectations on the ground that reform is about to begin—expectations that are often dashed, leaving potential reformers soured, by the time funding starts flowing years later. The long time lag precludes taking advantage of windows of opportunity that might arise from a newly appointed reformer, the jubilation after an election, or the push for change after a scandal. The planning process, circumscribed by congressional legislation and agency standard operating procedures, reinforces a tendency to see the rule of law as a problem of laws and institutions, rather than a problem of power and culture.

To measure their success, first-generation reforms will look at direct outputs, regardless of whether these have much effect on the rule of law. A police training program, for instance, will count the number of police trained, not the amount of crime reduced or perceptions of human rights among the populace. Anticorruption courses tend to measure attendance in U.S.-sponsored seminars, not payments of bribes among the local or foreign business communities. The quantitative focus is an unfortunate side effect of congressional oversight and demands. But the targets measured often have nothing to do with the desired outcomes or impact. No tourists worried about safety look up the number of police academy graduates in a potential vacation spot—they look at the country's crime statistics. So should rule-of-law reformers.

More sophisticated practitioners have fought against these constraints, struggling to create second-generation reforms within the confines of this first-generation system. The World Bank's judicial reform program in Venezuela, for example, followed the usual first-generation goal of seeking a "good quality justice system" rather than stating what that justice system should do for society. The program design showed an understanding that reform would require work across all rule-of-law institutions, but after paying lip service to the broader idea, the project zeroed in on court reform. Within the constraints of a first-generation court reform program, however, project designers considered second-generation concerns such as the importance of locating supporters and constituencies for change and determining likely resistance, the need for civil society demand, and the need to act when windows of opportunity opened. Eventually, though supposedly focused on court reform, the Venezuelan project ventured far afield into bottom-up efforts to affect social norms, such as media campaigns sponsored by civil society leaders and widespread societal educational efforts to build support for the rule of law.[5] Such programs show how thoughtful program designers, struggling within the constraints of a poor system, are working toward second-generation reform.

Second-Generation Reform Process

Second-generation rule-of-law reform makes a bold claim: that improving the rule of law within other countries does not require a series of institutions to be built that mimic those in the United States. Instead, it requires getting right the political and cultural relationships between a state and society. Because second-generation reform acknowledges the centrality of the particular politics and social norms of a unique country, it cannot offer a set of pre-sequenced mix-and-match program options. Instead of checking off laundry lists of laws and institutions that must be reformed in a predetermined sequence, adjusting power systems and culture requires a more sociological process that uncovers who will be in opposition and who will offer support, uses this knowledge to map the best ways to leverage change, and then looks for windows of opportunity to catalyze reform. The same process can be applied to each country—ideally by trained political scientists or sociologists—but the timing and tactics to leverage change will differ in each place.[6] The political and cultural terrain within a given state must determine actual activities.

Variations on this method are increasingly being adopted by second-generation practitioners throughout the governance arena.[7] As mentioned in the first chapter, the World Bank's Problem-Driven Governance framework, the OECD and DFID's analysis of drivers of change, and Norway's consideration of political economy, among others, are all moving toward a similar set of tools for analysis. The schema below is a basic outline of this second-generation reform methodology.

Step I: Start with the Problem

Before leaping to a solution, it helps to determine the actual problem. Often, the obstacle won't be obvious. It must be determined in the field in consultation with the constituencies the United States is trying to aid. This process has a second, crucial side benefit. Because outside reformers depend on local citizens to create lasting change, choosing a problem that is *seen* as a problem by locals helps gain supporters for reform.[8] Reforms that are chosen solely based on the notions of outside reformers, no matter how justifiable they may appear, are solutions looking for a problem, and they are unlikely to find local champions. Too often, first-generation reformers visit the community they claim to be helping and discover that they need to "create" demand. Reformers are left trying to convince the legal community that they need new bankruptcy laws, a judicial career system, or some other improvement.[9] Starting with a jointly determined end in a stakeholder-focused problem identification process ameliorates this problem. By choosing to solve a problem that is seen as problematic by the local community, reformers will find that they are already a step ahead in gaining a constituency for reform.

Thus, second-generation reform starts by looking at the problem and determining which rule-of-law ends society needs help with—rather than beginning with a mishmash of institutions to be "improved." Ends-based definitions force reformers to begin with the problem they are trying to solve and consider what it will actually take to address that problem, rather than jumping into institutional or legal solutions.

When a societal problem—or "end," in the language of ends-based reform, is considered at the beginning of program design, it quickly becomes apparent that it will require work across rule-of-law institutions—from police and courts to law enforcement. The Asia Foundation, for instance, sponsored a survey to consider the factors impeding Indonesia's business climate. The top issue respondents cited in the rule-of-law field was "legal certainty." The typical first-generation response would be to publish laws, and indeed, that was one part of the variable in the survey. But the preponderance of responses actually dealt not with commercial laws—but with law enforcement and corruption issues.[10] As a law school dean claimed, "The crooked judges often ask, 'Who wants to win?' and then whoever gives them the bigger bribe, they ask that lawyer to write the decision, and then they don't even necessarily check the logic. So not only is it corrupt, but it could just be badly written law that hurts the idea of precedent."[11] The survey also showed that security was quite important to foreign businesses and larger businesses. Other factors in the variable therefore included requiring courts to enforce verdicts; police to work effectively without corruption; and the legislative and executive branches of government to have a good working relationship. And, in fact, legal issues were not the top finding from that or other surveys. Instead, an entirely different rule-of-law issue—security—was viewed as a larger problem for businesses.[12] In other words, the business community felt it was more constrained by corruption or by organized criminals who "tax" any business that becomes moderately successful than by outdated bankruptcy procedures. When a problem, rather than an institution, is analyzed, these unexpected impediments and cross-institutional solution sets become more readily apparent.

Obviously, much turns on identifying the best rule-of-law goal for any country. What is the "best"? As discussed throughout the rest of the chapter, it helps to choose a goal that is focused on an actual problem that is viewed as a problem by local citizens—and that may have an indirect effect on other rule-of-law problems. An open mind, common sense, and rigorous empirical examination based on interviews with a wide range of the constituents within the target country are essential. The community may be foreign or local businesses, the poor, minorities, or any portion of society—but it will not initially be lawyers or judges. They are the means, not the end, of any rule-of-law reform. Actually understanding what people want is a specialized task that is well developed in the sociological field. As Benjamin Crosby discusses in his work on participation, group leaders are frequently unrepresentative of the group they supposedly represent; some participants will wish to block change; and numerous other well-known pitfalls await the unwary researcher.[13] However, once some basic sociological techniques are learned, they are not complex and are easy to structure into standard questionnaires.

Step 2: Determine the Institutional, Political, and Cultural Components of the Problem

Let's say that the problem identified in a country is a lack of equality under the law. In first-generation reform programs, this problem is immediately put into the solution set of "access to justice," because a lack of equality under the law means that poor individuals and those without connections don't bother to use courts under the assumption that they will not be treated equally. But the problem is usually much bigger than that. Politicians and rich businessmen are considered above the law and evade punishment by paying bribes or calling on well-placed contacts. Business contracts are shaky and can always be undone by more connected businesses, and thus development is constrained. The result is widespread disdain and cynicism about the justice system, which makes people feel that they have little legitimate recourse for their grievances. Moreover, the business climate suffers as everyone tries to work with a few well-connected companies and individuals, skewing the market and reducing competition.

The problem of lack of equality before the law has institutional components—bribery and corruption among the courts and police will need to be addressed. It also may have legal components—laws may be needed to protect minorities or give women an equal say in justice. It clearly has a crucial political component—politicians and connected, rich businessmen benefit from their above-the-law status and will want to protect it. They may even use physical threat to maintain their position, as with the connections Russian oligarchs forged with the Russian mafia. Finally, a cultural element often exists: social norms of deference based on gender, hierarchy, caste, or class that are hard to break. A largely female judiciary in a patriarchal society, for instance, can give the courts a weak and low-status reputation, making it more difficult for judges to stand firm in the face of driven businessmen or high-status politicians.[14]

Determining the many components of a problem requires mapping the problem, so that the best avenue for reform can be found. At this stage, reformers should not start looking for where to target their efforts—there may be many avenues by which to affect the problem, only a few of which are appropriate for any particular reform agency. They should simply try to identify where the problem resides and how many roots might need to be dug out to create change.

In Step 2 of an ends-based reform program, consultants are hired at the beginning of a project, to evaluate not institutions but society. Ideally, consultants will be versed in both the region and its political culture as well as the types of political and social problems that feed various rule-of-law imbalances. Through additional background readings, stakeholder interviews, meetings with academics specializing in the sociology and political science of that country, and by using well-developed sociological evaluation techniques attuned to culture and power relationships, consultants should be able to collect information on the various components of an identified problem. This work is best conducted in tandem with step 1's problem identification. A final mapping for lack of equality before the law may look something like table 7.1.

Obviously, this step could continue interminably. Time is a crucial opportunity cost, however, and should not be wasted attempting to compile a perfect list. It is enough to gain a broad sense of the problem areas that are the most important to the local community. There are no rewards for being clever or subtle in discovering new problems—the goal is to identify the areas for reform that are viewed as major issues by the local community. Thus, the issues that surface early and often are likely to be those most worth tackling.

It is essential, at this point, not to be looking for the answer or solution a particular agency will be working on. The goal of step 2 is simply to identify the problem and understand the various aspects that will need to be tackled for success, before ruling out one solution or another as outside a particular agency's jurisdiction. For that reason, external consultants can be particularly useful in providing a 360-degree view of the problem, without letting the restraints of the contracting agency fetter their judgment.

TABLE 7.1 **MAPPING LACK OF EQUALITY BEFORE THE LAW**

PROBLEM:
Lack of equality before the law is suppressing small business development and is harming the human rights and willingness of minorities and the poor to access justice

Political Component	Institutional/ Legal Component	Cultural Component
Executive, legislature, and wealthier business community directly benefit, fuel corruption	**Courts:** Corruption within courts **Police:** Corruption within police force **Laws:** Laws against corruption exist, but they are unenforced	Paying fees for speeding processes of government is so widespread that it is not regarded as corruption
Oligarchs with close ties to government also hold close ties to organized criminals who intimidate judges	**Courts:** Judicial fear of physical threat **Police:** Lack of enforcement of laws against intimidating judges	Female judiciary is low status, easily intimidated; judiciary isn't a respected institution
President's children have preferential access to government contracts	**Courts:** Judiciary formally independent of government but cannot prosecute government officials and friends for corruption **Laws:** Laws against corruption not written to cover this situation	Culture of nepotism and family self-help makes drawing bright lines on nepotistic practices difficult; people complain about president's children but are happy when their families obtain a nepotistic connection
President favors home region; proportional representation system means legislature does not represent rural regions directly; no political weight for rural areas	**Courts:** Courts too far away for easy access by rural population, contract enforcement low **Police:** Few police in rural areas, property theft high	Rural inhabitants largely illiterate, are intimidated by city itself and by written procedures of courts Police in rural areas have social/patronage ties with higher classes of those regions

Political Component	Institutional/ Legal Component	Cultural Component
Wealthy/businessmen will lobby for existing court fee structure	**Courts:** Court fees and cost in lost time too great for poor **Jails:** Overcrowded and dangerous; rich buy their way out while poor languish **Laws:** Legal arrangement requires losing plaintiff to pay court fees; this discourages poor from bringing suits	Poor are unorganized, few groups represent their interests
Politicians attack minority group to win popular appeal or to appear "tough on crime"	**Courts:** Few or no members of minority group on courts **Police:** Police drawn from groups especially inimical to minority population **Laws:** No laws on equal opportunity or anti-discrimination	Minority group subject to widespread private and public discrimination
Others...	Others...	Others...

Step 3: Locate Opposition and Support

A cardinal belief of second-generation programs is that rule-of-law reform involves change to power structures, big and small. One of the core changes the rule of law institutes is moving from a culture of privilege based on power to one of rights based on equality before the law. Reforms therefore inevitably create winners and losers within the government and within bureaucracies and can be expected to generate opposition.[15] Sometimes, it's easy to see who is losing a privileged position: Greater judicial independence reduces the power of the executive, for instance, which may generate executive opposition. Sometimes it is less clear. Take a supposedly "technical" reform like making courts more efficient by transferring administrative duties from judges to clerical staff. An outsider may assume that judges would be happy to cut their paperwork and spend more time on the law, reducing their case backlogs. But a judge who cannot control case assignments loses an opportunity to solicit bribes—and so corrupt judges might fight such a reform. An unwary reformer might be completely blindsided by such unexpected opposition. Even wholly apolitical reforms, such as rearranging the curriculum in a law faculty, may meet bureaucratic resistance from people who simply don't want to change their ways and who think they can outlast any external reformer. Even average citizens might not be on the side of rule-of-law reform when push comes to shove. What an outsider might see as a problem—such as a corruptible police officer—might be useful to locals who view bribes as easier to deal with than the slow court system.[16]

Second-generation reformers recognize that reform is going to meet resistance. They also know that no external reform program alone can bring about change—outsiders depend on individuals within a country to act as the fulcrums of change. The intensity and location of opposition and support matter. Choosing to work on an important problem for which there is no internal constituency for reform, where a high degree of organized opposition exists, is simply a recipe for failure. So before settling on a sequence of reforms, second-generation programs start by searching for areas where the greatest support and least opposition can be found. This is not a new concept: Similar interest-based analysis considering sources of support and opposition and the relative power of these forces was carried out by USAID in country assessments in Africa and the Middle East for use in democracy programming in the early 1990s.[17] It has become a part of most of the problem-based analysis and political structures thinking that are burgeoning now, twenty years later.

Finding supporters is just as subtle as locating opponents. For decades, reformers have been told to find local champions.[18] It is indeed crucial to locate champions—but, as discussed in chapter 4, the reality is that few people will be across-the-board reformers, or across-the-board opponents, to all change. Most people will be for reforms that will help them and against reforms that will hurt them or make their lives more difficult. In other words, they will want to protect their areas of privilege. For this reason, individuals who appear to be reformers often flip suddenly on their Westerns supporters and revert to unprogressive tendencies once they have gained some power—a reversal so embarrassing that Westerners are often slow to admit it is happening.

The motives of "reformers" are often mixed, and the more the mixture is understood, the greater the ability to leverage change. A Ministry of Justice may be for an anticorruption strategy—so long as it is focused on corruption in the courts rather than in the ministry. A Supreme Court justice campaigning for judicial independence may in fact be trying to gain autonomy and political power. Even reformers acting out of "pure" and non–self-interested motives may have blind spots that outside actors must be on the alert for—a progressive law school dean, for instance, may be more interested in the speaking opportunities, international junkets, and praise that comes with being singled out as a reformer than in the reforms themselves. In fact, most true across-the-board reformers are often outsiders in their own countries—the lack of acceptance by their own countrymen may give them the psychological need to seek approval and support from outsiders, or they may become more estranged from their own countrymen as they grow to be seen as overly associated with the West.

A serious, on-the-ground stakeholder analysis is thus necessary to map out likely sources of support and opposition for particular reform activities within the map of problems already identified.[19] The stakeholder set must extend beyond rule-of-law institutions to other areas of political and cultural power within a country—religious and civic institutions, the media, political parties, civil society, local business, foreign business, educational communities, and other such constituencies where support may be lurking. However, in choosing which constituencies to include and map, the opportunity cost of extra work and time for the researcher should be taken into account—mapping too many groups will add tedium and not necessarily value. The stakeholder analysis should therefore look at groups that are either already organized or are easy to organize. Crosby's rule of thumb is a good one to keep in mind: "Only those groups or actors with real and mobilizable resources that can be applied for or against the [policy reform] should be included."[20] Finally, stakeholder analysis should gauge the intensity of support and the level of power and influence a particular person or organization might have. Crosby's determinants of influence (information, economic resources, status, legitimacy/authority, coercion) are a good measure for this metric.[21]

Stakeholder analysis comes before program design because it has to influence whom to involve in program conception, as well as the programs chosen. Many first-generation rule-of-law programs undertake a cursory stakeholder analysis to gain "participation." But analyzing stakeholders after the reform tactics have been chosen undermines the whole purpose of the analysis. The idea at this point is not trying merely, or even primarily, to build support; it is to search for the best fulcrums of leverage through which to influence society. Say, for instance, USAID wants to tackle corruption in a country. If it finds that the judiciary is likely to oppose an anticorruption campaign, a good program won't start by working with the judiciary and then looking for support within it. Instead, it might begin by organizing anticorruption activities among lawyers, politicians who wish to make their names as "anticorruption" reformers, or local business owners too scared to speak out on the "corruption tax" alone but willing to join a coalition fighting it. Eventually, the program may want to tackle the power, professional culture, or institutional structure of the judiciary—but it would likely wish to begin by amassing another vertical or horizontal check on the court's power. Creating such checks on power requires meaningful participation, not just a name on a sign-in sheet. Because the entire point is to reform relationships between rulers and ruled, the latter need skin in the game. Real, meaningful participation of locals is often a missing element in rule-of-law assistance.[22] It is difficult, slows programming, and makes the reformers' lives harder—but without it, programs led and implemented by outsiders can rarely be sustained. Ultimately, after all, it is not the outsiders' country.

It is also important to undertake this research in the field, not to just make guesses about likely support or opposition. Many development organizations, for instance, believe that the business community is a source of support for rule-of-law reforms. They assume entrepreneurs want efficient, predictable commercial adjudication. Many businesses, particularly small ones, do. But, in fact, experience in Eastern Europe shows that first movers into the business realm are often oligarchs who want to entrench their preferences.[23] Entrepreneurs entering later may wish to change the system through a coalition—but they are just as likely to want to find a niche and gain the benefits they can gather to themselves, rather than trying to overcome the collective action problem of coming together to create change. Even many international businesses may prefer to work around a broken system by writing contracts that require foreign adjudication, for instance, rather than spend valuable time away from their business trying to change a country's method of justice.

The only way to determine which individuals and institutions support and oppose reform is to invest the time and money in a good stakeholder analysis, conducted by a knowledgeable and experienced sociologist or social scientist trained in interview techniques. The money and time it takes to conduct such a study are negligible compared with the costs in lost funds and time of a poorly chosen reform effort. If the same sociologist or consultant undertakes steps 1, 2, and 3, then ideas about stakeholders will begin to form during the earlier stages of analysis, and this step can progress more quickly once the problem is identified in step 2. While it will require additional effort and should continue after problem identification, the findings will overlap with those of steps 1 and 2, and therefore may be best undertaken by the same group of consultants who began the project. A sample stakeholder matrix might look like table 7.2.[24]

This matrix can then be mapped to determine systems of support and opposition that can be organized or diffused. Lines can be drawn between groups to suggest pre-existing organizational connections that make working together easier. This map can be useful to see likely alliances that can be made in support of reform—and may alert the reformer to alliances in opposition that may be formed or forthcoming. Different colors, font sizes, or bold can be used in the matrix to demonstrate the intensity and mutability of support, such as whether it is likely to alter if a charismatic individual is removed or if a government changes. Such a map can help reformers understand at a glance what areas of policy are likely to have support and opposition, who needs to be satisfied for policy to move forward, and whether opposition is dispersed and fragmented or entrenched and highly linked. Table 7.3 shows what a final stakeholder map generated from this analysis might look like.

TABLE 7.2	STAKEHOLDER MATRIX	
	Opposition (Institutional or Individual)	**Support** (Institutional or Individual)
Government		
President/prime minister		
Legislative		
Judiciary		
Key ministries (such as Justice, Interior)		
Local/provincial government		
Private Sector		
Local businesses, small to medium		
Local businesses, large		
Foreign business with local outpost		
Civil Society		
Religious		
Professional groups (lawyers, police, others)		
Single-issue pressure groups		
Educational System (teachers, students)		
Media		

Level of Support/ Opposition (Silent, Individual, Organized, Intense-Core)	Level of Power/ Leverage (High, Medium, Low) and (Steady or Subject to Change)	Resources That the Group/ Individual Brings to Bear

TABLE 7.3 STAKEHOLDER MAP

Equality Before the Law (reforms in police and judicial corruption, rural policing and access to justice for the poor)

Level of support	Supporters	Neutral	Opposition
Intense-Core	Clean-hands politicians Minister of Justice Minister of the Interior		Oligarchs–Corrupt politicians Organized crime Chief justices and heads of court
Medium	Journalist X U.S. foreign businesses	Magistrates' school New judges Bar association Small local businesses	Lower court judges
Low	Poor communities	Most media	

Step 4: Determine Evaluation Targets and Measurement Goals

By now, a program designer will have begun to understand the problem as a whole, where support and opposition lie, and where change might occur. It is now time to determine metrics for evaluating whether the problem is getting better or worse. It may seem odd to determine metrics for performance evaluation before a rule-of-law project for the country has even been devised, but that is precisely why this step is sequenced here. Once a project exists, evaluation will inevitably be

SAMPLE QUESTIONS TO ASK IN STAKEHOLDER ANALYSIS

Political: Is a high-level official willing to champion the cause? Has he/she invested political capital in the cause? Has he/she used a) rhetoric, b) funds, c) political capital to further the cause?

Ministries: Have they asked for greater funding for reform? Worked internally for reform even without funding? Requested donor assistance for reform? Devised a program for reform without outside help?

Private Sector: What are incentives for reform? What are disincentives? Is there a business champion who began working for reform before donor assistance?

Media: How do the media frame the issue? Are there journalists making a name for themselves with this issue? Is there an independent paper, magazine, radio, or television station making a name for itself based on its independence or muckraking?

Civil Society: Have any single-issue groups mobilized around this issue? Did they begin locally, or with donor support? Are their leaders respected by the public? Government? Businesses?

built around its tactics—and too often, that means choosing targets that measure narrow outcomes, such as the number of police trained or workshops held, rather than the actual goals a reform effort is trying to achieve. By determining what to evaluate before the program is devised, reformers are forced to focus on the problem—in other words, measure the end, not the program, which is the means.[25] Choosing these measurements at this stage of the process is also likely to influence program design and keep programs focused on goals that matter.

Metrics can be broken into three levels. **Output metrics** measure the direct activities of a program: the number of people trained, the number of trainings held, and so on. These are the most commonly collected metrics and are frequently demanded by program administrators trying to keep contractors to their terms of reference, or by Congress, which is trying to ensure that taxpayer money is well spent. However, such metrics are meaningless. Hundreds of one-hour workshops are unlikely to affect the rule of law anywhere. If thousands of judges are trained, but the training is of poor quality, the numbers will hardly affect any real problem. Meanwhile, meeting such predetermined programming goals can prevent programmers from taking advantage of moments of opportunity. A real reformer may arise who needs help—but because contractors are stuck carrying out ten more rote trainings, they cannot offer the time to assist with real reform. Wherever possible, program designers should not include output metrics—and certainly, they should not start with them.

Outcome metrics measure the actual effects of a program. For instance, if a reform is intended to train police in order to uphold human rights law, an outcome metric might survey those trained to find out if they believe more in human rights after the training than before, or feel they are more able to uphold the law. If a reform is geared at speeding up justice by reducing case backlogs, an outcome metric would look at whether caseloads have, in fact, gone down. Outcome metrics do not look at the full impact on society, which can have diffuse causes. They do not, for instance, measure whether citizens believe police brutality is down, in the first instance, or whether cases are being closed more quickly, in the second. Either of these outcomes could be influenced by things outside the scope of the reform program, such as the appointment of a new police commander who is tough on brutality or a sudden drop in the number of cases brought because people are so disgusted with the system. Instead, outcome metrics try to gauge whether a reform is actually accomplishing its stated purpose, stopping one step short of whether that reform's purpose is actually having an impact on society. These are far more important metrics to gather than output metrics—and once a program has been designed, the program creators should determine which outcome metrics would be useful to collect. These, not outputs, measure whether a reform is working as it was intended. Outcome metrics cannot be determined at this stage, before a program is devised. Instead, they should be part of step 5, when a program designer determines the program.

At this stage in the process, program designers need to determine **impact metrics**, which will show whether the program itself is having an impact on the actual problem. Ends-based performance metrics should measure the societal, not the institutional, level, despite the difficulty of tracing impact to the reform itself. They should be geared to measure real changes in how people experience their country, because the experience of individuals or businesses within a state is what rule-of-law reformers are ultimately working toward. If the goal is equality before the law, they may wish to measure the changing rates by which people in disadvantaged groups (impoverished, minority, female, low status) bring and win cases, or these groups' changing perceptions of court corruption, or the frequency with which they turn to local problem-solving methods to adjudicate disputes—not how many judges have been sensitized, or how many alternative dispute resolution programs have been created. Finding the proper metrics and measuring them is always an immensely difficult undertaking. However, because all programs inevitably end up working toward targets (the equivalent of teaching to the test), attempting to measure the right things, rather than the easy things, is essential.

Societal-level measurements are difficult, because such metrics inevitably are affected by many elements outside of the control of the rule-of-law reform program. Moreover, tracing the causality between a program and a societal-level effect is problematic. There is no simple answer—all metrics have their flaws—and it is for this reason that it is also important to determine outcome metrics in the final stage of program design. Two keys to choosing appropriate impact metrics for ends-based programs are to choose broadly, but humbly, and to be aware of time lags and unexpected side effects. On the former, if the goal is law and order, the measurements have to include crime rates, not police academy graduates. But many factors affect crime rates, such as demographic bubbles and economic downturns. The measurement therefore might best be the change from a linearly projected rate, rather than a percentage decline in the overall rate. Even after these steps, impacts should be expected to be minimal—any one program that appears to have had a huge, immediate effect would be suspect. On the second point, some counterintuitive side effects should be expected and built into the measurement model. In a good anticorruption program, perceptions of corruption tend to rise as a result of societal awareness campaigns before they fall. When police begin to do their jobs better, crime rates often increase, because more people report crimes that they previously would not have bothered to report.[26] Trained measurement professionals should be able to create well-conceived metrics to address these gaps.

Setting measurement targets is among the most difficult, and most important, elements of ends-based program design. Impact metrics are crucial to staying focused on the end goal. But achievement in any such societal-level targets may be marginal, and foundations and political bodies at home may demand more of their rule-of-law dollars. Outcome metrics are therefore also essential, so that designers and funders can tell whether a particular program is being well executed. However, wherever possible, program designers should fight against the collection of output metrics (the number of trainings held or equipment distributed) because such metrics can force reformers to follow predetermined programs that are no longer useful by the time the program is implemented. Impact metrics should be the measurements around which programs are designed, to ensure ends-based targets; outcome metrics should be created once programs are designed to measure effectiveness in carrying out the program itself.

Step 5: Design the Reform Program

At this point, a program designer has maps that show the various components of the problem, who wants to help solve it, and who will be in opposition. No agency could possibly tackle all the problem areas with all of the potential stakeholders—nor should it. Instead, based on an agency's mission, the political and social terrain inside the country, and the political terrain and interests among various U.S. government agencies, a program designer must now choose the most likely parts of the problem to tackle. If an aid agency such as USAID is undertaking the analysis, aid may form a portion of the programming—but any program designer would be wise to look at all the methods that could be pulled from across governmental and nongovernmental programs to work together to achieve reform goals. In making a choice, a program designer will wish to ask some questions:

- Which of these sub-problem areas must change for overall end-goal success? Which are primary, and which are secondary?
- Which areas are likely to be affected by changes made in other areas, and which must be addressed directly?
- Where will I have local support? Where is there a champion who will take up this cause, and who has the influence to lead it? Where is the opposition located, and how can I avoid it?
- How can I involve local sources of support meaningfully, so they own and continue their own reforms?
- What areas can my agency address, given our skills, expertise, and comparative advantages?
- Which areas must be addressed simultaneously by other organizations if success is to be achieved? Can I persuade other agencies in my government, or programs run by other governments, to assist with these additional areas of reform, so that our strategies are coordinated or complementary?
- Where might countervailing U.S. interests undermine my program? Can these be addressed and ameliorated in the interagency process?
- Does U.S. government action actually harm this goal because of countervailing interests? Should the program, or part of it, be executed in the form of a grant to a nongovernmental body less associated with the U.S. government to enable greater legitimacy or to avoid clashes with other national interests?

The program designer will also need to determine which areas can be addressed immediately, which could be added to the program in time, and which are outside the agency's ambit because of resource constraints, legal constraints, or lack of expertise. If, for instance, all the major areas of change require working with the police but the agency is legally constrained from working with the police, then either the program will not be able to achieve its objectives and meet its evaluation goals or a partner agency must be found that can tackle the police portion of the problem. In such a partnership approach, the agencies must coordinate their activities and work in tandem, in order to meet the evaluation metrics. Choosing impact evaluation targets ahead of program design should keep program designers honest in evaluating whether the programs they can do are likely to have an effect and drive partnerships. It also should serve to encourage program designers to abandon projects that simply cannot work. After designing the program, it is time to select outcome metrics.

Choosing Program Elements: Best Fit

As program designers choose reform targets, they should consider the sixteen tactics described in chapter 6. Their analysis is best conducted with a "best-fit" mind-set of looking at the type of institution or procedure that best solves the problem at hand, given the reality of the local situation. The best-fit concept evolved in response to failures of "best-practice" interventions, which often led to simply mimicking the shells of Western institutions, without any of the cultural or political context that enabled them to work.[27] The theory suggests that what best serves a system is not some "ideal" institution unmoored from cultural context or economic and political realities but a solution that fits the particular problem at hand, within that cultural and social world. As World Bank scholar Brian Levy explains, "The central issue is understanding country-specific constitutional structures and patterns of political, social, and economic interests and to aim for a good fit between efforts to strengthen administrative and accountability systems and these country-specific realities . . . rather than remaining preoccupied with politically unachievable comprehensive reforms, the focus is on more modest, viable initiatives, especially those for which results are observable."[28]

As discussed in step 2, the best-fit program to meet many rule-of-law needs will often not be found in institutional reform—but may be located in other areas altogether, such as when the intervention that would provide the most bang for the buck in the business sector is not commercial law reform, but better law enforcement against organized crime.

In other cases, the best fit may be a form of local problem solving that looks quite different from that of Western institutions. In many countries, for instance, reformers are starting to look at informal systems of justice. In Sierra Leone, 80 percent of the population turns to customary justice doled out primarily by chieftains and secret societies. Such justice is highly unaccountable and often illiberal—but it is also where people actually go to resolve their disputes.[29] A second-generation program designer cannot simply ignore this problematic reality and work to fix more liberal, government-sanctioned courts that only a fifth of the population uses. Instead, donors need to confront this problem, and they can do so in different ways. Scholars studying DFID's program in Sierra Leone note, for instance, that some local NGOs "work with a broader array of informal actors and engage with illiberal practices in order to reform them. Donors could learn from such approaches."[30] Best-fit programs face real moral and practical issues that must be navigated by each program to remain true to both donors' moral commitments and the actual needs of the country. However, it is worth keeping in mind that solutions that are too liberal, and out of keeping with local norms, are less likely to be sustained, and practices that work with institutions ignored by large segments of the population are unlikely to affect societal change—so a balance must be struck that helps countries move down a path while not being so far from current social mores.

Others fault best-fit programs for providing second-class services to another country: If Americans demand jails built to a certain standard, or lawyers with a certain education, why should another country have anything less? But it is worth looking at such an accusation from the perspective of the recipient. In Afghanistan, the U.S. government refused to offer cheap, local forms of distributed energy or power, but instead provided a U.S.-style power station. The end result cost three times the budgeted amount and its operating costs had skyrocketed as a result of the price of the fuel. As the Afghan Deputy Minister of Water and Energy remarked at the time, "Instead of giving me a small car, you give [*sic*] me really a Jaguar. . . . And it will be up to me whether I use it, or just park it and look at it."[31] The first-class power plant was simply too costly to fit the needs of the country. That made it worse than less advanced forms of energy provision that would actually have been used.

Over time, it will be inevitable as well as useful for a set of common reform options to grow around the various rule-of-law ends. There is always a problem with such pre-made "solutions"—but at least they will be chosen around ends, and not institutions. Eventually, scholars will help by assessing which reforms succeeded in tackling problems—rather than looking only at how to carry out reforms to institutions, as current rule-of-law scholarship does.[32] Until that time, ingenuity and thoughtfulness, as well as research into how other reformers in developed and developing countries have conquered similar problems, will provide ideas for potential program design.

Sequencing and Implementation

Strategy is not everything. As the Albania example in chapter 6 illustrated, implementation matters. In a first-generation reform program, projects are designed and budgeted years in advance. Implementation occurs along a pre-designed track in which supposedly apolitical, technical projects are sequenced and carried out in order.

To be successful, a second-generation approach to implementation must take political cycles and cultural moments into account. Second-generation reform recognizes that while time unfolds at the same rate of sixty seconds every minute, in politics and society there are punctuations, windows of opportunity in which sixty seconds can be worth far more than the same amount of time a few months down the road. A moment of political scandal over corruption can provide far greater impetus for an anticorruption program. A new administration might provide a salient moment to launch public administration reform. The appointment of a particularly well-respected judge could create a window of opportunity for action in the judiciary. The process of ends-based programming will, ideally, assist program implementers in recognizing these windows of opportunity when they occur. The stakeholder analysis, for instance, will help program designers recognize when a group of supporters (or those in opposition) has coalesced or when a particularly useful player has attained a high position of influence. The problem map will alert program designers to ripple effects as they begin to happen in other elements of society or in institutions that could allow a program to catapult forward.

Recognizing moments when action is possible means that second-generation programs require a different approach to budgeting. Well-designed programs will need the flexibility to respond with greater resources or manpower to moments of opportunity. Thus, second-generation reform programs must be able to adapt their plans on short notice. Similarly, such programs can operate within a set overall budget—but ideally, they will have maximal flexibility within those parameters to reprogram budget lines. If large-scale funding flexibility is impossible, such programs could have smaller pools of funds that could be used to take advantage of unexpected opportunities. USAID's Office of Transition Initiatives, for instance, has been able to respond with greater flexibility to dynamic situations thanks to its funding structure, and similar budgeting provisions should be sought for rule-of-law programs.

The demands of second-generation reform make the implementing partner extremely important. These are not rote projects that can be carried out wholesale. A great deal rests on the abilities of those who are spotting these windows of opportunity or determining the best local partners with whom to work. Ideally, U.S. government agencies would shift away from contractors and bring thousands of excellent people into government service to implement program after program, learning as they go. However, until the U.S. government implements better human resource practices for those who are serving in government and undertakes civil service reform so that the best civil servants can move up and be rewarded, it is likely to continue to have pockets of amazing people doing terrific work but is unlikely to get wide-scale, sustained excellence across government agencies. Thus, program designers will have to be particularly careful to choose extremely good contractors. In other cases, they will want to take programs out of the U.S. government ambit altogether—especially in countries or areas where U.S. national interests are likely to be so significant as to undermine the ability of the contractors to accomplish their goals because of countervailing forces or because they feel pressured to show results more quickly than a well-executed program could accomplish.

Enabling the most successful, fluid, politically attuned resource allocation and attracting the best human capital within development agencies are among the most difficult challenges for second-generation reform. It will mean occasionally having to abandon programs that are not working, despite being on the hook for metrics that will not look good as a result. And it will mean attaining success in areas that were not originally expected and thus not budgeted for or set to be measured. Particularly when a gap exists between the agency writing the terms of reference and the contractor carrying out the program, providing such flexibility is difficult—and will require a real cultural change within U.S. government agencies. However, only by fighting for a new organizational paradigm at home will America be able to successfully work to bring new organizational paradigms to other countries.

CHAPTER EIGHT

CONCLUSION

Above all, our lodestar was how to make the Iraqis help themselves. My mantra was, "Do everything as though we will be pulled from this station tomorrow." As the [Iraqi police] became more capable, we were increasingly able to simply stand back and watch. That's hard for Americans to do, but we understood that our metric for success was to render ourselves superfluous. How did we know when we had done our job? When we became capable of being bored.

– John Renehan[1]

In the 1980s, the corpses of nearly 200 murder victims were wheeled into the mortuary in Palermo, Sicily, each year. Outside its doors, the mafia operated with near impunity. Funds for schools were diverted to renovating the apartment houses of mafia bosses. Businesses were intimidated into silence and forced to pay for "protection." Political parties were riddled with mafia ties from top to bottom; even one of Italy's European parliamentarians was connected. The people were cowed into apathy by the strength of a system that appeared all-encompassing. At intervals, the government would organize itself to crack down. The police would make arrests—but their cases would founder on "insufficient evidence" thanks to the silence of citizens who feared mafia retribution more than they believed in the possibility of justice. The moment would pass, and the mafia violence would return.

But in the early 1980s, the mob overstepped. An internal war launched by a mafia family led to the killing of public officials who had previously been off-limits. The losing mob families went to the courts and confessed to magistrates, and in 1986, unprecedented trials began to unravel the mafia net. Such trials had happened before. What was different this time was the uprising among society. Disgust at the level of violence and at the "excellent cadavers" of innocent government officials finally broke through the apathy and fear. For the first time, the Catholic Church spoke against the mafia. Teachers began organizing students, creating curricula on lawfulness, civic renewal, and democratic ownership of their own society. Housewives began protesting, hanging bed sheets out of their windows with anti-mafia slogans to show their disgust and refusal to bow down any longer.

But all this would not have been enough, in itself. In January 1992, the trials had made their way to Italy's top court. In the past, it had handed out light sentences on legal technicalities, deflating any efforts to break the stranglehold of crime. Now, Giovanni Falcone, one of the magistrates who had led the early trials, was Minister of Justice. He had worked for a year to galvanize the government against the mafia. Perhaps the professional cultural shift was one of the reasons that this time, the Court of Cassation upheld the tough sentences of the lower courts. Leading *mafiosi* would be imprisoned for life. Suddenly, the courts were galvanized. The "clean hands" magistrates of Milan began bringing cases that would unravel a web of corruption claiming nearly all the major political parties. Space opened for "La Rete"—a new party with an anticorruption platform to win seats in parliament.

A few months later, in May 1992, a 500-kilogram bomb killed Falcone, his wife, and three police escorts as they drove through a tunnel in Palermo. The people of the city rose up as they never had before. Anguished at the death of a man in whom they had placed their hope, they took to the streets—demanding, for the first time, a society of lawfulness. Two months later, another bomb killed a second magistrate and five police escorts. The blast gutted the apartments on the lower stories of the building. Once again, the public took to the streets, and this time stayed there until the government passed a series of laws demanded by the magistrates that would allow mafia members to be captured and kept in prison.

Law enforcement did its part—and now the other parts of society had to do theirs. In the election the following year, La Rete won by a landslide in Palmero. The new mayor undertook a series of measures to uphold the civic renaissance of the city, so that the people could continue to feel that they owned their society. The city and teachers, schools, civic groups, and the church worked to make sure that the people of Palmero felt they belonged to a civic community. The relationship between state and society was being restored. While the mafia has not been eradicated, murders in Palermo averaged around ten a year by the late 1990s. Outside the mortuary's doors, a rule-of-law society had begun to take hold.[2]

Physician, Heal Thyself!

The story of Sicily is a story of internal renewal—of a people, their government, and brave members of the legal apparatus taking it upon themselves to restore the relationship between state and society. Hong Kong provides an equally heartening example—the small island successfully fought corruption so pervasive that accident victims had to bribe ambulance crews to take them to the hospital. In just two decades, from the 1960s to the 1980s, the city became one of the best-governed places on earth and an important financial hub. Catalyzing rule-of-law reform as an external actor is more difficult. There are many examples of failure, and fewer cases of broad-based success. But the difficulties stem as much from structural issues within the United States and other well-meaning governments and institutions as from rough terrain in other countries. Hard as it is to get these programs right, we would exponentially increase our chances if we stopped getting in our own way. Development practitioners must begin to think politically—less like technocrats and more like advocacy organizations. They must also be empowered with the tools to act politically, such as more flexible funding, simplified and expedited hiring ability, and the ability to make more decisions with less oversight, so that they can seize windows of opportunity. Members of the diplomatic community must take this work seriously, recognizing that they, too, often undermine the slow, punctuated bottom-up and top-down work of rule-of-law reform through more glamorous diplomatic activities that prop up a supposedly friendly government or help a reformer. Without the structures of a rule-of-law society, these short-term diplomatic actions often do little more than create brittle allies who sit atop an unstable political structure. Finally, the United States could greatly improve its chances of success by streamlining the number of agencies involved in rule-of-law programming—or, if that is too quixotic, at least forcing the coordination of the vast number of agencies engaged in this work within each country, so that we could craft strategies rather than execute tactics. The United States should also recognize where U.S. government fingerprints get in the way—and provide more separation, with consultation rather than coordination, for government-supported nongovernmental actors in these sensitive areas.

Such reforms are not simple. In the United States, they would require changes to legislation as well as cultural changes at home—particularly altering attitudes in Congress, USAID, the State Department, and myriad other agencies. But they do mean that greater success is within our control. We need not abandon all hope. Instead, we should abandon failing tactics and embrace a new way of looking at rule-of-law reform. The core takeaways from a second-generation methodology are:

1. **The rule of law is not about a set of institutions. It is about achieving a set of ends that determine the relationship between a state and its society.** This sounds obvious when written, but the logic often dissolves on the ground in the face of what appear to be broken organs of justice. In Kabul, for instance, prosecutors labor in an office with no computers. They work in coats near a wood stove that fails to fully heat the small room, strewn with papers, with no law books in sight. How can the United States not, at least, provide a proper office as part of its justice reforms? But pictures of prosecutor's offices in parts of England in the 1900s are remarkably similar to present-day conditions in many developing countries. And while England has made many gains in its understanding of justice since that time, it is equally clear that it had established the concept of the rule of law.

The rule of law is about establishing a government that is bound by, and governs through, pre-existing laws, which treat citizens as equal before the law, which respect human rights, ensure law and order, and provide for efficient settlement of disputes and regularized decisions. While institutions and laws can assist in these outcomes, they are the means, not the ends. They should never be confused for ends in themselves, and they are often not the most important levers of change.

2. **The most important elements to change are a country's power structure and its popular and professional norms.** When the United States and United Nations intervened in Haiti in 1995, they found that police lacked handcuffs.[3] Of course, the rule of law is unlikely to take hold unless the police have such fundamental equipment. But while such resources may be necessary, they will never be sufficient to bring about the rule of law. Second-generation reformers realize that the rule of law is not broken because police lack handcuffs—police lack handcuffs because powerful forces in the government or society have decided that rule-of-law institutions should be weak, subordinate, or underfunded. This is the key mental shift that distinguishes first-generation, institution-focused reform from second-generation, ends-based reform.

   No matter how badly it appears that equipment, buildings, and other material goods are needed, they are secondary to real reform. Second-generation reformers know that fixing the handcuff problem alone is inadequate; the same issues will reappear in different guises. But if the power structures and relationships are fixed, the handcuffs will come.

   Until power structures and professional and popular culture support the rule of law, politically powerful individuals can ignore laws and institutions will continue to malfunction. Therefore, laws and institutions are rarely the place to begin rule-of-law reforms unless they are being leveraged tactically to achieve more fundamental reforms to power structure and culture. When the power structure and cultural norms are better suited to the rule of law, more technical legal and institutional reform will come from inside the system; only then will "technical assistance" be helpful.

Reform programs should focus on creating structures of vertical and horizontal accountability that limit the power of any one part of government or society. Outside reformers can and should identify and assist domestic reformers to rise to positions where they can effect change—but that is only the first step. Domestic reformers should then be assisted and pressured into creating checks and balances, and they should not be supported in circumventing such measures simply because they are seen as reformers. Such mantles have a habit of slipping.

Meanwhile, working to change social norms—particularly professional cultural change, which outsiders can effect through top-down as well as bottom-up programs—is essential. Reformers should think more systematically about how to create reform in this arena, and scholars should begin to empirically examine these efforts.

3. **While many tactics will be needed to leverage reform, the United States should focus on bottom-up efforts—especially those at one remove that operate through grants to civil society.** In the cultural schism between diplomats and development workers, both win—the power structure is the most important element of reform, as diplomats like to believe—but one of the best ways to affect it is through bottom-up methods more favored by the development community.

   One of the most effective methods for affecting the power structure is by supporting civil society. Such efforts should involve not only NGOs but also businesses, religious groups, schools, university students, and the media, to name just a few other elements of a robust social effort. These groups will last long after outside reformers leave. They can pressure a government, or change their own societies, from inside, with local knowledge and local legitimacy. And simply by existing, they create a vertical check on the government, or a horizontal check on other powerful societal forces, becoming in and of themselves an important structure to support the rule of law.

A few proven approaches allow the United States to engage in successful bottom-up reform. One is via local organizations with the ability to disburse grant funds or provide local skill-building. Another is through U.S. or international organizations that have a deep, long-term presence on the ground in other countries, such as the Asia Foundation, the International Republican Institute, and the National Democratic Institute. These organizations are far from perfect. But they provide an excellent means for the U.S. government to take tools that are too blunt and to fine-tune them to adapt to the local marketplace. These organizations can take large government expenditures and parcel them into smaller grants that can be absorbed and put to good use by more lithe local organizations. Work can be conducted in the local language. Real reformers can be differentiated from self-interested individuals with good English and the ability to use development buzzwords. Evaluators can share the same local knowledge as those being evaluated. Moreover, these organizations can operate with less need to focus on short-term wins. That gives them the ability to pursue long-term U.S. interests, such as having stable, rule-of-law–based partner countries abroad, while insulating them from short-term government strategy that may require rewarding autocrats or otherwise acting in ways that diminish the U.S. rule-of-law credibility.

4. **The United States should also use strong enmeshment to greater effect and should greatly improve its weak enmeshment techniques.** Diplomats, National Security Council staff, politicians, and aid practitioners should begin thinking of organizations that can be used to enmesh other countries into rule-of-law systems—from NATO to the Community of Democracies. They must then begin using the membership process—the most important moment of leverage—as a way of catalyzing change, rather than treating membership as a diplomatic reward.

   Meanwhile, these same actors need to recognize the inherent weakness of exchange programs in sparking change in political systems and professional cultures inimical to reform. Instead, they can work more strategically to bring civil society actors from different reforming countries together. Often, local activists have more to learn from each other's efforts than they could be taught by Americans or Western Europeans. In the democratization field, organizations such as NDI frequently arrange for reformers from a country that has successfully brought down an autocrat to share lessons learned with those who are struggling to do the same. The United States could try similar activities in the rule-of-law arena. From Sicily to Chicago, Hong Kong to Los Angeles, examples of successful rule-of-law reforms abound. Pairing development practitioners with domestic reformers who have successfully improved their own country's rule-of-law systems is a relatively untried practice that is worth exploring.

5. **Reform does not occur along a steady timeline. It takes place during windows of opportunity. Therefore, the United States must provide more flexible budgets and program structures to take advantage of these moments when they arise.** Small amounts of money provided to savvy local groups at the right time can create much more impact than large amounts provided to U.S. contractors for slow programs focused on rebuilding institutions. Because reform largely involves power structures and cultural norms, it must take advantage of windows of opportunity when a country is in flux and open to change. To make bottom-up efforts effective, U.S. aid should be reformed so that it can be more easily provided to local sources without strings attached. Moreover, local groups should be allowed to disburse the aid in a fast, flexible manner that is in keeping with overall U.S. goals—rather than micromanaging locals through program line items that disable their unique abilities as domestic reformers. Altering the relationship between a state and its citizens is not an easy task. Attempts by Congress or a given administration to push money out the door to show quick results leads to laws passed through diplomacy with no constituency, hastily built Potemkin-like programs that have no sustainability, and activities that can actually undermine the rule of law. Today's U.S. aid programs are hamstrung to ensure accountability—and instead yield a minimal amount of greater assurance,

and an assurance of reduced impact. Metrics of efficiency must be replaced with metrics of efficacy.

6. **The rule of law is an interdependent system—all parts must function for any part to function. Therefore, if it is possible, U.S. government agencies working on different segments of the rule-of-law field within a given country should be streamlined and coordinated.** If police arrest criminals, but these lawbreakers are then released by weak courts, the rule of law fails. If modern business laws are passed and courts deliver sound judgments but plaintiffs are unable to collect on those judgments, the rule of law fails. If the poor have access to trained judges and trusted courts but are terrorized by corrupt police, the rule of law fails. The rule of law is an interdependent system that requires multiple rule-of-law institutions to function, or the entirety of the project fails.

   Thus, the organization of U.S. rule-of-law efforts is particularly problematic. More than two dozen U.S. entities cannot realistically coordinate in any given country. The existence of so many groups with equity in the outcome is part of the reason that America's first-generation rule-of-law programs focus on little more than police reform, or law reform, or court reform, rather than the rule of law as a whole. With so many entities at work, divvying up the field by legal institution is the only way to even attempt to stay out of each other's lanes. However, doing so renders actual reform almost impossible. It is not enough for each of these agencies to simply apply their own ends-based tactics—what is needed is overall strategy, and that requires coordination within countries.

   Where possible, Congress should amend legislation (such as the law barring Section 660 foreign aid from being used for police reform) so that all aspects of rule-of-law reform can come under one broad roof. Ideally, a small number of agencies—such as INL, USAID's Office of Transition Initiatives, and USAID's Democracy and Governance section—would undertake all aspects of rule-of-law reform. This would require creating winners and losers in the U.S. bureaucracy—ICITAP, for instance, would need to be moved from the Department of Justice into INL itself. The Office of

Transition Initiatives and the Democracy and Governance section of USAID could create better ties and coordination to allow a smoother handoff between short-term and long-term activities. The rule-of-law leaders within the Economics and Growth section of USAID would need to move to Democracy and Governance, infusing the importance of strong economies into a more robust understanding of democracy.

Such wholesale reform of the U.S. development bureaucracy is likely to be immensely difficult (a lesson the United States would do well to keep in mind when trying to do the same thing within other countries). If it cannot be accomplished, at least the United States could work toward better coordination of rule-of-law reform at the strategic level and on the ground within each country by setting up interagency teams focused on a problem: the rule of law, rather than their individual sectors such as police or court reform. Such coordination should work not simply to let each agency know what the others are doing, but to help each see the system as a whole and create strategic tactics that work together. The goal would be to view police, courts, lawyers, and laws as aspects of a rule-of-law system that is based in power structures and in culture, and to implement tactics that affect these larger objects of reform, rather than divvying up turf based on unhelpful distinctions between institutions.

7. **Be aware of the dangers of unintended side effects. Follow the Hippocratic oath: First, do no harm.** Using diplomacy to force law reform on a recalcitrant country can lead executives to bypass their parliaments. In countries with small pools of legal talent, a single reform issue can occupy all the best lawyers; the desired reform should be worth the opportunity cost. Bringing in lawyers from varied legal systems to rewrite laws creates a jumble of unused rules that can actually diminish respect for the law in general, and thus weaken the rule of law. Aid itself, when not monitored carefully, can easily lead to corruption—particularly when aid is given to capital-intensive activities such as prison building. In fact, studies have shown that even worse than receiving no aid at all is receiving

volatile and unpredictable influxes of aid that differ widely from year to year.[4] These unintended side effects are so common that they are now seen as simply part of the normal course of events for rule-of-law reform. They should instead be seen as unacceptable.

8. **In choosing more discrete elements for reform, focus on what citizens of the country need and want.** First-generation reform generally chose from a mishmash of standard reform measures. Second-generation reformers realize that success requires local support for reform to overcome inevitable opposition. Instead of choosing goals desired by outsiders and working to build a local support base, it is far simpler and smarter to begin with reforms desired by the local population. Such an approach builds credibility and can create a more successful track record of reform that can enhance support for later, more difficult, reforms. Focusing on what locals actually desire will likely lead to a greater focus on nontraditional and informal methods of dispute resolution that are used, rather than formal systems that are less frequented. It will require in-country knowledge rather than desk work from Washington, D.C. It will also require a different set of actors from abroad, leading us to the next point.

9. **Altering power structures and social norms requires adding anthropologists, sociologists, and political scientists alongside the lawyers and judges currently involved in rule-of-law efforts. It also requires teaching local political context and incentivizing the learning of such context.** Legal professionals have credibility within their professions. That is important to the rule-of-law field. But the rule of law is about far more than institutional reform—and therefore, it needs to augment these lawyers, police, and judges with practitioners who hail from other disciplines. The field should work to hire, and attract, a multidisciplinary base of talent—particularly from fields more accustomed to thinking in terms of power and culture. For all of these practitioners—lawyers, anthropologists, political scientists, and others—greater incentives to understand the local country context, including the politics

and sociology, are needed. These range from offering courses and incentivizing learning, to creating means for longer stints in the field, and greater time spent meeting and learning about the local country rather than filling out forms to meet congressionally mandated reporting requirements that too often get in the way of accomplishing effective work.

10. **As a new approach, second-generation, ends-based rule-of-law reform will require the sort of scholarly critique and investigative effort that is already too limited in first-generation, institution-based reform.** This is the first comprehensive attempt to offer a concept and methodology that should now be criticized and improved upon. Far more is needed. The U.S. military has invited academics to study its counterinsurgency efforts in Afghanistan. It has funded, as well as opened itself, to investigation, hoping to learn from the experience so that it can improve future programs. Too often, rule-of-law evaluations have been rote recitals paid for by implementing agencies to meet evaluation requirements, rather than rigorous scholarly exercises that could shed light on the larger issues in this difficult subject. Nor does the U.S. government bear the greatest responsibility—academics must begin to look beyond the theoretical arguments that make for interesting conversation among tenure boards and instead engage with real problems in the field that call for their talents. A generation of master's degree and doctoral students under the guidance of a handful of serious professors could transform far more than their academic fields—they could immeasurably improve the lives of people in countries throughout the world by illuminating the complex issues involved in governance reform abroad.

It takes courage to implement a new methodology for reform. It takes equal courage to admit that the current system is not working, when billions of U.S. tax dollars have been spent and careers have been invested in practicing the old method. But courage must be found. The rule of law is a crucial component of the foreign policy goals of the United States and many other countries. Rule-of-law reform is needed to pursue development, to improve global security, to bolster nascent democracies. Governments—in the United States and elsewhere in the developed world—owe it to their taxpayers to make rule-of-law programs as effective as possible. And as citizens who share a single planet, the success of these programs is important to our own security, and to the well-being of some of the world's most vulnerable people on earth. For our own good and the good of billions of people who could flourish under rule-of-law–based societies, let us begin.

NOTES

Chapter One

1 Anthony Kennedy, "Judicial Ethics and the Rule of Law," Issues of Democracy, United States Information Services (September 1999), http://usinfo.org/enus/government/branches/kennedy2.html.

2 See Rachel Stohl and E. J. Hogendoorn, "Stopping the Destructive Spread of Small Arms" (Washington, D.C.: Center for American Progress, March 10, 2010), 23–24.

3 David H. Bayley, *Changing the Guard: Developing Democratic Police Abroad* (New York: Oxford University Press, 2006), 109.

4 The General Accounting Office changed its name to Government Accountability Office in 2004.

5 U.S. General Accounting Office, "Foreign Assistance: U.S. Democracy Programs in Six Latin American Countries Have Yielded Modest Results" (Washington, D.C.: GAO, 2003); U.S. General Accounting Office, "Former Soviet Union: U.S. Rule of Law Assistance Has Had Limited Impact" (Washington, D.C.: GAO, 2001).

6 Wade Channell, "Grammar Lessons Learned: Dependent Clauses, False Cognates, and Other Problems in Rule of Law Programming," *University of Pittsburgh Law Review* 72(2) (Winter 2010): 171, citing Jan Stromsem et al., *Africa Regional Rule of Law Status Review* 15 (2007), http://pdf.usaid.gov/pdf_docs/PNADO804.pdf.

7 Channell, 172.

8 There are, of course, dozens of ways to classify definitions of the rule of law, depending on the purpose the definition is meant to serve, or what divisions it is intended to clarify. Brian Tamanaha divides the concept between pre-liberal and liberal ends; others divide it through formalist and substantivist definitions, or proceduralist and substantivist modes. I have chosen the following means of definition as best illuminating, I hope, the dilemmas faced by the rule-of-law building project. For a fuller discussion, see Rachel Kleinfeld, "Competing Definitions of the Rule of Law," in *Promoting the Rule of Law Abroad: In Search of Knowledge*, edited by Thomas Carothers (Washington, D.C.: Carnegie Endowment for International Peace, 2006), 31–73.

9 For more on this institutional isomorphism, see Federica Bicchi, "'Our Size Fits All': Normative Power Europe and the Mediterranean," *Journal of European Public Policy* 13(2), (2006): 286–303. Paul J. DiMaggio and Walter W. Powell, "The Iron Cage Revisited: Institutional Isomorphism and Collective Rationality in Organizational Fields," in *The New Institutionalism in Organizational Analysis*, edited by W. W. Powell and P. J. DiMaggio (Chicago, London: University of Chicago Press, 1991).

10 General Accounting Office, "Foreign Assistance: Rule of Law Funding Worldwide for Fiscal Years 1993–98," GAO/NSIAD-99–158 (Washington, D.C.: GAO, June 30, 1999), fn 1.

11 Stephen Golub, "A House Without a Foundation," in Carothers, ed., *Promoting the Rule of Law Abroad*, 108–19.

12 Dimitry Kochenov, "Behind the Copenhagen Facade: The Meaning and Structure of the Copenhagen Political Criterion of Democracy and the Rule of Law," *European Integration online papers (EioP)* 8(10), 2004, 20, http://eiop.or.at/eiop/texte/2004-010a.htm.

13 "Legal and Judicial Reform: Observations, Experiences, and Approach of the Legal Vice Presidency" (Washington, D.C.: World Bank, 2002), 65.

14 J. Clark, "Building on Quicksand: The Collapse of the World Bank's Judicial Reform Project in Peru" (Washington, D.C.: Human Rights First, April 2000).

15 See Mitchell A. Seligson and Siddhartha Baviskar, "Corruption in Albania: Report of Comparisons Between 2004 and 2005 Surveys," Casals and Associates, USAID, March 31, 2006, 73, 76.

16 Will Englund, "In Moscow, Biden Gets Specific on Corruption," *Washington Post*, March 10, 2011.

17 Aristotle, *Politics*, III, 15, 1286a-16, 1287a.; J. Barnes, ed., *The Complete Works of Aristotle* (Princeton, Princeton University Press, 1995).

18 See, for instance, John Locke, *Two Treatises of Government*, edited by Peter Laslett (New York: Cambridge University Press, 1994), 9:131, 353.

19 See A. V. Dicey, *Introduction to the Study of the Law of the Constitution* (London: Macmillan, 1885), 175–84.

20 Friedrich Hayek, *The Road to Serfdom* (Chicago: University of Chicago Press, 1944), 80.

21 See Judith Shklar, *Ordinary Vices* (Cambridge: Harvard University Press, 1984), and Judith Shklar, "The Liberalism of Fear," in *Political Thought and Political Thinkers*, edited by Stanley Hoffmann (Chicago: University of Chicago Press, 1998); and Fareed Zakaria, *The Future of Freedom: Illiberal Democracy at Home and Abroad* (New York: W. W. Norton, 2003).

22 Locke, "Treatise II," 131, 353.

23 Channell, 174.

24 Cargo cults are a Melanesian religious movement that skyrocketed during WWII, when Allied planes began to appear in the South Pacific. "Cargo Cult," *The Columbia Encyclopedia*, sixth ed. (2001), www.bartleby.com/65/ca/cargocul.html.

25 This work is being mainstreamed through documents such as "How-To Note: Political Economy Assessments at Sector and Project Levels," World Bank, March 2011; "Tools for Institutional, Political and Social Analysis of Policy Reform: A Sourcebook for Development Practitioners," Social Development Department, World Bank, 2007; "The Political Economy of Policy Reform: Issues and Implications for Policy Dialogue and Development Operations," Social Development Department, World Bank, 2008.

26 "Reforming Public Institutions and Strengthening Governance: A World Bank Strategy," Public Sector Group, Poverty Reduction and Economic Management Network, World Bank, November 2000, 11, 17, 33.

27 Eli Moen and Stein Sundstol Eriksen, "Political Economy Analysis with a Legitimacy Twist," Norwegian Agency for Development Cooperation, December 2010; Tom Dahl-Ostergaard et al., "Lessons Learned on the Use of Power and Drivers of Change Analyses in Development Co-operation," OECD DAC Network on Governance, September 2005; Department for International Development. Political Economy Analysis, How-To Note, DFID Practice Paper, July 2009.

28 Sue Unsworth, "What's Politics Got to Do with It? Why Donors Find It So Hard to Come to Terms with Politics, and Why This Matters," *Journal of International Development* 21:6 (August 2009): 883–94; Verena Fritz, Kai Kaiser,

and Brian Levy, "Problem-Driven Governance and Political Economy Analysis: Good Practice Framework," World Bank, September 2009.

29 Sue Unsworth, "Is Political Analysis Changing Donor Behavior?" Unpublished paper prepared for the Conference of the Development Studies Association, London, September 29, 2008.

30 Thomas Carothers, "The Rule-of-Law Revival," in Carothers, ed., *Promoting the Rule of Law Abroad*, 3–13.

31 See Center for Democracy and Governance, "Democracy and Governance: A Conceptual Framework," Dan Turello, ed., PN-ACD-395 (Washington, D.C.: USAID, November 1998), 7.

32 Madeline Albright, "Statement on the Rule of Law," New York, September 19, 2000, http://secretary.state.gov/www/statements/2000/000919.html.

33 Peter Slevin, "Powell Decries Putin's Policies," *Washington Post*, January 26, 2004.

34 Channell, 175.

35 GAO 1999, 36–37.

36 See GAO 1999, 5, which shows spending of $970 million for the years 1993–1998 alone. For recent figures, see Bayley 32–33; both tables together demonstrate the programs counted as rule of law reform. These numbers do not count the totality of Support for East European Democracy (SEED) program funding, which would add $400,000, or the Department of Defense's exchange program for foreign militaries known as IMET, for International Military Education and Training. Nor does it count all of the vast spending by DoD on rule of law programs in Afghanistan and Iraq, both of which have grown significantly since these data were collected in 2008.

37 Contractors are independent entities, of course, though from a funding standpoint, they can look more like arms of the U.S. government. According to its Securities and Exchange Commission disclosure reports in 2010, DynCorp International, which has built a profitable business working on everything from police training in Iraq to judicial programs in Eastern Europe, received "substantially all of our revenue from contracts or subcontracts with the US Government and its agencies." DynCorp International Form 10K annual report for the Securities and Exchange Commission, p. 17. The disclosure also lists all major current contracts, all of which are with the U.S. government, p. 14.

38 David Steinberg and C. P. F. Luhulima, "On Democracy; Strengthening Legislative, Legal, Press Institutions and Polling in Indonesia," Final Evaluation, USAID Grants 497-0336-G-SS-0041, 497-0364-G-SS-1089, and 497-0364-G-SS-2091, January 5, 1994.

39 In 1989, the U.S. Congress passed the Support for East European Democracy Act, Public Law 101–179 (augmented in 1992 with the Freedom Support Act, Public Law 102–511), which created an Office of the Coordinator of U.S. Assistance to Europe and Eurasia within the State Department to coordinate all aid within the former Soviet Union. No similar department was created to do the same in other regions of the world.

40 In some countries the local embassy controls the process; in others, Washington has the final word. Personal relationships tend to determine how much USAID is consulted. The process for creating these strategies changes every few years, and the strategies themselves have only a loose relationship to funding amounts, given how much money flows through agencies outside the State Department.

41 GAO 1999, 5.

42 David H. Bayley, *Changing the Guard: Developing Democratic Police Abroad* (New York: Oxford University Press, 2006), 43.

43 "Strengthening and Coordinating United Nations Rule of Law Activities," Report of the Secretary-General, August 6, 2008, United Nations, A/63/226, 4. "Strengthening and Coordinating United Nations Rule of Law Activities," Report of the Secretary-General, August 20, 2010, United Nations, A/65/318, 3.

44 United Nations 2008, 16.

45 David Trubek, "The 'Rule of Law' in Development Assistance: Past, Present, and Future," Occasional Papers, CALE, September 2004, 1; and "Initiatives in Justice Reform, 2009," Legal Vice Presidency of the World Bank, 2009, 3.

46 "Initiatives in Justice Reform, 2009," 1.

47 Japan International Cooperation Agency website, www.jica.go.jp/english/operations/thematic_issues/governance/activity.html.

48 "Statistics on International Development 2005/06–2009/10," UK National Statistics, October 2010, Annex 2.

49 See Thomas Carothers, "Democracy, State and AID: A Tale of Two Cultures," *Foreign Service Journal,* (February 2001), 23, available at www.carnegie.ru/publications/?fa=631. We're not alone; the EU has a similar cultural separation between its Commission, Council, and Parliament, and EuropeAid.

50 United Nations Office on Drugs and Crime, "Global Study on Homicide," October 2011.

51 Meanwhile, a book on the unique issues of operating within the few post-conflict states already exists: Jane Stromseth, David Wippman, and Rosa Brooks, *Can Might Make Rights? Building the Rule of Law After Military Interventions* (New York: Cambridge University Press, 2006).

52 There is a growing literature on the interaction between international actors and domestic reform, most of it centered around democratization. For an overview, see Geoffrey Pridham, "International Influences and Democratic Transition: Problems of Theory and Practice in Linkage Politics," in *Encouraging Democracy: The International Context of Regime Transition in Southern Europe*, edited by Geoffrey Pridham (Leicester: Leicester University Press, 1991), 1–30. See also, Laurence Whitehead, "Democracy by Convergence: Southern Europe," in *The International Dimensions of Democratization: Europe and the Americas*, expanded edition, edited by Laurence Whitehead (New York: Oxford University Press, 2001).

53 Benjamin L. Crosby, "Organizational Dimensions to the Implementation of Policy Change," USAID, Implementing Policy Change Project, Monograph no. 2, September 1996, 2. Marc M. Lindenberg and Noel Ramirez, *Managing Adjustment in Development Countries* (San Francisco: International Center for Economic Growth), 1989.

54 Archimedes, quoted by Pappus of Alexandria in "Collection" (*Synagoge*, Book VIII, c. AD 340, edited by Hultsch, Berlin: 1878), 1060.

Chapter Two

1 See J. R. R. Tolkien, *The Hobbit* (New York: Houghton Mifflin, 1997); and the *Lord of the Rings* trilogy.

2 General Accounting Office, "Foreign Assistance: Meeting the Training Needs of Police in New Democracies," GAO NSIAD-93-109 (Washington, D.C.: GAO, April 1993), 5.

3 Thomas Carothers, "The Rule-of-Law Revival," in *Promoting the Rule of Law Abroad: In Search of Knowledge*, edited by Thomas Carothers (Washington, D.C.: Carnegie Endowment for International Peace, 2006), 13.

4 Robert M. Perito, *Where Is the Lone Ranger When We Need Him? America's Search for a Postconflict Stability Force* (Washington, D.C.: U.S. Institute of Peace Press, 2004), 52–60.

5 General Accounting Office, "Foreign Aid: Police Training and Assistance," GAO NSIAD 92–118 (Washington, D.C.: GAO, March 1992), 1.

6 While the security concern was focused on America, it coincided with domestic security concerns felt by local Latin American governments and business elites. Thus, while not rule of law reform, it was actually more "demand" focused than many later rule of law reforms.

7 United States Foreign Assistance Act, December 1974, Public Law 93-559, Section 660.

8 For instance, the World Bank's comprehensive survey of 20,000 poor men and women worldwide found security to be a major, and growing, concern. Deepa Narayan, et al., *Voices of the Poor: Crying Out for Change* (New York: Oxford University Press published for the World Bank, 2000), 151–77.

9 United States International Security and Development Assistance Authorizations Act of 1983, Public Law 98–151.

10 United States International Security and Development Cooperation Act of 1985, Public Law 99–183. This act has been periodically updated, and greater allowances were made for broader training as time went on.

11 GAO, 1992, 8. See also United States International Security and Development Cooperation Act of 1981, Public Law 97–113.

12 GAO, 1992, 8–9. While EU strategy sounds more organized, its procurement and implementation systems are so slow and cumbersome that it has its own problems.

13 GAO, 1992, 9. Assistance was stopped after fiscal year 1987.

14 Public Law 98–151.

15 GAO, 1992, 8–9.

16 Bayley cites a host of studies supporting this finding. See David H. Bayley, *Changing the Guard: Developing Democratic Police Abroad* (New York: Oxford University Press, 2006), 65.

17 DoD training was allowed in fiscal years 1986 and 1987 for pinpoint trainings only in El Salvador and Honduras, and then that, too, was curtailed.

18 U.S. Department of Justice, International Criminal Investigative Training Assistance Program, "About ICITAP," United States Department of Justice, http://www.justice.gov/criminal/icitap/about/.

19 GAO, 1992, 1. However, because ICITAP early on was a small, largely academic program, most of this activity remained grounded in the traditional security paradigm, rather than the emerging rule-of-law conception of security.

20 United States Urgent Assistance for Democracy in Panama Act of 1990, Public Law 101–243.

21 GAO, 1992, 14.

22 For a description of the growth of this thinking in the Clinton administration, see Matthew Spence, "The Impact of American Democracy Promotion in

Post-Soviet Russia, Ukraine, and Kyrgyzstan, 1991–2003," (Unpublished D. Phil. dissertation, Oxford University, 2004).

23 United States White House, International Crime Control Strategy, "Foster International Cooperation and the Rule of Law," June 1998, www.fas.org/irp/offdocs/iccs/iccsi.html.

24 Ralf Mutschke, Assistant Director, Criminal Intelligence Directorate, International Criminal Police Organization (Interpol General Secretariat), "The Threat Posed by the Convergence of Organized Crime, Drugs Trafficking and Terrorism" (Written Testimony, U.S. House Committee on the Judiciary Subcommittee on Crime, December 13, 2000); Bill Gertz, "Hijackers Connected to Albanian Terrorist Cell," *Washington Times*, September 18, 2001.

25 USAID, "Albania Revised Strategic Plan FY 2001–2004," PD-ABS-947, December 2000, 7.

26 For more on this history, see James Gardner, *Legal Imperialism: American Lawyers and Foreign Aid in Latin America* (Madison: University of Wisconsin Press, 1980).

27 See David Trubek and Marc Galanter, "Scholars in Self-Estrangement," *Wisconsin Law Review* (1974): 1065, 1074; and John Henry Merryman, "Comparative Law and Social Change: On the Origins, Style, Decline & Revival of the Law and Development Movement," *American Journal of Comparative Law* 25: 3 (1977): 457–89.

28 William Douglas, "Lawyers of the Peace Corps," *American Bar Association Journal* 48:10 (1962): 909, 913.

29 Trubek and Galanter; Merryman.

30 A. David Adesnik, "Reagan's 'Democratic Crusade': Presidential Rhetoric and the Remaking of American Foreign Policy" (D. Phil. dissertation, Oxford University, 2005).

31 General Accounting Office, "Foreign Assistance: Promoting Judicial Reform to Strengthen Democracies," GAO/NSIAD-93-149 (Washington, D.C.: GAO, 1993), 14.

32 GAO, "Promoting," 1993. Accusatorial systems also tend to follow the rule that defendants are innocent until proven guilty, while inquisitorial systems in which the judge acts as both decider and investigator often presume guilt.

33 Joel Migdal, *Strong Societies, Weak States* (Princeton: Princeton University Press, 1988).

34 For a history of aid theories and attempts, see William Easterly, *The Elusive Quest for Growth* (Boston: MIT Press, 2001).

35 See John Williamson, "Development and the 'Washington Consensus,'" in *World Development* 21 (1993): 1239–1336; and *World Development Report 1991: The Challenge of Development* (Washington, D.C.: World Bank, 1991), http://wdronline.worldbank.org/worldbank/a/c.html/world_development_report_1991/front_matter/WB.0-1952-0868-4.frontmatter.

36 The debate on aid raged through anecdotal reports and newspaper accounts for more than a decade, bolstered by a series of studies, culminating in Craig Burnside and David Dollar, "Aid, Policies, and Growth," Policy Research Working Paper 1777, World Bank, 1997, which found that there was essentially no association between aid and improvements in development indicators. See Henrik Hansen and Finn Tarp, "Aid Effectiveness Disputed," and Ravi Kanbur, "Aid, Conditionality, and Debt in Africa," in *Foreign Aid and Development: Lessons Learnt and Directions for the Future*, edited by Finn Tarp (London: Routledge, 2000), 103–28 and 409–22, for a taste of this debate.

37 Douglass North, *Institutions, Institutional Change, and Economic Performance* (Cambridge: Cambridge University Press, 1990), 92–104. See also Paul Milgrom, et al., "The Role of Institutions in the Revival of Trade," *Economics and Politics* 2:1 (1990): 1–23. North drew on an earlier tradition, as Hobbes first linked the inability to enforce contracts with a lack of market development: Thomas Hobbes [1651] *Leviathan* (New York: Collier Books, 1962), while justice systems' link to capitalism and growth was also noted by Max Weber and Adam Smith. See Richard E. Messick, "Judicial Reform and Economic Development," *World Bank Research Observer* 14, no. 1 (February 1999).

38 Hernando de Soto, *The Other Path: The Economic Answer to Terrorism* (New York: Harper & Row, 1989).

39 The good governance paradigm began in the Africa section of the World Bank, in papers such as "Sub-Saharan Africa: From Crisis to Sustainable Growth" (Washington, D.C.: World Bank, 1989), and was cemented as common wisdom by Daniel Kaufmann, et al., "Governance Matters," Policy Research Working Paper 2196, World Bank, October 1999. The growth of the rule of law within the good governance agenda is traced in Ibrahim Shihata, "Good Governance and the Role of Law in Economic Development," in *Making Development Work: Legislative Reform for Institutional Transformation and Good Governance*, edited by Ann Seidman et al. (Germany: Kluwer Law International, 1999), XVII.

40 Author's interview with Robert Picciotto, former director of the Operations Evaluation Department of the World Bank, December 2003.

41 See Wade Channell, "Lessons Not Learned about Legal Reform," in Carothers, ed., *Promoting the Rule of Law Abroad*, 137–60, for descriptions of law and court reform. For police reform to improve economies, see D. H. Wulf, *Security Sector*

Reform in Developing Countries (Bonn: GTZ, 2000), www.ssrnetwork.net/document_library/detail/3214/security-sector-reform-in-developing-countries-an-analysis-of-the-international-debate; Michael Ignatieff, "Nation-Building Lite," *New York Times Magazine*, July 28, 2002, 22 ff.

42 Alan Greenspan, "Market Economies and Rule of Law," Remarks delivered to the Financial Markets Conference of the Federal Reserve Bank of Atlanta, Sea Island, Georgia, April 4, 2003, www.federalreserve.gov/BoardDocs/Speeches/2003/20030404/default.htm.

43 "Rule of Law," USAID Democracy and Governance website, www.usaid.gov/our_work/democracy_and_governance/technical_areas/rule_of_law.

44 USAID's Economic Growth section would undertake reforms generally described as "commercial law reform" rather than "rule-of-law reform," an issue discussed later in this chapter.

45 See Frank Upham, "Mythmaking in the Rule-of-Law Orthodoxy," in Carothers, ed., *Promoting the Rule of Law Abroad*, 75–104.

46 Arjan de Haan and Max Everest-Phillips, "Can New Aid Modalities Handle Politics?" United Nations University Research Paper no. 2007/63, October 2007, 8.

47 European Parliament, "Cooperation in the Area of Justice and Home Affairs in the Enlargement Process," Briefing no. 25 (March 30, 1990): 5–6.

48 Malcolm Anderson, Monica den Boer, and Gary Miller, "European Citizenship and Cooperation in Justice and Home Affairs," in *Maastricht and Beyond: Building the European Union*, edited by Andrew Duff, John Pinder, and Roy Price (London: Routledge, 1996), 112, 115; Jackie Gower, "EC Relations with Central and Eastern Europe," in *The European Community and the Challenge of the Future*, edited by Juliet Lodge, second edition (London: Pinter, 1993), 289.

49 Peter Van Ham, *The EC, Eastern Europe, and European Unity: Discord, Collaboration and Integration Since 1947* (London: Pinter, 1995), 183.

50 "A Survey of European Union Enlargement," *Economist*, May 19, 2001, 5.

51 In the early 1990s, a growing literature supported the idea of enlargement as a means of security; see, for instance, Jack Snyder, "Averting Anarchy in the New Europe," *International Security* 14:4 (1990): 5–41.

52 Monica den Boer and William Wallace, "Justice and Home Affairs," in *Policy-Making in the European Union*, edited by Helen Wallace and William Wallace, fourth edition (Oxford: Oxford UP, 2000), 493–522; Wallace, 496; Enzo R. Grilli, *The European Community and the Developing Countries* (Cambridge: Cambridge UP, 1994), 211–13.

53 European Parliament, *Cooperating in the Area of Justice and Home Affairs in the Enlargement Process*, Briefing no. 25, March 30, 1990, 4–5; Wallace, 494.

54 European Commission, "Agenda 2000: For a Stronger and Wider Union," DOC 97/6, Strasbourg, July 15, 1997, 39.

55 European Commission, "A New Partnership With South East Asia," Communication from the Commission, COM (2003) 399/4, http://eeas.europa.eu/library/publications/2004_seasia_en.pdf 12.

56 See Matthew Stephenson, "A Trojan Horse in China?" in Carothers, ed., *Promoting the Rule of Law Abroad*, 196–97, citing Secretary of State Madeleine K. Albright, "Remarks to U.S. Business Representatives," Sheraton International Club, Beijing, April 30, 1998; Interview by Bob Schieffer with Secretary of State Madeleine K. Albright, "Face the Nation," CBS, June 28, 1998.

57 Laure-Hélène Piron, "Review of the UNDP Rule of Law and Security Programme Somalia, 2004–2005," Overseas Development Institute, 2005.

58 Bruce M. Wilson and Roger Handberg, "Opening Pandora's Box: The Unanticipated Political Consequences of Costa Rican Legal Reform," Paper presented at the Midwest Political Science Association, Palmer House Hilton, Chicago, Ill., April 23–25, 1998. See also Bert Hoffmann, "Why Reform Fails: The 'Politics of Policies' in Costa Rican Telecommunications Liberalization," *European Review of Latin American and Caribbean Studies*, 84, April 2008, 3–19.

59 Thomas Carothers, "The Many Agendas of Rule of Law Reform in Latin America," in *Rule of Law in Latin America*, edited by Pilar Domingo and Rachel Sieder (London: Institute of Latin American Studies, 2001), 14.

Chapter Three

1 For a fascinating, if controversial, discussion, see Antony Anghie, *Imperialism, Sovereignty, and the Making of International Law* (Cambridge: Cambridge University Press, 2005).

2 It is not only the United States that is guilty: For instance, in 2001, the EU held up opening two chapters of its *acquis communautaire* that were necessary for Romania to join the Union. EU lawyers had lobbied Brussels to strong-arm Romania into overturning a law that forced foreign law firms to partner with Romanians if they wished to do business locally, and the EU refused to continue the progression toward accession until Romania complied. No one expects the EU to try something similar in China, despite its far more stringent laws on partnership. European Commission, "2001 Regular Report on Romania's Progress Towards Accession," SEC (2001) 1753, Brussels, November 13, 2001, 8, mentions

the problematic law at the report's beginning, a highly unusual occurrence in these reports; and the author's interview with Aurel Ciobanu-Dordea, pre-accession adviser, EU delegation; former chief negotiator, Romanian Department of EU Accession; former government agent for the European Court at Strasbourg; Bucharest, September 19, 2001, and September 21, 2001, provided a firsthand account of the threat to not open two *acquis* chapters.

3 "The People Come to Court," *Economist*, March 4, 2004; Roland Buerk, "Japan Urged to End 'False Confessions,'" BBC News, October 5, 2009.

4 See Ann Wise, "The Mafia Is Italy's Biggest Business," ABC News, Rome, November 12, 2008.

5 International Crisis Group, "Albania: State of the Nation," Balkans Report no. 87, March 1, 2000, 20.

6 For the classic model of postcolonial exploitation of the "periphery" by the "core," see Immanuel Wallerstein, *The Modern World-System*, vol. 1 (New York: Academic Press, 1974). James Rosenau's penetrated state theory, first articulated in *Linkage Politics* (New York: Free Press, 1969), began the attempt to understand the more complex, porous nature of sovereignty in "penetrated" states.

7 For a summary of the seminal studies that prove this finding, see "Ownership—What Money Cannot Buy," in *Assessing Aid: What Works, What Doesn't, and Why* (Washington, D.C.: World Bank, November 1998), 50–53.

8 This split personality is not unique to America. In the EU, for instance, the 2000 Cotonou Agreement, which governs the relationship between the EU and ACP (African, Caribbean, and Pacific) states, stresses a "participatory approach," claiming that the EU no longer imposes unilateral development policies but formulates goals with the developing country. Yet Cotonou simultaneously introduced political conditionality: All "ownership" takes place under the threat of aid suspension for countries that violate the "democracy, rule-of-law, and human rights" criteria. See Martin Holland, *The European Union and the Third World* (Basingstoke: Palgrave, 2002). See also Geographical Partnerships, "Overview of the Agreement 2000," December 2008, http://ec.europa.eu/development/geographical/cotonou/cotonou2000_3_en.cfm#Heading4.

9 William Wise, "Indonesia's War on Terror," U.S.-Indonesia Society, August 2005, 25–26.

10 Wise, 30.

11 Megawati was the last president to be chosen by parliament, not by popular vote. Her parliamentary base was narrow, and she owed her presidency to the support of Islamist parties. She did begin to act after the Bali bombings—but even then was accused by these Islamist parties of pandering to foreign pressure.

12 Susilo Bambang Yudhoyono, the next president, had a preexisting interest in rooting out terror, since his days as minister of political and security affairs. After a string of bombings had decimated the country's tourist sector, Yudhoyono was able to act not from U.S. pressure, but from the obvious economic impact that terrorism was having on Indonesia's weak economy—and the strong public mandate to rebuild that economy.

13 See Abram Chayes and Antonia Handler Chayes, *The New Sovereignty* (Cambridge, Mass.: Harvard University Press, 1995); and the findings in Milada Vachudova, "The Leverage of International Institutions on Democratizing States," European Forum Series 33, Florence: European University Institute, 2001.

14 See Wade Channell, "Urgency and Legitimacy: Tension in Rebuilding the Legal Structure for Business in Post-Conflict Countries," Center for International Private Enterprise, Economic Reform, July 30, 2010. www.cipe.org/publications/fs/pdf/073010.pdf.

15 David Mednicoff, "Middle East Dilemmas," in *Promoting the Rule of Law Abroad: In Search of Knowledge*, edited by Thomas Carothers (Washington, D.C.: Carnegie Endowment for International Peace, 2006), 263, discusses the strangeness of these ideas in the Middle East. Author's interview with Professor Hikmahanto Juwana, dean of the Faculty of Law, University of Indonesia, in which he cited the difficulty Balinese artists had with seeing copying, long viewed as a compliment, as a legal infraction; Jakarta, July 7, 2003.

16 Gustavo Gozzi, "Rechtsstaat and Individual Rights in German Constitutional History," in *The Rule of Law: History, Theory, and Criticism*, edited by Pietro Costa and Danilo Zolo (The Netherlands: Springer, 2007), 237–59, and Alain Laquièze, "État de Droit and National Sovereignty in France," in Costa and Zolo, *The Rule of Law*, 261–91.

17 Emily Wax, "Ethiopian Rape Victim Pits Law Against Culture," *Washington Post*, June 7, 2004, A1.

18 "Darfur at a Crossroads: Global Public Opinion and the Responsibility to Protect," event transcript, Brookings Institution, Washington D.C., April 5, 2007, 5. Survey conducted by worldpublicopinion.org in conjunction with the Chicago Council on Global Affairs.

19 Commodore Perry anchored with four steamships at Edo (present-day Tokyo), Japan, in July 1853, to open Japanese ports to U.S. trade and to gain docking rights for U.S. ships. After nearly nine months, he negotiated the first treaty opening Japanese trade to the West. While Perry did not fire a shot, the presence of the military steamships, unknown in Japan, was a powerful bargaining chip.

20 Juwana interview.

21 For an account of EU assertiveness of its own identity in the Middle East, see Richard Youngs, "Transatlantic Cooperation on Middle East Reform: A European Misjudgement?" 2004 (draft memo prepared for the Center on Democracy, Development, and Rule of Law Conference, Stanford University, October 4–5, 2004).

22 European Commission, "TACIS Regional Strategy 2004–2006," Section 4.2.

23 Laure-Hélène Piron, "Rwanda Justice Mission," Overseas Development Institute, 2003.

24 See "Voices of the Poor" study, Poverty Reduction and Management, World Bank, 2000: http://web.worldbank.org/WBSITE/EXTERNAL/TOPICS/EXTPOVERTY/0,,contentMDK:20622514~menuPK:336998~pagePK:148956~piPK:216618~theSitePK:336992,00.html.

25 The problem is often one of divvying up a small economic pie, rather than growing the pie as a whole. Locals who see that prisoners in foreign-built prisons are living with a more consistent supply of heat, electricity, and water than the rest of the population can become cynical about rule of law reform efforts. People accustomed to the extreme order of authoritarian and communist regimes can be particularly troubled by crime and feel that the West is being callous or soft by its choice of reforms. See Laurence Whitehead, "Institutional Design and Accountability in Latin America" (paper presented at the Carter Center, Atlanta, Georgia, October 16–18, 2000), 13–14.

26 Ioannis Michaletos and Stavros Markos, "Security and Politics in Albania: A Limitation of Civil Liberties?" Balkanalysis.com, March 25, 2007, www.balkanalysis.com/2007/03/25/security-and-politics-in-albania-a-limitation-of-civil-liberties.

27 See Michaletos and Markos. It is also only fair to say that these laws were far more sweeping than foreign audiences had desired. Moreover, U.S. leverage is quite slight in Albania. America is far away—Albania's future is clearly with the EU—and the United States is only Albania's seventeenth-largest trading partner, while it stands behind Italy, Greece, and most multinational aid bodies as a donor. Moreover, Albania was among the first countries to contribute troops to combat in Iraq and Afghanistan, repaying any favors it might have owed America. However, Albania has always liked America. Albanians credit Woodrow Wilson with protecting their sovereignty after World War I and praise NATO for saving their countrymen in Kosovo. Almost a seventh of their population lives in America. In 2007, Albanians gave visiting President George W. Bush a hero's welcome. Their own feelings are more likely to have affected this decision than any U.S. diplomacy. See aid tables and U.S. Department of State, "Background Note: Albania," Bureau of European and Eurasian Affairs, www.state.gov/r/pa/ei/bgn/3235.htm.

28 See Douglass North, *Institutions, Institutional Change, and Economic Performance* (Cambridge: Cambridge University Press, 1990), 92–104. See also Seymour Martin Lipset, "Some Social Requisites of Democracy," *American Political Science Review* 53:1 (1959): 69–105; Seymour Martin Lipset, *Political Man: The Social Bases of Politics* (Garden City, N.J.: Doubleday, 1960); and Samuel Huntington, *Political Order in Changing Societies* (New Haven, Conn.: Yale University Press, 1968). Huntington believes culture can change but generally only through cataclysmic events such as war.

29 Daniel Treisman, "The Causes of Corruption: A Cross-National Study," *Journal of Public Economics* 76:3 (2000): 402. Edward Banfield, *The Moral Basis of a Backward Society* (Chicago: Free Press, 1958), 85. Ironically, Douglass North, the new institutional economist who catalyzed the rule-of-law field, also leaned toward this view.

30 A. E. Dick Howard, "Constitutionalism and the Rule of Law in Central and Eastern Europe" (paper for the Conference on Challenges to European Stability, S'Agaro, Spain, September 2000).

31 Treisman, 401.

Chapter Four

1 Enzo lo Dato, "Palermo's Cultural Revolution and the Renewal Project of the City Administration," *Trends in Organized Crime* 5:3 (2000): 12.

2 Such as the large literature on whether civil or common law is more conducive to the rule of law, or ongoing debate over the most effective form of constitutional court.

3 Wade Channell, "Grammar Lessons Learned: Dependent Clauses, False Cognates, and Other Problems in Rule of Law Programming," *University of Pittsburgh Law Review* 72:2, Winter 2010, 145.

4 John Henry Merryman, "Comparative Law and Social Change: On the Origins, Style, Decline and Revival of the Law and Development Movement," *American Journal of Comparative Law* 25:3 (1977): 462; David Trubek and Marc Galanter, "Scholars in Self-Estrangement," *Wisconsin Law Review* (1974): 1072, 1079.

5 For discussions of these efforts, see John Dower, *Embracing Defeat: Japan in the Wake of World War II* (New York: Norton, 2000); Carl Friedrich, *The Impact of American Constitutionalism Abroad* (Boston: Boston University Press, 1967); Ivo Duchacek, *Rights and Liberties in the World Today: Constitutional Promise and Reality* (Santa Barbara, Calif.: Clio Press, 1973); Edward McWhinney, *Federal Constitution-Making for a Multinational World* (Leyden: A.W. Sitjhalf, 1966); and

Charles Howard McIlwain, *Constitutionalism: Ancient and Modern* (Ithaca, N.Y.: Cornell University Press, 1947). In Eastern Europe, see *Constitutional Reform and International Law in Central and Eastern Europe*, edited by Rein Mullerson et al. (London: Brill, 1998).

6 Giovanni Sartori, *Comparative Constitutional Engineering* (New York: New York University Press, 1994). See also Donald P. Kommers' review of András Sajó, "Limiting Government—An Introduction to Constitutionalism," in *East European Constitutional Review* 9:1/2 (2000), www.law.nyu.edu/eecr/vol9num_onehalf/reviews/limiting.html.

7 See, for instance, Scott Mainwaring and Matthew Soberg Shugart, "Juan Linz, Presidentialism, and Democracy—A Critical Appraisal," *Journal of Comparative Politics* 29:4 (1997); Alfred Stepan and Cindy Skach, "Constitutional Frameworks and Democratic Consolidation: Parliamentarism and Presidentialism," *World Politics* 46 (1993): 1–22; and Douglas Greenberg et al., eds., *Constitutionalism and Democracy: Transitions in the Contemporary World* (Oxford: Oxford University Press, 1993).

8 Walter F. Murphy, "Constitutions, Constitutionalism, and Democracy," in Greenberg et al., eds., 7.

9 James Madison, speech of June 8, 1789, 1 *Annals of Congress* 440ff; quoted in Murphy, 7.

10 Murphy, 7.

11 Such views have been held for centuries, such as in the Thibaut-Von Savigny debate in the early 1800s in which Thibaut saw codifying German law along French lines as a way of achieving various social objectives. See Merryman, 462.

12 See Douglass North, *Institutions, Institutional Change, and Economic Performance* (Cambridge: Cambridge University Press, 1990); Douglass North and Robert Paul Thomas, *The Rise of the Western World* (Cambridge: Cambridge University Press, 1973); and Mancur Olson, "Dictatorship, Democracy, and Development," *American Political Science Review* 87:3 (1993): 567–76. Olson also sees courts arising to protect democracy itself.

13 See Jeffrey Sachs, "Understanding 'Shock Therapy,'" Occasional Paper no. 7 (London: Social Market Foundation, 1994).

14 For more on the "Trojan horse" theory, see Matthew Stephenson, "A Trojan Horse Behind Chinese Walls?: Problems and Prospects of US-Sponsored 'Rule of Law' Reform Projects in the People's Republic of China," Center for International Development Working Paper no. 47, May 2000. Carol Rose, "The 'New' Law and Development Movement in the Post–Cold War Era: A Vietnam Case Study," *Law and Society Review* 32:1 (1998): 93–139. As Stephenson writes, "I know of

no theoretical work that gives a solid foundation to this hypothesis," though both Rose and Stephenson have noted how in Vietnam and China, the government works to corral rule-of-law reforms to the commercial sphere, while reformers hope that they will snowball into human and civil rights.

15 Guido de Ruggiero, *The History of European Liberalism* (Boston: Beacon Press, 1959), 25.

16 Armin Hoeland, "The Evolution of Law in Eastern and Central Europe," in *European Legal Cultures*, edited by Volkmar Gessner et al. (Aldershot, U.K.: Dartmouth, 1996), 482–84.

17 Quoted in Robert Sharlet, "Legal Transplants and Political Mutations: The Reception of Constitutional Law in Russia and the Newly Independent States," *East European Constitutional Review* 7:4 (1998), www1.law.nyu.edu/eecr/vol-7num4/107.html, 118.

18 Channell, 141.

19 Julio Faundez, "Legal Reform in Developing and Transition Countries—Making Haste Slowly," *Law, Social Justice and Global Development Journal*, 2000, www2.warwick.ac.uk/fac/soc/law/elj/lgd/2000_1/faundez, 37–38.

20 Ulrich Preuss, *Constitutional Revolution*, trans. Deborah Lucas Schneider (Atlantic Highlands, N.J.: Humanity Books 1995), 2 (emphasis added).

21 Cass Sunstein, "On the Expressive Function of Law," *University of Pennsylvania Law Review* 144:5 (1996).

22 Quoted in Hannah Arendt, *On Revolution* (New York: Viking Press, 1965), 145.

23 Faundez 2000, 34. Bolivia has legalized customary courts alongside national law, see "Bolivia: Double or Quits," *Economist* (December 15, 2007): 44.

24 Sharlet, 107.

25 The World Bank came to this conclusion after years of work to change commercial laws. Between 1990 and 2001, the World Bank launched 95 projects in the former Soviet Union alone that contained some legal reform elements. After 1997, the World Bank began turning more to judicial institutional reform, finding that its desired laws were passing but were not being implemented as desired. See Poonam Gupta, Rachel Kleinfeld, and Gonzalo Salinas, "Legal and Judicial Reform in Europe and Central Asia," World Bank Operations Evaluation Department, 2002.

26 See Stephen Golub, "A House Without a Foundation," in *Promoting the Rule of Law Abroad: In Search of Knowledge*, edited by Thomas Carothers (Washington, D.C.: Carnegie Endowment for International Peace, 2006), for his deconstruction

of the rule-of-law orthodoxy for a listing of these types of projects and their shortcomings.

27 North, 1990, 3.

28 Robert Putnam, *Making Democracy Work: Civic Traditions in Modern Italy* (Princeton, N.J.: Princeton University Press, 1994).

29 Elez Biberaj, *Albania in Transition* (Colorado: Westview Press, 1998); Miranda Vickers and James Pettifer, *Albania* (London: Hurst and Company, 1997), 33–54.

30 USAID, "Albania: Review and Resource Allocation (R2) 1998," 47–48.

31 International Crisis Group, "Albania: State of the Nation," Balkans Report no. 87, March 1, 2000, 18–19.

32 Author's interview with Kathleen Imholz, adviser, Council of Ministers of the Republic of Albania, OSCE representative, Tirana, Albania, December 3, 6, and 13, 2001.

33 Harry Blair and Gary Hansen, "Weighing In on the Scales of Justice: Strategic Approaches for Donor-Supported Rule of Law Programs," USAID Program and Operations Assessment Report no. 7, Washington, D.C.: USAID, February 1994, Executive Summary, 5.

34 "Legal and Judicial Reform: Observations, Experiences, and Approach of the Legal Vice Presidency" (Washington, D.C.: World Bank, 2002), 65.

35 Linn Hammergren, "Use of Empirical Research in Refocusing Judicial Reforms: Lessons from Five Countries" (Washington, D.C.: World Bank, 2003), 2.

36 See Golub for a damning indictment.

37 David H. Bayley, *Changing the Guard: Developing Democratic Police Abroad* (New York: Oxford University Press, 2006), 62.

38 See András Sajó, "How the Rule of Law Killed Hungarian Welfare Reform," *East European Constitutional Review* 5:1 (1996): 31–56, which addresses the tension between progressive, populist policies often favored by elected governments and the inability to pass such reforms that can occur with increased judicial power and independence (particularly because judiciaries worldwide tend to temperamentally favor conservative, incremental change).

39 "Reforming Public Institutions and Strengthening Governance: A World Bank Strategy," Public Sector Group, Poverty Reduction and Economic Management Network, World Bank, November 2000; Brian Levy. "Governance and Economic Development in Africa: Meeting the Challenge of Capacity Building," in *Building State Capacity in Africa: New Approaches, Emerging Lessons,* edited by Brian Levy and Sahr Kpundeh (Washington, D.C.: World Bank Institute, 2004). David

Booth. "Governance for Development in Africa: Building on What Works," Policy Brief 1, Africa Power and Politics, Overseas Development Institute, April 2011.

40 Carothers, 2006, 4.

41 Karon Cochran-Budhathoki, "Calling for Security and Justice in Nepal: Citizens' Perspectives on the Rule of Law and the Role of the Nepal Police" (Washington, D.C.: United States Institute of Peace, 2011), 45–46, 60–61, 65–67, 109–12.

42 The reluctance of the rule-of-law field to consider power structures is even more surprising because power structures have been a central theme in the related democratization literature. See Dankwart Rustow, "Transitions to Democracy: Toward a Dynamic Model," *Comparative Politics* 2:3 (April 1970): 337–63, which was the progenitor of a pact-based theory of democratization. Weingast takes a game-theoretic model to show the impact of political pacts. See Barry Weingast, "The Political Foundations of Democracy and the Rule of Law," *American Political Science Review* 91, 245–63. Guillermo O'Donnell and Schmitter suggest that transitions to democracy result from negotiations between state and opposition elites as well as civil society; see Guillermo O'Donnell, Philippe Schmitter, and Laurence Whitehead in their four-volume work *Transitions from Authoritarian Rule* (Baltimore: Johns Hopkins University Press, 1986). Michael Burton, Richard Gunther and John Higley, "Introduction: Elite Transformations and Democratic Regimes," in John Higley and Richard Gunther, eds., *Elites and Democratic Consolidation in Latin America and Southern Europe* (London: Cambridge University Press, 1992). Jerzy J. Wiatr, "Executive-Legislative Relations in Crisis: Poland's Experience, 1989–1993," in *Institutional Design in New Democracies*, edited by Arend Lijphart and Carlos Waisman (Boulder, Colo.: Westview Press, 1996), suggests that the relative strength of various powers in society, as well as the initial legal structure, accounted for the differences between Poland and Hungary in their path toward democracy.

43 Sue Unsworth, "What's Politics Got to Do with It? Why Donors Find It So Hard to Come to Terms with Politics, and Why This Matters," *Journal of International Development* 21:6, August 2009: 883–94.

44 See Gordon Barron, "The World Bank and Rule of Law Reforms," Working Paper no. 05-70, Development Studies Institute, London School of Economics, December 2005, 17, 19–20.

45 Verena Fritz, Kai Kaiser, and Brian Levy, "Problem-Driven Governance and Political Economy Analysis: Good Practice Framework," World Bank, September 2009.

46 See Patrick Chabal and Jean-Pascal Daloz, *Africa Works: Disorder as a Political Instrument* (Oxford: The International African Institute, 1999), which argues that

political actors in a number of African countries seek to maximize their returns from the confusion, uncertainty, and disorder that characterize many African states.

47 Author's interview with Fatos Lubonja, independent journalist, former dissident and political prisoner, Tirana, Albania, October 2006.

48 In Indonesia, for instance, an evaluation of USAID rule of law projects under the Suharto government found that work with NGOs and legal institutions would be allowed to continue until it began to threaten the authoritarian legal culture, at which point the state would step in to limit change. See David Steinberg and C. P. F. Luhulima, "On Democracy; Strengthening Legislative, Legal, Press Institutions and Polling in Indonesia," Final Evaluation, USAID Grants 497-0336-G-SS-0041, 497-0364-G-SS-1089, and 497-0364-G-SS-2091, January 5, 1994, 24–26.

49 Sajó, 1996, 31–56.

50 Blair and Hansen, 1994, 51.

51 For an overview of how USAID conceptualized this issue in the late 1990s, see Linn Hammergren, "Political Will, Constituency Building, and Public Support in Rule of Law Programs," PN-ACD-023, USAID, August 1998.

52 Thomas Carothers, "Democracy, State, and AID: A Tale of Two Cultures," *Foreign Service Journal* (February 2001); Matthew Spence, "The Impact of American Democracy Promotion in Post-Soviet Russia, Ukraine, and Kyrgyzstan, 1991–2003," (D. Phil. diss. Oxford University, 2004); and Matthew Spence, "Kyrgyzstan's Lesson to the West: Reform Follows Function," *New Republic Online*, March 30, 2005.

53 Fred Abrahams, "Albania," *Foreign Policy in Focus* 2:33 (May 1997): 2.

54 See Spence, 2005.

55 Kenneth D. Ackerman, *Boss Tweed: The Rise and Fall of the Corrupt Pol Who Conceived the Soul of Modern New York* (New York: Carroll & Graf, 2005). In fact, there is a growing body of research suggesting that, as the old saying goes, power really does corrupt. It is not simply that bad apples pursue power, but that the actual workings of power tend to make people feel more self-important, above the law, and less likely to curb antisocial behavior. See the innovative studies of Joris Lammers and Adam Galinsky as written in "The Psychology of Power," *Economist*, January 21, 2010.

56 When many former Securitate were forced to retire in 1990, many spent three years in military police school, graduated in law, and then became prosecutors. This was one reason that the creation of the National Institute of Magistracy as the only path to the prosecutorial and judicial careers was a particularly important

reform. See ARD Inc, "Democracy and Governance Assessment of Romania," submitted to United States Agency for International Development Mission to Romania, September 24, 2001, 16–18.

57 Alina Mungiu-Pippidi, "Romania," *Nations in Transit* (Washington, D.C.: Freedom House, 2006).

58 European Commission, "1999 Regular Report from the Commission on Romania's Progress Towards Accession," Brussels, October 13, 1999, 13.

59 Stoica also introduced a law to improve judicial enforcement by privatizing bailiffs.

60 Author's interview with Valeriu Stoica, former minister of justice and president, PNL Party, Bucharest, September 19, 2001; author's interview with Nicolae Idu, director general, European Institute of Romania, Bucharest, September 2001. The obvious alternative interpretation—levied by his successor—suggests that Stoica packed the court with "his" people, weakened judicial standards, and buttressed his political base. My interpretation emerged after multiple interviews with Stoica, his top secretaries, and the subsequent administration, and from analyzing the overall thrust of ministers' agendas rather than actions in isolation. While Stoica is a contradictory figure, I believe this is the most correct interpretation of his actions.

61 Author's interview with Elena Tanasescu, task manager, Justice and Home Affairs and Public Administration, European Commission Delegation to Romania, Bucharest, September 12, 2001.

62 "Monitoring the EU Accession Process: Judicial Independence," Open Society Institute (2001), 365–66, www.eumap.org/reports/2001/judicial.

63 "Constitution Watch," *East European Constitutional Review* 10:2–3 (2001), www1.law.nyu.edu/eecr/vol10num2_3/constitutionwatch/romania.html.

64 Guillermo O'Donnell, "Horizontal Accountability in New Democracies," in *The Self-Restraining State*, edited by Andreas Schedler, Larry Diamond, and Marc Plattner (Boulder, Colo.: Lynne Rienner, 1999), 29–62.

65 Culture is a notoriously messy catchall term that is wrestled with in "Legal Culture and Judicial Reform," Topic Brief, World Bank.http://siteresources.worldbank.org/INTLAWJUSTINST/Resources/LegalCultureBrief.pdf. In modern times, culture was revived as a variable in political science literature in the writings of Almond and Verba. See Gabriel Almond and Sidney Verba, *The Civic Culture: Political Attitudes and Democracy in Five Nations* (Princeton: Princeton University Press, 1963).

66 A culture-based theory of rule-of-law reform animates the Culture of Lawfulness projects of the National Strategy Information Center, an NGO

that the U.S. State Department has contracted with to improve the rule of law everywhere from Mexican border towns to Iraq by training police and citizens to each do their part in upholding the rule of law, www.cultureoflawfulness.org. For full disclosure, the author consulted for the Culture of Lawfulness project on rule of law reforms in Colombia and Mexico. The cultural theory of rule-of-law development is explored in the Spring 2000 issue of *Trends in Organized Crime*, which is completely devoted to the idea of a culture of lawfulness. It has its mirror in democratization literature in Samuel Huntington, *The Third Wave* (Norman: University of Oklahoma Press, 1991), which emphasizes the importance of ideology, culture, religion, and socioeconomic structures in pushing countries toward democracy. See also Harry Eckstein, "A Culturalist Theory of Political Change," *American Political Science Review* 82:3 (September 1988): 789–804, and Harry Eckstein, *Regarding Politics: Essays on Political Theory, Stability, and Change* (Berkeley: University of California Press, 1992). While in democratization, a cultural theory of change has been faulted for being unfit to describe rapid revolutions given the slow speed of cultural change (a charge itself disputed by cultural proponents), this criticism fails to function in the rule-of-law field, where no scholar claims that rapid change is possible.

67 A century after Max Weber suggested that Asia's Confucianism would restrain its economic development in *The Religion of China* (New York: Free Press, 1951), scholars such as Ezra Vogel, *The Four Little Dragons* (Cambridge: Harvard University Press, 2006), and Roy Hofheinz Jr. and Kent E. Calder, *The East Asia Edge* (New York: Basic Books, 1982), argued for its pro-development impact.

68 See Lawrence E. Harrison and Samuel P. Huntington, eds., *Culture Matters: How Values Shape Human Progress* (New York: Basic Books, 2000), for a book-length exploration of the role culture plays in political, economic, and rule-of-law development.

69 Alexis de Tocqueville, *Democracy in America*, translated by George Lawrence, J.P. Mayer, ed. (New York: Harper Collins, 1969), 308–09.

70 Paula Dobriansky, U.S. Undersecretary of State for Global Affairs, "Promoting a Culture of Lawfulness" (address at Georgetown University, September 13, 2004).

71 International Crisis Group, "Albania: State of the Nation," Balkans Report no. 111, May 25, 2001, 7.

72 See Nathan Thornburgh, "Looking for a Few Good Snitches," *Time*, February 19, 2006.

73 Most of us for instance, don't need to know that we are likely to go to jail to be prevented from murdering someone—we simply do not go around killing people. The sociologist Emile Durkheim writes of the movement from repression to democracy being concomitant with growing civilization and acceptance of the rule of law. See Steven Lukes, *Emile Durkheim: His Life and Work* (Harmondsworth:

Penguin, 1975), quoted in Laurence Whitehead, ed., *The International Dimensions of Democratization: Europe and the Americas*, expanded edition (New York: Oxford University Press, 2001), 167.

74 Joel Migdal, *Strong Societies and Weak States* (Princeton: Princeton University Press, 1988).

75 Channell, 146–48.

76 Wade Channell notes the Bulgarian folk story of Andreshko, whose protagonist is a hero because he resists the state's law enforcement in favor of loyalty to a friend. Channell points out that such deep-seated cultural predilections cannot be wiped out solely by writing new laws—the cultural factor itself must be addressed. Channell, 147.

77 IRSOP Market Research and Consulting, "Romanian and European Values and Beliefs: Are They Different or Not?" June 2005.

78 Amity Shlaes, *The Forgotten Man: A New History of the Great Depression* (New York: Harper Perennial, 2007), 197.

79 Robert Scalapino, *The Politics of Development* (Cambridge: Harvard University Press, 1989), quoted in Susan Rose-Ackerman, *Corruption and Government: Causes, Consequences, and Reform* (Cambridge: Cambridge University Press, 1999), 106.

80 Author's interview with Professor Hikmahanto Juwana, dean of the Faculty of Law, University of Indonesia, Jakarta, July 7, 2003.

81 Author's interview with Santiago, Department of Justice ICITAP program developer, Jakarta, July 11, 2005.

82 Roy Godson, "Guide to Developing a Culture of Lawfulness," *Trends in Organized Crime* 5:3 (2000): 91–102.

83 John H. Merryman, *The Civil Law Tradition* (Stanford: Stanford University Press, 1969), 2.

84 Montesquieu, *The Spirit of the Laws*, translated and edited by Anne M. Cohler et al. (Cambridge: Cambridge University Press, 1989), 315.

85 Cheryl Gray and Kathryn Hendley, "Developing Commercial Law in Transition Economies," Policy Research Working Paper 1528, World Bank, November 1995.

86 Nader Fergany et al., "Towards Freedom in the Arab World," Arab Human Development Report, United Nations Development Program, 2004, http://hdr.undp.org/en/reports/regionalreports/arabstates/name,3278,en.html.

87 Weingast, 245–62.

88 William Culberson, *Vigilantism: Political History of Private Power in America* (New York: Praeger, 1990), 2, argues that "vigiliantism arose from practical needs in the absence of foundations regulating social order."

89 "Legal Culture and Judicial Reform."

90 Stace Lindsay, "Culture, Mental Models, and National Prosperity," in Harrison and Huntington, eds., *Culture Matters*, 284.

91 Lawrence Harrison, "Promoting Progressive Cultural Change," in Harrison and Huntington, eds., *Culture Matters*, 299.

92 In 2010, Teach for America hired more college seniors from Yale, Georgetown, Dartmouth, and Duke than any other employer. See Michael Winerip, "A Chosen Few Are Teaching for America," *New York Times*, July 11, 2010.

93 Alex Inkeles and David H. Smith, *Becoming Modern: Individual Change in Six Developing Countries* (Boulder, Colo.: Westview Press, 1998), 29.

94 Two programs funded by USAID and the American Embassy, respectively.

95 See Lyla Mehta and Synne Movik, eds., *Shit Matters: The Potential of Community-Led Total Sanitation* (Practical Action Publishers, July 1, 2010).

96 "Albania Country Report," First Quarter, 1998, Economist Intelligence Unit (1998), 12; author's interview with Kathleen Imholz, December 3, 6, and 13, 2001.

Chapter Five

1 David Finkel, "U.S. Ideals Meet Reality in Yemen," *Washington Post*, December 18, 2005.

2 In the democratization field, these four methods have been better delineated and researched. For accounts of international actors' roles in democracy promotion, see Peter Burnell, ed., *Democracy Assistance: International Co-operation for Democratization* (London: Frank Cass, 2000).

3 Simply describing each potential method of change already shows some of the fissures. It is unlikely that many countries would hold up the U.S. model of government transparency as ideal; nor is it likely that corruption will frequently make the top talking points of senior officials speaking with government leaders of other countries if that other country is strategically important at all.

4 Author's interview with Santiago, Department of Justice ICITAP program developer, Jakarta, July 2005.

5 See the three-part, front-page *Washington Post* series by David Finkel on democratization programs in Yemen run by the National Democratic Institute for International Affairs: "U.S. Ideals Meet Reality in Yemen," December 18, 2005; "A Struggle for Peace in a Place Where Fighting Never Ends," December 19, 2005; and "In the End, a Painful Choice," December 20, 2005.

6 Wade Channell, "Grammar Lessons Learned: Dependent Clauses, False Cognates, and Other Problems in Rule of Law Programming," *University of Pittsburgh Law Review* 72(2) (Winter 2010): 181–92.

7 Julio Faundez, "Legal Reform in Developing and Transition Countries—Making Haste Slowly," *Law, Social Justice and Global Development Journal*, 2000, www2.warwick.ac.uk/fac/soc/law/elj/lgd/2000_1/faundez, 36.

8 See Harry Blair and Gary Hansen, "Weighing In on the Scales of Justice: Strategic Approaches for Donor-Supported Rule of Law Programs," USAID Program and Operations Assessment Report no. 7 (Washington, D.C.: USAID, February 1994); and Linn Hammergren, "Political Will, Constituency Building, and Public Support in Rule of Law Programs," PN-ACD-023, USAID, August 1998.

9 Author's interview with Marcellus Rantatena, Partnership for Governance Reform, Jakarta, July 5, 2005.

10 Interview with Ronan MacAongusa, First Secretary, European Commission Delegation to Indonesia, Jakarta, July 2005.

11 Civil society actors working in the judicial field largely considered Manan an honest justice with few management skills presiding over a deeply corrupt institution. However, the acquittal of high-profile individuals brought to court on corruption charges, as well as accusations of bribery, have tainted Manan in the eyes of some members of the public. The truth, as it so often is, is murky.

12 Thomas Carothers, "The Rule-of-Law Revival," in *Promoting the Rule of Law Abroad: In Search of Knowledge*, edited by Thomas Carothers (Washington, D.C.: Carnegie Endowment for International Peace, 2006), 7–8, calls this "type three" rule-of-law reform. The "fourth wave" of democratization theory is explored by Michael McFaul, "The Fourth Wave of Democracy and Dictatorship," *World Politics* 54:2 (January 2002): 212–44, and Valerie Bunce, "Rethinking Recent Democratization," *World Politics* 55:2 (January 2003): 167–92, who suggest that mass movements of citizens coordinated into constituencies and sharing organizing techniques, rather than the third wave's elite pacts, broke the back of authoritarian regimes in the most recent democratization wave. While the history of the current wave of democratization in the Middle East is yet to be written, it is clear that citizen movements organized on a shoestring played a pivotal role—though

they had to rely on military acquiescence, the change that occurred in Egypt and other countries would not have happened without such bottom-up pressure.

13 "Civil society" is a term frequently used by practitioners. Originally meant to describe social activities not directed by the government or undertaken for profit, from political parties to Masonic clubs, it has unduly narrowed to mean the realm of legally incorporated NGO institutions. I use the term in the traditional sense to imply citizen organizations, whether legally incorporated or not, including religious organizations, businesses, and mass movements. I also include efforts to educate journalists or use the media to highlight rule-of-law information that would spur such groups to form or to advocate for change.

14 Alexis de Tocqueville, *Democracy in America*, translated by George Lawrence, edited by J. P. Mayer (New York: Harper Collins, 1969), 513. A flowering of writings lauding civil society, such as Robert Putnam's *Making Democracy Work: Civic Traditions in Modern Italy* (Princeton, N.J.: Princeton University Press, 1994), as well as George Soros' Open Society Institutes throughout Eastern Europe, contributed to the civil society focus of funding efforts. Civil society was not always embraced in America; the Founding Fathers were skeptical of factions, and established religion was also inimical to early civil society movements that ate into their monopolies in different states.

15 For an example, see David Finkel's 2005 *Washington Post* series on the National Democratic Institute for International Affairs program for conflict resolution in Yemen.

16 MacAongusa interview; author's interviews with Gerald Colledani, EURALIUS Head of Mission, Tirana, Albania, October 2006, and Luisa Rizzo, European Commission Delegation project manager, Justice and Home Affairs, Tirana, October 2006.

17 Rizzo and Colledani interviews.

18 MacAongusa interview.

19 Stephen Golub, "The Legal Empowerment Imperative," in Carothers, ed., *Promoting the Rule of Law Abroad*, 169.

20 Hammergren, 1998, 4.

21 For the non-linear nature of evaluating effective advocacy work in the United States—findings that also hold true abroad, see Steven Teles and Mark Schmitt, "The Elusive Craft of Evaluating Advocacy," *Stanford Social Innovation Review*, May 2011.

22 Steven Sampson, "The Social Life of Projects: Importing Civil Society to Albania," in *Civil Society: Challenging Western Models*, edited by Chris Hann and Elizabeth Dunn (New York: Routledge, 1996), 129–42.

23 Author's interview with Eglantina Gjermeni, director, Gender Equality for Development, Tirana, October 2006.

24 See, for example, "Russian MPs Approve NGO Controls," BBC News, December 23, 2005, http://news.bbc.co.uk/2/hi/europe/4554894.stm; "Putin Warning Over 'Puppet' NGOs," BBC News, January 31, 2006, http://news.bbc.co.uk/2/hi/europe/4664974.stm; "Uzbek Government Exerting Pressure on Local NGOs to Close Voluntarily," Eurasianet, October 3, 2005, www.eurasianet.org/departments/civilsociety/articles/eav100405.shtml.

25 In Indonesia, Islamists decry Asia Foundation civil society reforms aimed at supporting moderate Islam for being "U.S. supported" (author's interviews with Asia Foundation staff in Indonesia). In Iran and Egypt, reformers have refused U.S. funding for democracy because of its taint. See Laura Secor, "Keep Away: The Case for Doing Nothing," *New Republic*, April 23, 2007.

26 In fact, U.S. covert funding to support civil societies that would press for the rule of law helped to create the EU itself: In the 1950s, CIA funds helped to support a variety of NGOs in Europe speaking against communism and for liberalism, the Marshall Plan, and European integration. Richard J. Aldrich, *The Hidden Hand: Britain, America and Cold War Secret Intelligence* (London: John Murray, 2001). See also Greg Behrman, *The Most Noble Adventure: The Marshall Plan and the Time When America Helped Save Europe* (New York: Free Press, 2007), 240–42.

27 Kimberly Gould Ashizawa, "The Evolving Role of American Foundations in Japan," in *Philanthropy and Reconciliation: Rebuilding Postwar U.S.-Japan Relations*, edited by Tadashi Yamamoto, Akira Iriye, and Makoto Iokibe (New York: Japan Center for International Exchange, 2006), 116–22.

28 In the mid-1980s, Congress created the governmentally funded National Endowment for Democracy (NED) as an independent foundation to encourage the development of civil society organizations promoting democracy in their countries, including rule-of-law programs. However, NED continues to face accusations of CIA involvement (further backed by its association with civil society organizations connected with the Iran-contra affair). The ongoing taint of covert funding can undermine impact if not carefully diffused. See David Lowe, "Idea to Reality: A Brief History of the National Endowment for Democracy," National Endowment for Democracy, www.ned.org/about/nedhistory.html, for these early congressional battles between covert and overt funding.

29 Author's interview with Agus Loekman, Asia Foundation Indonesia, Jakarta, July 11, 2005.

30 Loekman interview.

31 As Laurence Whitehead correctly points out, civil society is not neutral—it can just as easily be a negative influence on rule of law as a positive one, and therefore finding supportive locals is crucial. Laurence Whitehead, ed., *The International Dimensions of Democratization: Europe and the Americas*, expanded edition (New York: Oxford University Press, 2001), 82.

32 ARD Inc., "Democracy and Governance Assessment of Romania," submitted to USAID/Romania, September 24, 2001, 11, 15, 28.

33 For a case study of such effects in Kazakhstan, see Pauline Jones Luong and Erika Weinthal, "Environmental NGOs in Kazakhstan: Democratic Goals and Nondemocratic Outcomes," in *The Power and Limits of NGOs: A Critical Look at Building Democracy in Eastern Europe and Eurasia*, edited by Sarah E. Mendelson and John K. Glenn (New York: Columbia University Press, 2002), 152–76.

34 Richard Holloway, "NGOs: Losing the Moral High Ground—Corruption and Misrepresentation," paper delivered at the Eighth International Anti-Corruption Conference, Lima, 1997. M. H. Khan, "The Role of Civil Society and Patron-Client Networks in the Analysis of Corruption," Corruption and Integrity Improvement Initiatives in Developing Countries, UN Development Program, 1998, 111–27.

35 ARD, 11, 15, 28.

36 The same methods hold true for evaluating U.S. organizations. See Steven Teles and Mark Schmitt, "The Elusive Craft of Evaluating Advocacy," May 31, 2011, www.hewlett.org/library/grantee-publication/elusive-craft-evaluating-advocacy.

37 George Shultz, *Turmoil and Triumph: Diplomacy, Power, and the Victory of the American Ideal* (New York: Simon and Schuster, 1982), 970, quoted in David Adesnik and Michael McFaul, "Engaging Autocratic Allies to Promote Democracy," *Washington Quarterly* 29:2 (Spring 2006): 18.

38 The statement did not, however, eliminate mixed messages, a problem with diplomacy as a method that is discussed later in this section. The Reagan administration endorsed five UN resolutions critiquing Pinochet's human rights record, but it also abstained on three and voted against one. Quoted in Adesnik and McFaul, 22.

39 This summation is drawn from Adesnik and McFaul, 17–19.

40 See Adesnik and McFaul for a series of cases of diplomatic action to enhance democracy.

41 NATO, the EU, the Council of Europe, and the Organization of American States all require the rule of law within their membership criteria. The EU also has a rule-of-law clause for trade agreements. See also Peter Van Ham, *The EC,*

Eastern Europe, and European Unity: Discord, Collaboration and Integration Since 1947 (London: Pinter, 1995), 176.

42 Millennium Challenge Corporation, "Selection Indicators," Millennium Challenge Corporation, United States of America, www.mcc.gov/selection/indicators/index.php.

43 Adesnik and McFaul, 23.

44 The conditionality barred all development aid to governments that engage "in a consistent pattern of gross violations of internationally recognized human rights."

45 The less defined the policy goal, the less successful the sanctions. See Gordon Crawford, "Foreign Aid and Political Conditionality: Issues of Effectiveness and Consistency," *Democratization* 3:4 (1997), and Olav Stokke, *Aid and Political Conditionality* (London: Frank Cass, 1995).

46 Crawford 1997, 81–82. See also Larry Diamond, *Promoting Democracy in the 1990s: Actors and Instruments, Issues and Imperatives* (Washington, D.C.: Carnegie Commission on Preventing Deadly Conflict, 1995), and Stokke 1995.

47 Since 1979 the U.S. has provided around $1.3 billion annually to Egypt and nearly $3 billion to Israel (nearly one-third from the foreign aid budget, the remainder from the military budget) to keep the peace between Egypt and Israel, regardless of either country's rule-of-law record. Gordon Crawford, *Foreign Aid and Political Reform: A Comparative Analysis of Democracy Assistance and Political Conditionality* (London: Palgrave, 2001), 11–12. Some of the most damning inconsistencies occurred in Latin America during the Cold War; see Walter LaFeber, *Inevitable Revolutions: The United States in Central America*, second edition (New York: Norton, 1993).

48 U.S. Department of State, "Background Note: Romania," Bureau of European and Eurasian Affairs, April 2008. Romania sponsored the April 2000 resolution that "member states also have a solemn responsibility to promote and protect human rights by working together to consolidate democracy." Harold Hongju Koh, "The Right to Democracy," *Issues of Democracy*, U.S. Department of State, May 2000, http://usinfo.state.gov/journals/itdhr/0500/ijde/koh.htm. Romania also hosted the November 2003 regional conference of the Community of Democracies, even as the government sought to undermine press freedom and the rule of law at home.

49 USAID/Romania, "R2 FY 2002, March 2000," 4.

50 Claudiu Degeratu, "Romania's Participation in the Fight Against International Terrorism," in *The Evolution of Civil-Military Relations in South East Europe*, edited by Philipp H. Fluri et al. (Heidelberg, Germany: Physica-Verlag, 2005),

185–96; "U.S. Bank Officials to Thank Romanians for Shutting Down Fraud Operations," U.S. Embassy Press Release, July 16, 2004.

51 United States Department of State, "Romania," U.S. Country Reports on Terrorism, 2004, 51.

52 Thomas Fuller, "Romania Dangles Use of a Sea Base to Woo U.S.," *International Herald Tribune*, June 18, 2003. The movement of troops through Romania also pumped more than $30 million into the impoverished local economy.

53 U.S. Department of State, "Background Note: Romania," Bureau of European and Eurasian Affairs, April 2008.

54 USAID/Romania, "R4 FY 2001," March 1999, 40.

55 Laurel Miller and Robert Perito, "Establishing the Rule of Law in Afghanistan," Special Report 117, U.S. Institute of Peace, March 2004, 5–7, 15–16.

56 Crawford 2001, 42–45.

57 See the Foreign Operations Appropriations Act of 2002, Public Law 105–115. See also the House Concurrent Resolution 240 "Condemning the Massacre of East Timorese Civilians by the Indonesian Military." Passed by the U.S. House of Representatives, November 14, 1991.

58 Author's interview with Agung Laksono, Speaker of the House, Jakarta, July 7, 2005.

59 Peter Gelling, "New Report Sheds Light on 2002 Papua Shooting," *International Herald Tribune*, April 8, 2007. In 2004, a U.S. grand jury indicted one Indonesian for these slayings, but Indonesia failed to extradite or indict any perpetrators and spent eight months delaying the entrance of an FBI investigative team, which needed to enter Indonesia to collect evidence for the U.S. case.

60 For a full account of this strategic difference, see the various interpretations offered in congressional testimony, "Indonesia in Transition: Recent Developments and Implications for U.S. Policy," hearing before the Subcommittee on Asia and the Pacific, House Committee on International Relations, 109th Congress, First Session, March 10, 2005.

61 Scott Morrissey, "U.S. Lifts Indonesian Arms Embargo," *Arms Control Today* (January/February 2006), www.armscontrol.org/act/2006_01-02/JANFEB-indonesia.asp.

62 Bill Guerin, "Indonesia-Russia: Arms, Atoms and Oil," Asia Times Online, December 12, 2006, and John Haseman and Eduardo Lachica, *Toward a Stronger U.S.-Indonesia Security Relationship* (Washington: U.S.-Indonesia Society, 2005), 16.

63 In a similar vein, it is worth noting the case of the Inter-Governmental Group on Indonesia (IGGI), a mechanism formed in 1967 to coordinate donor assistance and originally led by the Dutch. In 1992, the Dutch development officer used particularly strong language to criticize the Suharto regime's human rights record. With the economy booming and great disdain for its former colonizer's arrogance, President Suharto simply called the IGGI's bluff, saying that Indonesia would no longer accept aid from the IGGI so long as the Netherlands chaired the organization. The international community didn't wish to cut itself out of the fast-growing country. Instead, it regrouped as the Consultative Group on Indonesia (CGI), with the Netherlands no longer a member. Meanwhile, even the Netherlands wanted to provide aid and was reduced to doing so through various international institutions such as the IMF. So much for the powers of persuasion. Loekman interview and Library of Congress, "Indonesia: Area Handbook Series Glossary," 2007, June 5, 2008.

64 The problem is not the use of an executive order in and of itself—this is a common tool of democratic governments. The difficulty for the rule of law lies in the use of such measures to avoid the parliamentary process.

65 This is not a far-fetched case: Canada and Britain tried exactly this to defend their companies, when Indonesian courts misused bankruptcy laws to declare Manulife, a major (and solvent) Canadian insurance company, bankrupt—and then did the same to Britain's PT Prudential Life. Bill Guerin, "Who's Bankrupt? Foreign Firm or Jakarta Court?" Asia Times Online, April 30, 2004, www.atimes.com/atimes/Southeast_Asia/FD30Ae02.html.

66 Haseman and Lachica, 8.

67 Laurence Whitehead calls this process "convergence," meaning the ability of the EU to interact with acceding states on a multitude of levels, in which individuals and domestic institutions are enmeshed in a web of political expectations, cultural norms, twinning programs, aid, and technical assistance until they alter to resemble their Western counterparts. See Whitehead, *International Dimensions*, 261–84.

68 Jack Snyder, "Averting Anarchy in the New Europe," *International Security* 14:4 (Spring 1990): 5–41.

69 Antoaneta Dimitrova and Geoffrey Pridham, "International Actors and Democracy Promotion in Central and Eastern Europe," *Democratization* 11:5 (2004): 91–112, have an excellent breakdown of the various organizations that could carry out democratization through integration (their term for enmeshment), the tools available to each, and their varied levels of success. Also see Martha Finnemore, *National Interests in International Society* (Ithaca: Cornell University Press, 1996). For other studies on the usefulness of the EU enlargement process for democratization, see Diamond, 1995; K. Smith, "Western Actors and the

Promotion of Democracy," in *Democratic Consolidation in Eastern Europe: International and Transnational Factors*, vol. 2, edited by Alex Pravda and Jan Zielonka (Oxford: Oxford University Press, 2001), 31–57; Geoffrey Pridham, "EU Enlargement and Consolidating Democracy in Post-Communist States—Formality and Reality," *Journal of Common Market Studies* 40:3 (2002): 953–73; Jiri Pehe, "Consolidating Free Government in the New EU," *Journal of Democracy* 15:1 (2004): 36–47; Jan Zielonka, "Challenges of EU Enlargement," *Journal of Democracy* 15:1 (2004): 22–36; Heather Grabbe, "How Does Europeanization Affect CEE Governance?" *Journal of European Public Policy* 8:6 (2001): 1013–31; and Geoffrey Pridham, *Designing Democracy; EU Enlargement and Regime Change in Post-Communist Europe* (Basingstoke: Palgrave, 2005).

70 Ironically, since the United States was a prime mover behind EU integration and enmeshment; see Behrman 2007, 112, 336–337.

71 The debate on whether NATO was useful for democratic strengthening was fierce and high profile. See William Perry, "The Enduring Dynamic Relationship That Is NATO," *Defense Viewpoint* 10:9 (1995), Strobe Talbott, "Why NATO Should Grow," *New York Review of Books* 42:13 (August 10, 1995): 27–30; Richard Holbrooke, "America, A European Power," *Foreign Affairs* 71:2 (March/April 1995): 38–51; Dan Reiter, "Why NATO Enlargement Does Not Spread Democracy," *International Security* 25:4 (2001): 41–67; Vaclav Havel, "NATO's Quality of Life," *New York Times* (May 13, 1997), A21; Robert O. Keohane and Stanley Hoffmann, "Conclusion: Structure, Strategy, and International Roles," in *After the Cold War: International Institutions and State Strategies in Europe, 1989–1991*, edited by Robert Keohane et al. (Cambridge: Harvard University Press, 1993), 381–406.

72 For a skeptical reading, see Peter Feaver, "The Clinton Administration's China Engagement Policy in Perspective," paper presented at the Conference on War and Peace, Duke University, Durham, North Carolina, 2006, www.duke.edu/web/cis/pass/pdf/warpeaceconf/p-feaver.pdf.

73 Paula Dobriansky, U.S. Undersecretary of State for Global Affairs, "Promoting a Culture of Lawfulness," address at Georgetown University, Washington, D.C., September 13, 2004.

74 Peter Haas, "Introduction: Epistemic Communities and International Policy Coordination," *International Organization* 46:1 (Winter 1992): 1–35; Martha Finnemore, "International Organizations as Teachers of Norms," *International Organization* 47:4 (Autumn 1993): 565–97.

75 Author's interview with Tim Smith, Political Cone, U.S. Embassy in Jakarta, Indonesia, July 2005.

76 The divergent predilections of Congress and the State Department regarding these methods appear as well in the debate throughout the 1990s over whether the United States should engage or sanction China.

77 Aurelia Brazeal, "U.S. Relations with Indonesia," testimony of the deputy assistant secretary of state for East Asian and Pacific Affairs, before the Subcommittee on Asia and the Pacific, House Committee on International Relations, July 5, 2007.

78 Many argue that human rights abusers have been trained in these programs, often due to the failure of norm spreading rather than as a deliberate act. See, for example, Victor Alba, "Spain's Entry Into NATO," in *NATO and the Mediterranean*, edited by Lawrence S. Kaplan et al. (Wilmington, Del.: Scholarly Resources, 1985), 101.

79 Vincent Lingga, "Big Challenges of Improving Investment Climate," *Jakarta Post*, July 8, 2005. See also the conference on "Investment for Asian Development: Lessons So Far, Challenges for the Future," Jakarta, Indonesia, July 5–6, 2005.

80 U.S. Department of State, "Embassy Press Release," Office of Defense Cooperation Mission, Bucharest, Romania, November 13, 2006.

81 Jeffrey Simon, "NATO's Membership Action Plan (MAP) and Prospects for the Next Round of Enlargement," Woodrow Wilson Center White Paper, no. 58, November 2000, 10–11, www.wilsoncenter.org/topics/pubs/ACF45B.pdf.

82 Chris Cooper and Mikhael Johansen, "An Evaluation of Completed Twinning Projects," report presented to the National Contact Points' Meeting, Brussels, January 30–31, 2003, 22–23.

83 USAID/Romania, "R4 FY 2001," 5.

84 ARD, 27–28.

85 ARD, 27–28.

86 Dimitrova and Pridham, 99.

87 Jon Pevehouse, "With a Little Help from My Friends? Regional Organizations and the Consolidation of Democracy," *American Journal of Political Science* 46:3 (July 2002): 611–26.

88 Romano Prodi, "A Wider Europe: A Proximity Policy as the Key to Stability," address at "Peace, Security and Stability: International Dialogue and the Role of the EU," Sixth ECSA-World Conference, Jean Monnet Project, Brussels, December 5–6, 2002.

89 "The Pull of Brussels," *Economist*, October 12, 2011.

90 U.S. Ambassador to China Clark T. Randt Jr., "U.S.-China Relations and Rule of Law Developments" (address at Yale University's China Law Center, New Haven, Connecticut, September 17, 2003).

91 Karen Halverson Cross, "China's WTO Accession: Economic, Legal, and Political Implications," *Boston College International and Comparative Law Review* 27:2 (2004): 339–47. Cross argues that the WTO's effect on legal reform differs significantly from the lack of effect of the General Agreement on Tariffs and Trade in Eastern Europe.

92 José Toharia, "Judicial Independence in an Authoritarian Regime," *Law and Society Review* 9:3 (Spring 1975): 475–96. See Matthew Stephenson, "A Trojan Horse Behind Chinese Walls?: Problems and Prospects of US-Sponsored 'Rule of Law' Reform Projects in the People's Republic of China," Center for International Development Working Paper no. 47, May 2000, for an overview of the potential lack of spillover in China.

93 Iulian Muresan, "Maintaining an Independent Justice System in Romania," Network Europe, May 18, 2007; "Justice for Some," *Economist*, November 3, 2007. While the Romanian Parliament did pass an EU-desired law to create an agency to monitor public officials' wealth, the law passed has been changed to make it less useful by raising the limit at which declared assets can deviate from official salary.

94 M. R. Sukhumbhand Paribatra, deputy minister of foreign affairs of the Kingdom of Thailand, "Engaging Myanmar in ASEAN," address at the conference "Engaging Myanmar in East Asia," organized by the Institute of Strategic and Development Studies Inc., the Republic of the Philippines, and Konrad Adenauer Stiftung, Manila, Philippines, November 29, 1998.

95 Adem Copani, "The New Dimensions of Albania's Security Posture," *NATO Review* 44:2 (March 1996): 24–28, www.nato.int/docu/review/1996/9602-6.htm. Elez Biberaj, "Albania's Road to Democracy," *Current History* 92:577 (November 1993): 384. Julie Kim, "Albania: Country Background Report," Congressional Research Service 98-974 F, June 29, 2000, 4–5.

96 Kim, 5. In 2002, Albania's request for membership was turned down, but U.S. Secretary of State Colin Powell signed the Adriatic Charter promising eventual membership in NATO for Albania, Croatia, and Macedonia if they attained the political criteria.

97 Enika Abazi, "Defense Reform of the Albanian Armed Forces," *Quarterly Journal* 3:3 (September 2004): 35. For more on Albania's experience with NATO, see Albanian Ministry of Defense, "Action Plan for Membership of Republic of Albania in NATO," Tirana, 2001; and G. Robertson, "NATO-Albania Relations Strong and Growing Stronger," U.S. Embassy in Italy, www.usembassy.it/file2001_05/alia/a1051815.htm, May 18, 2001.

98 Copani, 24–28. Abazi, 32. However, Albania had never been threatened by coups; civilian meddling in the military had been a more significant problem.

99 Ryan Hendrickson et al., "Albania and NATO's 'Open Door' Policy," *Journal of Slavic Military Studies* 19 (2006): 251.

100 Ryan Hendrickson and Brian Fornernis, "Albania and NATO's Strategic Partnership," *Low Intensity Conflict and Law Enforcement* 9, no. 1 (2000): 21, also make a fair point in claiming that NATO undercut the rule of law through omission in 1997 when it kept its distance as Albania descended into anarchy, neither imposing order nor exerting any normative framework or socializing influence.

101 Hendrickson et al., 2006, 248–57.

102 Hendrickson et al., 2006, 257.

103 Adrian Pop, "Romania's Challenge," *NATO Review* 1 (Spring 2003), www.nato.int/docu/review/2003/issue1/english/summaries_pr.html.

104 USAID/Romania "Annual Report FY 2004," June 15, 2004, 3.

105 Ibid.

106 Thomas Carothers, "Democracy, State, and AID: A Tale of Two Cultures," *Foreign Service Journal* (February 2001).

107 Crawford, 2001.

108 Adesnik and McFaul, 21.

109 Sarah Mendelson, "Democracy Assistance and Political Transition in Russia: Between Success and Failure," *International Security* 25:4 (2001): 94–95.

Chapter Six

1 J. Alexander Thier, "Reestablishing the Judicial System in Afghanistan," CDDRL Working Papers, Number 19, September 1, 2004, 11.

2 Richard Posner, "Creating a Legal Framework for Economic Development," *World Bank Research Observer* 13:1 (Washington, D.C.: World Bank, 1998), 7.

3 John Henry Merryman, "Comparative Law and Social Change: On the Origins, Style, Decline & Revival of the Law and Development Movement," *American Journal of Comparative Law* 25:3 (1977).

4 Harry Blair and Gary Hansen, "Weighing In on the Scales of Justice: Strategic Approaches for Donor-Supported Rule of Law Programs," USAID Program and

Operations Assessment Report no. 7 (Washington, D.C.: USAID, February 1994), 40.

5 USAID, "Albania Revised Strategic Plan FY 2001–2004," October 2000, 33.

6 Author's interview with Kreshnik Spahiu, Director, Citizens Advocacy Office, Tirana, October 2006. Checchi Consulting, "The Women's Legal Rights Initiative, Quarterly Progress Report, April 1, 2006–June 30, 2006," July 26, 2006, 13.

7 Author's interview with Artan Hoxha, president, Institute for Contemporary Studies (ISB), Tirana, October, 2006; Spahiu interview; author's interview with Ardian Dhima, program director, Institute for Policy and Legal Studies, Tirana, October 2006.

8 "Romania," in *Nations in Transit 2001*, edited by Adrian Karatnycky, Alexander Motyl, and Amanda Schnetzer (Washington, D.C.: Freedom House, 2001), 316–17.

9 USAID/Romania, "FY 2002 Annual Report," March 4, 2002, 8.

10 USAID/Romania, "Strategic Plan 2002–2006," 41.

11 Aliana Mungiu-Pippidi, "Romania," in *Nations in Transit* (New York: Freedom House, 2004). See also Alina Mungiu-Pippidi, "The Coalition for a Clean Parliament," *Journal of Democracy* 16:2 (April 2005): 154–55.

12 Mungiu-Pippidi, 2004.

13 The IMF and World Bank particularly use conditionality for legal change. See Poonam Gupta, Rachel Kleinfeld, and Gonzalo Salinas, "Legal and Judicial Reform in Europe and Central Asia," World Bank Operations Evaluation Department, 2002; Devesh Kapur and Richard Webb, "Governance-Related Conditionalities of the International Financial Institutions," unpublished manuscript prepared for the XII Technical Group Meeting of the Intergovernmental Group of 24 for International Monetary Affairs held in Lima, Peru March 1–3, 2000.

14 Gupta et al., 19.

15 Author's interview with Leonard Orban, Secretary of State, Government of Romania Ministry of European Integration, Bucharest, September 2001. Author's interview with Vasile Puscas, Chief Negotiator for European Union Accession, Ministry of European Integration, Government of Romania, Bucharest, September 2001. Author's interview with Aurel Ciobanu-Dordea, Pre-accession Adviser, EU delegation; former chief negotiator, Romanian Department of EU Accession; former government agent for the European Court at Strasbourg; Bucharest, September 19, 2001, and September 21, 2001.

16 Orban interview.

17 IRSOP Market Research and Consulting, "Romanian and European Values and Beliefs: Are They Different or Not?" June 2005.

18 Author's interview with Eglantina Gjermeni, director, Gender Equality for Development, Tirana, October 2006.

19 In the end, Romania and Bulgaria were postponed, largely for rule-of-law reasons, until 2007—though their entrance is still considered by the EU to be part of this "big bang."

20 Leonardo Morlino and Amichai Magen, "EU Rule of Law Promotion in Romania, Turkey and Serbia-Montenegro," prepared for the Workshop on "Promoting Democracy and the Rule of Law: American and European Strategies and Instruments," CDDRL, SIIS Stanford University, October 4–5, 2004, 18–20.

21 Mungiu-Pippidi, 2004; Sorana Pârvulescu, Ana Demsorean, and Bogdan Vetrici-Soimu, "Evaluating EU Democratic Rule of Law Promotion: Country Report, Romania," Bucharest, October 2005, 38.

22 The release to the press of transcripts of a party executive meeting in 2003 revealed plans to blatantly manipulate the judiciary, including "telephone justice," plans to bribe journalists, and a desire to amend the transparency law. See excerpts in Pârvulescu et al., 75–78.

23 For descriptions of such institution-building projects, see General Accounting Office, "Foreign Assistance: Rule of Law Funding Worldwide for Fiscal Years 1993–98," GAO/NSIAD-99–158 (Washington, D.C.: GAO, June 30, 1999); General Accounting Office, "Foreign Assistance: Promoting Judicial Reform to Strengthen Democracies," GAO/NSIAD-93-149 (Washington, D.C.: GAO, 1993); European Commission, "Final Report: Evaluation of the PHARE and TACIS Democracy Programme, 1992–1997," prepared by ISA Consult. For an overview of USAID's early experiences with institutional reform, see Linn Hammergren, "Institutional Strengthening and Justice Reform," PN-ACD-020, USAID, August 1998, and Linn Hammergren, "Judicial Training and Justice Reform," PN-ACD-021, USAID, August 1998.

24 Thomas Carothers, "Democracy Assistance: The Question of Strategy," *Democratization* 4, no. 3 (Autumn 1997): 11.

25 Javier Ciurlizza, "Judicial Reform and International Legal Technical Assistance in Latin America," *Democratization* 7, no. 2 (Summer 2000) 224.

26 Author's estimate based on EuropeAid programs described.

27 Investment Development Consultancy (IDC) and Development Strategies, "Evaluation of EC Country Strategy; Albania 1996–2001," September 2001, 37.

28 Private cars were banned under communism, and most Albanians did not drive until the early 1990s.

29 Investment Development Consultancy, 25–26.

30 International Crisis Group, "Albania: State of the Nation," Balkans Report no. 87, March 1, 2000, 18.

31 Thomas Carothers, "The Problem of Knowledge," in *Promoting the Rule of Law Abroad: In Search of Knowledge*, edited by Thomas Carothers (Washington, D.C.: Carnegie Endowment for International Peace, 2006), 22.

32 Stephen Golub, "The Legal Empowerment Imperative," in Carothers, ed., *Promoting the Rule of Law Abroad*, 169.

33 David Steinberg and C.P.F. Luhulima, "On Democracy; Strengthening Legislative, Legal, Press Institutions and Polling in Indonesia," Final Evaluation, USAID Grants 497-0336-G-SS-0041, 497-0364-G-SS-1089, and 497-0364-G-SS-2091, January 5, 1994, 11.

34 An evaluation as late as 1998 found that political will for rule-of-law reform was so low that the consultant could not recommend a full project. Chemonics International, "Legal Reform in Indonesia," USAID, February 1998. These views echoed findings by evaluators Steinberg and Luhulima, 3.

35 Steinberg and Luhulima, 6, 11. The Asia Foundation was created in 1951 as the Committee for a Free Asia, an ostensibly private body that was originally supported by covert indirect CIA funding to counter communist influence in Asia. As discussed earlier, covert funding ended in the 1960s. Joel Waldman, "The Asia Foundation: Past, Present, Future," U.S. Congressional Research Service (Washington, D.C.: Government Printing Office, February 1983).

36 Steinberg and Luhulima, 3, 6, 11.

37 Author's interview with Isa Gartini, USAID Democracy and Governance officer, Jakarta, July 2005.

38 Author's interview with Zacky Husein, attorney and former Rule-of-Law Program Director, Asia Foundation, Jakarta, July 21, 2005.

39 Author's interview with Bivintry, executive director of PSHK, Jakarta, July 15, 2005.

40 Bivintry interview.

41 Husein interview.

42 The Asia Foundation, "Executive Summary," Second Semi-Annual Report Institutional Development and Advocacy for Legal Reform in Indonesia (Grant No. 497-G-00-00-00058-00), March 2001–August 2001, 2–3.

43 Bivinitry interview.

44 Douglas Ramage,"Indonesia in Transition" congressional testimony before the Subcommittee on Asia and the Pacific, House Committee on International Relations, 109th Congress, First Session, March 10, 2005.

45 Author's interviews with Agus Loekman, Asia Foundation Indonesia, Jakarta, July 11, 2005, and with Husein.

46 Husein interview.

47 Pierre Landell-Mills, "Mobilizing Civil Society to Fight Corruption in Bangladesh," PREM Notes, no. 30, Public Sector, World Bank, October 1999.

48 David Dollar, "Aid and Reform in Africa: Lessons from Ten Case Studies," remarks made at a news conference at the World Bank in Washington, D.C., March 27, 2001.

49 Peter Janssen, "Indonesia's Spider Web," *Foreign Direct Investment*, June 2, 2004, www.fdimagazine.com/news/fullstory.php/aid/703/Indonesia_92s_spider_web.html.

50 Author's interview with Elena Tanasescu, task manager, Justice and Home Affairs and Public Administration, European Commission Delegation to Romania, Bucharest, September 12, 2001.

51 USAID/Romania, "Strategic Plan 1998–2000," 9, 15.

52 Guillermo O'Donnell, "Horizontal Accountability in New Democracies," in *The Self-Restraining State*, edited by Andreas Schedler, Larry Diamond, and Marc Plattner (Boulder, Colo.: Lynne Rienner, 1999), 29–62.

53 Jennifer Widner, "Building Judicial Independence in Common Law Africa," in Schedler et al., eds., *The Self-Restraining State*, 177–93.

54 David Mednicoff, "Legalism *Sans Frontières*? U.S. Rule-of-Law Aid in the Arab World," Carnegie Endowment for International Peace, Democracy and Rule of Law Project, Working Paper 61, 2005, 11–16.

55 USAID Mission to Romania, "USAID Cooperative Agreement no. DHR-0032-A-00-5053-00 with World Learning Inc. to Provide Support for the Democracy Network Program in Romania," May 12, 1995, 1.

56 USAID/Romania, "Strategic Plan 1998–2000," 9, 15.

57 World Learning, "Democracy Network Program in Romania, 1995–1999," Summary Assessment for USAID, 1999, 11, 15; ARD Inc., "Democracy and Governance Assessment of Romania," submitted to USAID/Romania, September 24, 2001, 10, 15; USAID/Romania, "R4 FY 2002," 41.

58 ARD, 10, 15.

59 USAID/Romania, "R2 FY 2002," March 2000, 37.

60 USAID/Romania, "Country Strategic Plan 2002–2006," 35.

61 *Nations in Transit*, 2005; Mungiu-Pippidi, 2005, 154–55.

62 This type of diplomatic incentive restructuring is commonly analyzed in democratization theory. See Guillermo O'Donnell, Philippe Schmitter, and Laurence Whitehead in their four-volume work on democratic transitions, *Transitions from Authoritarian Rule* (Baltimore: Johns Hopkins University Press, 1986). See also Larry Diamond, "Introduction: Political Culture and Democracy," in *Political Culture and Democracy in Developing Countries*, edited by Larry Diamond (Boulder, Colo.: Lynne Rienner, 1994), 4, and Barbara Geddes, "Initiation of New Democratic Institutions in Eastern Europe and Latin America," in *Institutional Design in New Democracies: Eastern Europe and Latin America*, edited by Arend Lijphart and Carlos H. Waisman (Boulder, Colo.: Westview Press, 1996), 6.

63 Author's conversation with Lt. Gen. Paul Monroe, Los Angeles, Calif., January 29, 2011.

64 The author has served as a consultant to this project, which is run by the National Strategy Information Center in Washington, D.C.

65 Wahid ended perhaps the most critical roadblock to the rule of law: the system of dwifungsi (dual function), in which the military paralleled the civilian government from the local to national levels, had reserved seats in parliament, and maintained control over the main political party, Golkar. "A Matter of Law . . . and, of course, Order," *Economist*, July 6, 2000.

66 Author's interviews with Cliff Keeling, Department of Justice ICITAP instructor, Jakarta, July 5, 2005; Santiago, Department of Justice ICITAP program developer, Jakarta, July 11, 2005; Harbin Marular, ICITAP Program, Jakarta, July 11, 2005.

67 Marular interview.

68 U.S. Department of Justice, "Indonesia," ICITAP Project Overview.

69 Santiago interview.

70 Author's interview with Heather Roche, ICITAP Program Director, Washington, D.C., July 2001.

71 Santiago interview.

72 See John Dower, *Embracing Defeat: Japan in the Wake of World War II* (New York: Norton, 2000), 247–49; Author's interview with Zainab al-Suwaij, executive director of the American Islamic Congress, the organization that won the contract to rebuild the educational system of Basra, Iraq, Washington, D.C., September 15, 2003.

73 Franca Brilliant, "Civic Education Assessment—Stage II: Civic Education Programming Since 1990," no. 3158–011, Management Systems International, December 1999.

74 Author's interview with Marcellus Rantatena, Partnership for Governance Reform, Jakarta, July 5, 2005.

75 The Partnership had a unique edge in bringing these large, feuding organizations together; its executive director, H. S. Dillon, is a Sikh, and thus one of the few Indonesians unaffiliated with either organization.

76 Interview with Ronan MacAongusa, First Secretary, European Commission Delegation to Indonesia, Jakarta, July 2005. Tellingly, however, the EU refused to fund the project, and it is not clear whether the U.S. government could have, had it been approached. In keeping with Muslim norms, NU and Muhammadiyah had created their anticorruption activities for men. The strategy made sense for rural, patriarchal Indonesia, but the EU's gender-equity criteria meant it could not support the initiatives.

77 See "Justice Denied for East Timor," Human Rights Watch Backgrounder, December 20, 2002. Also see David Cohen, "Intended to Fail: The Trials Before the Ad Hoc Human Rights Court in Jakarta," International Center for Transitional Justice, August 2003.

78 Author's interview with Laksamana Sukardi, former minister of state-owned enterprise, in charge of privatization, Jakarta, July 8, 2005. The claim that human rights had colonial overtones appeared in multiple interviews, including those with Loekman, Akbar Tadjung, Member of Parliament and former Speaker of the House, Jakarta, July 2005, and Tudang Mulya Lubis, attorney and founder of what was then called the Indonesian Legal Aid Institute, Jakarta, July 12, 2005.

79 Diamond, 1995.

80 Author's interview with Fatos Bundo, European Union Project Implementation Unit, Tirana, December 2001.

81 Juwana interview.

82 USAID, "Albania Revised Strategic Plan, FY 2001–2004," PD-ABS-947, December 2000, 29.

83 Unfortunately, this corruption effort often appeared more politically savvy in strategic concept than it was in implementation. Contractors generally just repurposed existing programs to fit the new anticorruption focus, meaning that the implementation of the strategy left much to be desired and may have played a role in its general ineffectiveness. Dhima interview.

Chapter Seven

1 USAID Data Sheet 654-006, "Civil Society Strengthening," Angola Mission, FY 2004 Program.

2 USAID, Angola, Activity Data Sheet, "Civil Society Strengthening," www.usaid.gov/our_work/democracy_and_governance/regions/afr/angola.html.

3 Stephen Golub, "A House Without a Foundation," in *Promoting the Rule of Law Abroad: In Search of Knowledge*, edited by Thomas Carothers (Washington, D.C.: Carnegie Endowment for International Peace, 2006), 108–109.

4 The United States is not alone in this problem. EU reform efforts in Eastern Europe also lurched from issue to issue, usually based on what mattered to the European state in charge of the EU presidency, not local needs. Under the Austrian presidency, for instance, the far-right government pushed for a harder line on immigration and exported that focus to all the countries in line for enlargement. Earlier, a pedophilia scandal in Belgium led to a drive within accession countries against smuggling people for sexual purposes and pornography. After September 11, all the acceding countries had to pass a raft of antiterrorism measures. Meanwhile, the actual needs of the acceding countries were secondary. Monica den Boer and William Wallace, "Justice and Home Affairs," in *Policy-Making in the European Union*, fourth edition, edited by Helen Wallace and William Wallace (Oxford: Oxford University Press, 2000), 504, 516.

5 Waleed H. Malik, "Challenges of Forging Civil Society Partnerships for Judicial Reform," LCSPS World Bank, www.worldbank.org/publicsector/legal/venezuelapaper.doc.

6 The second-generation approach is similar to problem-oriented policing processes in proposing a methodology rather than a set of solutions. See "The Key Elements of Problem-Oriented Policing," Center for Problem-Oriented Policing, www.popcenter.org/about-keyelements.htm.

7 See, for example, Verena Fritz, Kai Kaiser, and Brian Levy, "Problem-Driven Governance and Political Economy Analysis: Good Practice Framework,"

World Bank, September 2009; and Adrian Leftwich, "Thinking and Working Politically," Discussion Paper, Developmental Leadership Program, March 2011.

8 Benjamin L. Crosby, "Participation Revisited: A Managerial Perspective," USAID Implementing Policy Change Project, Monograph no. 6, April, 2000, 8, elucidates this benefit of participation, as well as other implementation benefits. Although there remains little empirical work, the scant quantitative research available suggests that participation in identifying problems yields greater project success. The field of participation in executing projects is more diverse in its findings, since participation slows programs and can divert focus as well. See Michael Cernea, "The Building Blocks of Participation: Testing a Social Methodology," in *Participatory Development and the World Bank*, edited by Bhuvan Bhatnagar and Aubrey Williams, Discussion Paper no. 183 (Washington, D.C.: World Bank, 1992), which analyzes 25 World Bank projects.

9 For instance, USAID devotes a section of its Indefinite Quarterly Contracts (IQCs) for rule-of-law reform to "constituency building."

10 The study's list of variables corresponds well to the style of problem analysis suggested here. "Regional Investment Attractiveness, A Survey of Business Perception, Indonesia 2003," Regional Autonomy Watch, Asia Foundation, and USAID, 2003, 6–7, 30, 67–69, 74–75.

11 Author's interview with Professor Hikmahanto Juwana, dean of the Faculty of Law, University of Indonesia, Jakarta, July 7, 2003.

12 In fact, in this broad, USAID-sponsored survey of ordinary individuals in Indonesia, legal issues did not register as a priority issue among the problems facing Indonesia, although security concerns were raised by some participants. Rising consumer prices and cost of living were cited as the main problems. See AC Nielsen/Asia Foundation, "Survey Report on Citizens' Perceptions of the Indonesian Justice Sector" (August 2001).

13 Crosby, 2000, 6.

14 In many Eastern European judiciaries, the high percentage of female judges is not a reflection of women's liberation but rather reflects the low status of jobs in the civil service judiciary. The presence of a preponderance of women both creates this low status and perpetuates it. The rule of law could benefit in such societies from cultural changes to gender perception (hardly part of the standard first-generation rule-of-law tool kit).

15 European Stability Initiative, "Reshaping International Priorities in Bosnia and Herzegovina: Part Two, International Power in Bosnia," Berlin: March 30, 2000, April 5, 2002, www.esiweb.org, 10.

16 David H. Bayley, *Changing the Guard: Developing Democratic Police Abroad* (New York: Oxford University Press, 2006), 96.

17 Thomas Carothers, "Democracy Assistance: The Question of Strategy," *Democratization* 4:3 (Autumn 1997): 127.

18 USAID has even codified the need to find a "champion" of reform in order to achieve legitimacy and a reform constituency—important needs, but not necessarily attuned to this problem of self-interested reformers. See Center for Democracy and Governance, *USAID Policy Implementation: What USAID Has Learned* (Washington, D.C.: USAID, January 2001), 5.

19 For detailed recommendations on how to conduct good stakeholder analysis, see Benjamin L. Crosby, "Management and the Environment for Implementation of Policy Change, Part One," USAID, Technical Note no. 4, April, 1992.

20 Benjamin L. Crosby, "Stakeholder Analysis: A Vital Tool for Strategic Managers," USAID, Technical Note no. 2, March 1991, 2.

21 Crosby, 1992, 9–10.

22 Wade Channell, "Grammar Lessons Learned: Dependent Clauses, False Cognates, and Other Problems in Rule of Law Programming," *University of Pittsburgh Law Review* 72(2) (Winter 2010): 176.

23 Even Adam Smith recognized this problem, writing: "People of the same trade seldom meet together, even for merriment and diversion, but the conversation ends in a conspiracy against the public, or in some contrivance to raise prices," and "To widen the market and to narrow the competition is always the interest of the dealers.... The proposal of any new law or regulation of commerce which comes from this order, ought always to be listened to with great precaution, and ought never to be adopted, till after having been long and carefully examined. . . . It comes from an order of men, whose interest is never exactly the same with that of the public, who have generally an interest to deceive and even to oppress the public, and who accordingly have, upon many occasions, both deceived and oppressed it." Adam Smith, *An Inquiry Into the Nature and Causes of the Wealth of Nations*, edited by R. H. Campbell and A. S. Skinner, Glasgow edition (Indianapolis: Liberty Classics, 1981), 145, 267.

24 Crosby locates the government in the center, with opposition on either side. I believe that frequently, elements of the government are arrayed against reform—including, occasionally, the supposed interlocutor of reform agencies. Therefore, I prefer to map support and opposition without *a priori* assumptions regarding the nexus of power within a society, or the support base within the government.

25 Some useful ideas for evaluation of such projects can be found in Robert Picciotto's thinking on policy coherence and development evaluations, drawn

from decades of service to the World Bank's Operations and Evaluation Department. See, for instance, Robert Picciotto, "Background Paper: Policy Coherence and Development Evaluation: Concepts, Issues and Possible Approaches," OECD Workshop: Policy Coherence for Development, Paris, May 18–19, 2004, 21–22.

26 Discussion with police sergeants and academics, "Culture of Lawfulness Training Workshop," National Strategy Information Center, Washington, D.C., April 2005.

27 See David Booth, "Governance for Development in Africa: Building on What Works," Policy Brief 1, Africa Power and Politics, Overseas Development Institute, April 2011. Some of the challenges of a best-fit approach are addressed in "Better Results from Public Sector Institutions," World Bank Approach to Public Sector Management 2011–2020, Extended Working Draft for Consultation, World Bank, April 2011. Most of these are failures on the part of development agencies, not compelling reasons to refrain from this sort of reform.

28 Brian Levy, "Governance and Economic Development in Africa: Meeting the Challenge of Capacity Building," in *Building Capacity in Africa: New Approaches, Emerging Lessons*, edited by Brian Levy and Sahr Kpundeh (Washington, D.C.: World Bank Institute, 2004).

29 Leni Wild and Marta Foresti, "Politics into Practice: A Dialogue on Governance Strategy and Action in International Development," Conference Report, Overseas Development Institute, May 2011, 8.

30 Wild and Foresti, 8.

31 Brett J. Blackledge, Deb Riechmann, Richard Lardner, "After Years of Rebuilding, Most Afghans Lack Power: A U.S.-Led Effort Could Do More Harm than Good," Associated Press, July 19, 2010, www.msnbc.msn.com/id/38303355/ns/world_news-south_and_central_asia.

32 Contrast, for example, the solution set offered by the Center for Problem-Oriented Policing, based around identified problems and various sets of tested solutions, with the solution set offered by the comprehensive World Bank website on rule-of-law reform that is centered around institutions. See Center for Problem-Oriented Policing, www.popcenter.org/default.htm; the World Bank's Legal Institutions for the Market Economy, www.worldbank.org/publicsector/legal/index.cfm. While the World Bank site is one I have worked on, and which I consider among the most comprehensive in the field, it is intended to respond to practitioner demand and is thus largely focused on institutional reform rather than solutions to real problems. The Center for Problem-Oriented Policing provides a set of questions and potential solutions that can assist local areas in solving their actual needs.

Chapter Eight

1 John Renehan, "The Business They've Chosen: Dispatches from a Police Transition Team in Ramadi," *American Interest*, vol. 4, no. 2, November/December 2008, 106.

2 Enzo lo Dato, "Palermo's Cultural Revolution and the Renewal Project of the City Administration," *Trends in Organized Crime* 5:3 (2000): 10–34.

3 David H. Bayley, *Changing the Guard: Developing Democratic Police Abroad* (New York: Oxford University Press, 2006), 64.

4 See "Aid Predictability: Synthesis of Findings and Good Practices," OECD DAC Working Party on Aid Effectiveness, October 2011.

INDEX

ABOUT THE AUTHOR

Rachel Kleinfeld is the co-founder and CEO of the Truman National Security Project, an organization dedicated to promoting smart, strong, and principled national security policy for the twenty-first century. Her passion lies in issues at the interstices of national security, human security, and development.

Kleinfeld has consulted for the World Bank, the EU, OECD, government agencies, and private organizations, to promote the rule of law in weak states, work that she continues as a nonresident associate of the Carnegie Endowment for International Peace. Her writings have appeared in multiple books, including: *Promoting the Rule of Law* (2005); *With All Our Might* (2006); *The Future of Human Rights* (2008); *Relocating the Rule of Law* (2009); and *Promoting Democracy and the Rule of Law: American and European Strategies* (2009).

Previously, as a Senior Consultant at Booz Allen Hamilton, Kleinfeld worked on energy security, terrorism, homeland security, and trade and security issues. As a consultant at the Center for Strategic and International Studies, she has written on citizen preparedness for bioterrorism. She has also worked in human rights and economic development in India, Israel, and Eastern Europe, and has served as an elections monitor in Pakistan and Bangladesh. Her writings on energy security in the developing world recently appeared in *Let There Be Light: Electrifying the Developing World through Markets and Distributed Energy*.

Named one of the "Top 40 Under 40" Rising Political Leaders by *Time Magazine* in 2010, Kleinfeld appears regularly on national radio and television and has been widely published in newspapers and journals. She serves as a national security expert for the *National Journal* and was a regular blogger for the *New York Times* during the 2008 campaign.

Kleinfeld is a founding member of the U.S. Department of State's Foreign Affairs Policy Board. A Rhodes Scholar and Truman Scholar, Kleinfeld has served on the Rhodes Selection Committee and on the Board of Trustees for the Blue Fund, a mutual fund. She received her B.A. from Yale University and her M. Phil. and D. Phil. in International Relations from St. Antony's College, Oxford. Kleinfeld was born and raised in a log house on a dirt road in her beloved Fairbanks, Alaska.

Carnegie Endowment for International Peace

The **Carnegie Endowment for International Peace** is a private, nonprofit organization dedicated to advancing cooperation between nations and promoting active international engagement by the United States. Founded in 1910, its work is nonpartisan and dedicated to achieving practical results.

As it celebrates its Centennial, the Carnegie Endowment is pioneering the first global think tank, with flourishing offices now in Washington, Moscow, Beijing, Beirut, and Brussels. These five locations include the centers of world governance and the places whose political evolution and international policies will most determine the near-term possibilities for international peace and economic advance.